FIFTY YEARS AFTER BRETTON WOODS

Fifty Years After Bretton Woods

The New Challenge of East–West Partnership
for Economic Progress

Edited by Miklós Szabó-Pelsőczi
Foreword by H.J. Witteveen

Avebury

Aldershot • Brookfield USA • Hong Kong • Singapore • Sydney

Published by
Avebury
Ashgate Publishing Limited
Gower House
Croft Road
Aldershot
Hants GU11 3HR
England

Ashgate Publishing Company
Old Post Road
Brookfield
Vermont 05036
USA

British Library Cataloguing in Publication Data

Fifty years after Bretton Woods: the new challenge of
    east–west partnership for economic progress
    1. International finance 2. Monetary policy 3. International
    economic relations
    I. Szabó-Pelsőczi, M. (Miklós), 1924–
    332.4'6

ISBN 1 85972 224 5

Library of Congress Catalog Card Number: 96-84106

Printed and bound in Great Britain by
Ipswich Book Co. Ltd., Ipswich, Suffolk

Contents

Contents

Contents

Contents

Foreword

H.J. Witteveen

The Robert Triffin–Szirák Foundation chose an important subject for its Sixth Conference in November 1994. It was the year in which the Bretton Woods institutions, the World Bank and the IMF, celebrated their fifty-year existence. So the focus had to be on the international monetary system in line with Robert Triffin's interest and work.

It is in this context that the Conference also studied East-West partnership in the transition process of Central and Eastern Europe from central planning to a market system. That is the crucial problem at the present time, and many speakers have given penetrating comments on it.

It is very stimulating to look at the subject both from Central and Eastern European and Western European viewpoints. The experience and insight of the World Bank and of the IMF was particularly enlightening, showing both how much these Bretton Woods institutions have been doing and how serious and deep-seated some of the transition problems are.

Mr Selowsky of the World Bank pointed out in conclusion that there may be a growing diversity in performance by the different countries. This will create a need for flexibility in the World Bank's means of assistance. It will be a major challenge, also for the European Union. Mr Odling-Smee of the IMF reported on this beginning diversity. He noted that all the more successful countries in Central and Eastern Europe have adopted IMF-supported economic programmes.

It depends on internal political considerations how far countries have been able to do this. It is an interplay between such different internal conditions and the available monetary resources that will be decisive for the success of this unprecedented historic economic transition process.

In this conference and the present volume, this fascinating subject is studied from many different angles. This provides a penetrating insight into these developments which are so important for Europe's future.

Preface by the Editor*

Miklós Szabó-Pelsőczi

I would like to express my special thanks to Mr Árpád Göncz, President of the Republic of Hungary and the High Patron of this Conference; to Mrs Triffin, our guest of honour; to Mr Philippe Maystadt, Minister of Finance of Belgium, Chairman of this Conference and of its Organizing Committee; to the government of Belgium and especially to Former Deputy Prime Minister and Minister for Foreign Affairs Willy Claes and to his successor, Minister Jan Vandenbroucke for placing at the disposal of the Conference the facilities of the Egmont Palace; to our host, the European League for Economic Cooperation; to our Sponsors; to my colleagues in the Organizing Committee; to Mr Bernard Snoy, whose tireless energy, combined with his innate tact, was among the main ingredients of the successful preparation of this Conference; and to the members of the Conference.

In my Preface to the collected papers presented at the Fifth Robert Triffin –Szirák Conference I have expressed the view, that 'the recessionary bias of the floating rate regime would not survive the stress of the tectonic changes brought by the collapse of the Soviet Empire'.

I am still holding that view. Because of the recessionary, and at the same time inflationary characteristics of the current exchange rate regime, industrial countries cannot respond as flexibly and generously to exogen shocks and challenges reaching them from the transition and developing countries, as the United States could with respect to Western Europe after World War II. Therefore, we are still in the period of 'tectonic changes' and can only work for the eventual realization of stability and non-inflationary growth. This book, explicitly or implicitly, is about techniques and strategy to reach this goal.

* *Opening address, November 17, 1994 (partial excerpts)*

Preface

I would like to use this opportunity to thank my associates in preparing the Conference and in editing this book: first of all Ms Regine Mandy, the Foundation's Representative in Brussels; chief editorial associate Mr Péter Sarkadi and technical editor Ms Erzsébet Deme; my secretaries Mrs Andrea Ánosi-Kárpáti and Mrs Klára Róma-Sass; as well as Avebury, a member of Ashgate Publishing Group and its editor, Ms Sarah Markham.

December 1995
Bedford, N.Y. and Budapest

Part I

The New Challenge
Fifty Years after Bretton Woods

1 The International Monetary System and the Responsibilities of the Economics Profession*

Miklós Szabó-Pelsőczi

Robert Triffin, one of the major actors of international monetary developments during the last fifty years, was praised for 'his power of analysis, for his conviction and courage, for his institutional imagination and for his pragmatism' (de Larosière). I would like to praise him today both for his personal humility and for his professional pride rooted in the great responsibilities of the economics profession.

It is important to stress the double virtues of personal humility and professional pride at the beginning of this Conference, whose multi-dimensional task is to examine, in the light of the experience gained during the last fifty years, the present state of our monetary institutions and their ability to respond constructively, in the spirit of their original purpose, to history's current challenge.

This semi-centennial anniversary coincides with an epochal structural change in human and economic affairs, rare in history. The disintegration of the Soviet Empire brings to a spectacular end a five-hundred-year period, which began with the discovery of the New World. This discovery opened up for Western Civilization all continents formerly untouched by its commerce and technology. From now on, there will be no, even relatively, free economic goods: land, labour, air, water, or nature. All of them will be available at a price – a rather high price. This is the real global structural change we are now witnessing, of which the structural change of Central and Eastern Europe is only one, albeit very important, part.

Structural changes are expensive. Yet, they must be financed.

The only good, which is left almost free, is human intellect. This was the chief driving force behind the invention of money, private banking, national

* *Opening address, November 17, 1994*

3

banking systems and the effort of creating a well-functioning global monetary system at Bretton Woods. Once more, we must stimulate the human
mind, the mind of economists, bankers, statesmen, and public opinion to
devise a global monetary system which would answer the needs of the
global real economy now and in the distant future.

In this century, it was Keynes and later Triffin who stressed that any
region's and the global economy will turn out only suboptimal performance
unless its monetary system is organized around a supranational currency
anchor. It was Triffin, following in the footsteps of Eugène Delacroix,
Prime Minister of Belgium after World War I, and of Keynes, who cham-
pioned the establishment of regional and global clearing mechanisms, and
applied these principles to the establishment of the European Payments
Union, to the introduction of the Special Drawing Rights, and to the
formation of the European Monetary System. His influence is felt in the
Maastricht Treaty, the European Monetary Institute, and eventually in the
European Economic and Monetary Union. Triffin was 'working for a world
where logic and morality would reign... for a world where international
savings would be employed rationally to achieve harmonious development,
for a world where the great powers would submit to discipline based on
international co-operation' (de Larosière).

The Purposes of the International Monetary Fund were and are only
partially realized. Still, the gold-dollar standard as a proxy for a supranational currency supported by other international undertakings, like the
Marshall Plan, functioned tolerably well for a quarter century. It helped
create a high growth/low inflation economy in the United States and in the
world. This was in fact, and not in fancy, the golden age of the post-war
economy, because the relatively successful global monetary management
created a relatively elastic economy, in which the GDP/Price elasticity was
several times higher than during the next quarter of a century.

The golden age was followed by the current period characterized by
floating rates, liberalization and globalization of the banking and financial
industries, the freeing of both short- and long-term capital movements and
the virtual explosion of derivative trading. As the banking and financial
industries had become global, national governments lost almost all control
over them. Prudential standards for banks have been elaborated under the
aegis of the Bank of International Settlements. Comparable standards for
derivative trading are under preparation in Basle. If the net effect of these
efforts will not be more than to make speculation safer, they might encourage an even larger proportion of savings to be engaged in speculation than

before. Not only budget deficits can crowd out productive investments, excessive demand for speculative funds has the same effect.

The anniversary of the Bretton Woods institutions inspired many comments and recommendations. These range over a large field. Those are the most valuable, which recommend to 'major industrial countries... to achieve greater economic convergence... and a more formal system of co-ordination... to avoid excessive exchange rate misalignments and volatility... and in time, commitments to flexible exchange rate bands' (The Bretton Woods Commission), or even the conversion of 'the present *de facto* (exchange rate) regime into a *de jure* system of announced target zones among the major currencies' (Dr C. Fred Bergsten). While these ideas incubate, we must give serious consideration and support to constructive short-term measures, like the IMF Management's proposal for a 36 billion SDR allocation and for the setting up of Co-financing Trust Accounts (CTAs).

Changes in the real economy often create demand for new banking services supplied with some time-lag by the banking industry. Today, the financial markets are already globalized, and we must trust that the international monetary institutions will adjust their practices to the new demand on their energies and creative imaginations. This world-wide structural change must be financed with adequate non-inflationary monetary creation leading to the expansion of non-inflationary real economic activity to new savings, financing further growth. To provide uncontrolled liquidity, simply to fuel speculation while clamping down on real growth, is clearly counterproductive. The management of world liquidity, in the spirit of the Purposes of the Fund and of its First Amendment, must go hand in hand with the regulation of destabilizing hot-money flows. This regulation should lead to a global monetary system which would exclude the underlying conditions generating these flows in the first place.

Industrialized countries are already working toward the creation of new monetary rules. In addition, an eventual greater economic and payments co-operation among certain transition countries in harmony with their efforts to join the European Community show that today the 'realists' and not the 'visionaries' are those who want convergence, and a more rationally functioning global monetary system.

Only if the industrial countries' economy is flexible, can the developing and transition countries overcome their own rigidities. Therefore, in the struggle for greater monetary co-operation, industrial countries must be increasingly dynamic leaders. *Noblesse oblige.* The transition and the developing countries, often representing great ancient and now newly emerging civilizations, can be expected to co-operate in their own interest. Only combined global political will can create the desired results. It is admittedly difficult to achieve this. The trade-off is a systematically disorganized global monetary market-place for which no economist should wish to accept responsibility, and probably none of us will.

Security, stability, peace, and prosperity are closely linked.

Because of this, I firmly believe that the future of humanity is not in star-wars but in a well-functioning global monetary system.

The task of this Conference is to bring the latter's realization closer.

It is in this spirit, in the spirit of the original intentions of Bretton Woods, that I open this conference and wish success to its deliberations.

2 The Marshall Plan from Today's Perspective*

Fred L. Hadsel

The background of the Harvard talk

Bretton Woods, as this conference knows, was a principal international response to the post-war financial situation of the world. The Marshall Plan, which followed soon after, inaugurated the co-operative search for European prosperity – a search that today holds new possibilities in view of the current situation.

It would be folly, in these brief introductory remarks, to try to survey the course of European recovery.

Instead, arising in part from my background in history and diplomacy, but more especially from my direction of the George C. Marshall Foundation for more than a decade, my remarks will take a different direction.

I invite you to reflect on the brief talk entitled merely 'Remarks', which George Catlett Marshall gave at Harvard University on 5 June 1947. Two aspects of this talk give it a unique quality.

In a biographical sense, it marked Marshall's transformation from soldier to statesman. In a historical sense, it marked a turning point in history.

Marshall's emergence as a statesman was not a mysterious act of alchemy. During his forty years of military service – which earned him the sobriquet of 'The Organizer of Victory' – Marshall not only displayed qualities of absolute integrity, selfless service, and a genius of command which stamped him with greatness. These years also brought him experience in the economics of mobilization and the politics of congressional relations. Moreover, as the only military leader to be a chief of staff throughout the war, he took part in all of the allied conferences on the future of Europe. His

* *Opening address, November 17, 1994*

7

diplomatic experience underwent a further stringent education after the war when he sought to establish peace between Communist and Nationalist China.

Soon after becoming Secretary of State, Marshall attended the Moscow meeting of the foreign ministers in March and April 1947, where he experienced at first hand the intransigence of Molotov and plunged into the bewildering problems of post-war Europe. His wry comment, at the end of April, that the patient (Europe) was declining, while the doctors (the Great Powers) deliberated, forecasted a new phase in the American effort to deal with the European crisis.

May 1947 was the critical month. It challenged his phenomenal ability to analyse problems and find feasible solutions. The policy which emerged in these weeks combined his personal convictions with the best advice of his advisors. It was both principled and pragmatic. It confirmed his emergence as a world statesman.

Late in May, Marshall concluded that an American response to Europe's desperate situation was extremely urgent. Despite Dean Acheson's fear that university commencements were the graveyard of good speeches, Marshall chose the Harvard ceremonies, only a week away, as the best occasion. He was still working on the draft when he and Mrs Marshall flew to Cambridge the day before the ceremony.

There was nothing in the local circumstances that would forecast the immortality of what Marshall still labelled merely Remarks. It was a pleasant June afternoon; a number of honorary degrees had been granted; and several persons spoke to the congenial academic assemblage held outdoors in the Harvard yard. Marshall's Remarks were very brief, less than fifteen minutes long. Almost by accident, a local radio station preserved a recording, and from this transcript, it is clear that Marshall was not comfortable in reading a text. His voice was flat; his speaking manner brusque. His whole delivery was unemotional, matter-of-fact, and unadorned. The talk was twice all but drowned out by overhead airplanes. The applause was routine, and the audience seemed unaware of the significance of his Remarks.

Summary of the talk

The talk addressed two problems. The first part – almost half of the text – was directed to his own countrymen. Marshall made a special effort to explain the existing situation in Europe in terms that the American people could understand. From his long experience, he recognized the cardinal importance of public support for any new policy. Only through grasping clearly the crisis in Europe, would the people of the United States escape the danger of isolationism and make the proper decision on which 'the whole world of the future' depended. This was so important to him that he repeated the point in extemporaneous comment at the end of his Remarks.

Toward Europe, Marshall extended his now famous proposal of an American commitment to break the cycle of despair and restore the confidence of the Continent. You are all familiar with his principal points:

Assistance should be a basic cure, not piecemeal. It should be open to all countries crippled by the war, not just a few. The initiative should be European, not just American.

At the same time, any country opposing the programme could not expect help. Efforts to undermine this assistance would be opposed.

Relevance to today

What has made these Remarks enduring is not only the fact that they initiated the economic recovery of Europe and contributed to the remaking of the Continent. It is also the fact that they invoked principles of American policy which are relevant to the situation facing Europe today, and to the problems which this conference is addressing.

The first principle is very practical: it is the inextricable relationship in the United States between domestic and foreign policy, in which only a well-informed public leads to sound decisions. For four decades, American policy has been determined by the cold war. Even though present policy may be subject to new distractions, the importance Marshall placed on this relationship remains entirely valid in the present, though different, circumstances.

The second principle is at heart philosophical. Policy must be directed toward economic goals and not be distracted by political divisions. That this imperative takes on new and different aspects does not, in any way, diminish its continuing relevance.

The third principle is geopolitical. The initiative in searching for European prosperity must lie in Europe. Only when European nations hammer out proposed solutions to their problems can the United States respond effectively.

The acceptance of these three guiding principles – formulated by Marshall at Harvard and currently relevant to the problems facing Europe – does not guarantee easy success. But if our reflections have any validity, these principles must be recognized as essential as this conference discusses the future of European partnership.

3 Robert Triffin and the Concept of a Managed Global Monetary Reserve System*

Bernard Snoy

The most remarkable thing about the work and personality of Robert Triffin was the combination of three aspects: his power of analysis, his conviction and courage, and his institutional imagination and pragmatism.

First, his power of analysis. Before all others, Robert Triffin understood the inherent fragility of the gold exchange standard and announced its ineluctable demise. To replace it, he proposed a plan aimed at regulating the creation of world liquidity avoiding the shortcomings of both a return to the gold exchange standard and the weaknesses of floating exchange rates. The concept of a managed reserve system as an instrument for exerting a stabilizing influence on the behaviour of the global economy will probably remain the most important point in Triffin's intellectual legacy.

Second, Robert Triffin was a man with a heart, a man of conviction, enthusiasm, and courage and finally an indefatigable reformer determined to change things and prepared to begin all over again as often as need be. As Jacques de Larosière puts it in his address to the Robert Triffin Jubilee in 1988, Robert Triffin was 'working for a world where logic and morality would reign, where international savings would be employed rationally to achieve harmonious development, for a world where great powers would submit to discipline based on international co-operation'. Triffin was a true citizen of the world and fought tirelessly for international rules safeguarding more generously the interest of the developing countries and ensuring a better symmetry in the adjustment obligations of both industrial and developing countries. There is no doubt that he would have shown the same conviction, dedication, and perseverance for the search of an appropriate

* *Opening address, November 17, 1994*

11

international response to the problem faced by Eastern European countries in transition.

Third, Robert Triffin combined the bold thinking and outspoken humour that academics can afford with a demonstrated practical sense and a remarkable institutional imagination. Like his friends Jean Monnet and Robert Marjolin, he knew that institutions are the key to improving the workings of the system in practice. Hence his insistence on proposing solutions based upon such bodies as the IMF, the OECD, and the European Commission. We all know that Robert Triffin was the instigator of the European Payments Union, which played such a crucial role in the restoration of external convertibility and prosperity in Western Europe in the 1950s. Under the Kennedy and the Johnson Administrations, he was the key advocate of the First Amendment to the IMF Articles of Agreement which created the Special Drawing Rights (SDRs). He played an important role too in the design of the European Monetary System. This economist with his world-wide outlook saw clearly that the reform of the international system called for the decentralization of co-operation at the regional level. Today, I am sure, he would have had high expectations for the EBRD and regional arrangements in Eastern Europe.

Taking with us the inspiration of this man of vision, of high ethical standards, and with a knack for creative institutional arrangements, let us turn to the new challenge of East-West partnership following the collapse of the Soviet Empire. Let us try to imagine what Robert Triffin would tell us if he was with us today.

I think he would first remind us of the urgency of reordering the international monetary system and of pressing ahead with the construction of the European Monetary Union. Indeed, in Robert Triffin's view, our present system of floating exchange rates is both inefficient and inequitable. He would point to the detrimental impact on growth in general, as well as for transition and developing countries in particular, of the high level of exchange rate volatility and the recurrent misalignments of the key currencies. Indeed, both developing and transition countries need a stable exchange system to which they can anchor their own currencies. Also, Robert Triffin never stopped repeating how grossly unfair the present system is in allocating the benefit of seigniorage to countries which are already the richest in the world.

Preoccupied to provide a solid growth environment for the countries in transition, Robert Triffin would draw attention to the contribution which floating exchange rates, with the ensuing elimination of the sanction of devaluation and the uncontrolled proliferation of world liquidity, have made to the laxity of fiscal policies since the 1970s, as exemplified by the increase from 36 to 67 per cent between 1974 and 1993 of the public debt/GDP ratio in the G-7 countries. Jacques de Larosière was recently echoing Robert Triffin's views when he declared in Madrid on September 29, 1994 at the conference on 'Fifty Years after Bretton Woods: the Future of the IMF and the World Bank' that 'the world has not yet finished paying for the consequences of 15 years' disregard of the external stability of currencies'. We paid heavy prices in the 1970s and the 1980s. We paid again in the recession of the early 1990s and even today, despite the hopeful signs of recovery. There is, no doubt, a link between the heavy debt burden of OECD countries, their reduced margin of manoeuvre for fiscal policies, their more restrictive monetary policies, and the higher real interest rates that we are observing with possible dampening effects on growth and productive investment at a crucial moment for the transition in Eastern Europe.

But we know that Robert Triffin was a positive reformer. Rather than complaining, he would have offered concrete and constructive proposals:

–   First, he saw the collapse of the Soviet Empire as a crucial new opportunity to act on his proposal of moving towards a global management of the international monetary system with a central authority issuing and controlling an international currency, the SDR, and with the external use of reserve currencies being kept within set limits. Now that the Bretton Woods institutions have become genuinely universal, the fundamental issue for Triffin's disciples is whether the world can afford to continue operating in an international economic and monetary system characterized by erratic fluctuations between its most important currencies, ill-defined mechanisms of economic policy co-ordination, and unregulated international financial markets in which speculative activities overshadow the primary functions of savings mobilization and allocation.

–   If these reforms are not feasible at the global level for lack of political will in the major industrial countries, Triffin would have turned to existing institutions to capitalize on their performance: first, to the IMF to seriously strengthen its authority procedures and its methodology in multilateral surveillance and second, to the European Commission and to the European Monetary Institute, charged with the preparation of the

European Central Bank, to implement at the European level what could not be achieved at the world level.

Therefore, Robert Triffin would surely have enjoyed attending our conference which will precisely deal with these two broad topics:

1 How can we create a global economic and monetary environment conducive to a successful transition of the former centrally planned economies?

2 Is the international monetary system fit for the task of Eastern European reconstruction?

Robert Triffin was a great supporter of the international financial institutions. He worked at some point for the International Monetary Fund and held assignments for the Organisation for European Economic Cooperation, the predecessor of OECD, and for the European Commission. He would, therefore, have asked the questions such as the following: are the current approaches of international financial institutions to the transition problem the right ones? Do they take sufficiently into account the profound, systemic nature of the transformation of Eastern Europe? Are we not transposing in a too simplistic way macroeconomic approaches or project financing techniques used in other parts of the world, without sufficient attention to structural problems? Besides liberalization, stabilization, and privatization, do we give sufficient attention to the creation of the legal, institutional, and human bases of market economy? How can true entrepreneurs be created to run the former state assets in an efficient way? Is the path these countries are following socially and politically sustainable? Has the international community provided enough assistance and has that assistance been of the right nature? How did our response compare to the vision and generosity which presided over the post-World War II reconstruction of Western Europe and Japan? Did we pay enough attention to the possibilities of mitigating the pains of adjustment by the revival of some forms of regional co-operation and externally financed modernization of the infrastructure? Did we correctly grasp the true nature of the transition challenge with dimensions that extend beyond the realm of pure economics?

Then comes the specific European dimension. Robert Triffin was a true believer in European integration as a step towards a more just international economic and monetary system. He would surely have given us insights on further questions such as:

1　How should Europe modify its integration strategy to facilitate the transition process and ultimately allow the Central and Eastern European countries to take their legitimate place in the European construction?

2　More immediately, are the European Union technical assistance instruments, the PHARE and TACIS programmes, and its financial assistance instruments, well designed, well implemented, and well adapted to the transition needs and to a progressive integration strategy of Eastern Europe?

Last but not least, what are the new initiatives that may be called for? Initiatives of the European Union, the G-7, the G-10, or a new G-24? Should we rather encourage the countries in transition themselves to take initiatives and organize regional customs unions, economic unions, clearing unions, or even payments unions with external financial support?

The fundamental message of Robert Triffin was a message of peace and of European and international co-operation.

In the conclusion of his fundamental book *Europe and the Money Muddle* published in 1957, he wrote, 'the fundamental dilemma of international economic relations in this twentieth century lies in the inadequacy of national sovereignty as a framework for policy decisions and their administrative implementation in an interdependent world'.

Perhaps more than any other economist, Robert Triffin has contributed to find imaginative ways to structure and implement international co-operation. Fifty years after Bretton Woods, we need the same constructive and creative spirit to address the new challenge of East-West partnership for economic progress.

4 The Challenge of Creating a Global Economic and Monetary Environment Conducive to a Successful Transition of the Former Centrally Planned Economies*

Philippe Maystadt

I am very pleased to welcome the Triffin–Szirák Foundation in Brussels for its conference on 'The New Challenge of East-West Partnership for Economic Progress'. Five years after the fall of the Berlin wall, it is indeed a most timely initiative to take stock of the international community's initial approaches to the historic mandate of transition and to clarify our views on the challenges which lie ahead. This has been a time of great expectations, disillusionment, and mixed results. Above all, we should remember the courage and determination of those political leaders who continued to defend the principles of democracy and market reform, despite the initial disarray of their countries' social and economic fabric. How did the rest of the world react? Which of the many solutions that have been tabled worked and which did not?

General lessons from the first five years

A first general observation is that no new Marshall Plan has been set up to support an economic reconstruction which is even more encompassing than the one facing Western Europe after World War II. A number of bold initiatives, announced for geopolitical reasons, fell short of expectations because they were ill-timed or because the conditions attached to the disbursement of funds were only partially fulfilled.

Instead, the international community has been relatively successful in responding to emerging financing needs with *ad hoc* solutions: the European Union took the lead in mobilizing exceptional assistance, both on its

* *Keynote address, November 17, 1994*

16

own and in the wider G-24 context; the EBRD is becoming a central catalyst for private investment flows; the OECD added a new dimension to its promotion of market economic principles; and the IMF and the World Bank adapted their lending instruments to the initial requirements of economic transformation.

Regional trade and payments arrangements have so far not played a decisive role in the transition from command to market systems. Despite the intellectual appeal of these proposals, the transition countries have been reluctant to step into any formal arrangement which could have perpetuated the dependency structure imposed by the prescriptions of intra-COMECON trade. They have, instead, insisted on a rapid integration in the world trade and payments system as their principal vehicle for attracting foreign investment and wealth accumulation.

However, world economic developments have so far not been favourable to the integration of the former command economies: rapid successes have been delayed because the transition countries had to implement the initial stages of reform during a period of weakness in world activity, which has been especially severe in Europe. It would have required much higher levels of international demand or much larger resource transfers to create from the outset conditions for a rapid expansion in mutual trade and income creation between the East and the West.

Radical liberalization measures have not worked in those countries where price mechanisms could not fulfil their equilibrating role of supply and demand, in the absence of efficient and competitive markets. The transition has been most successful in those cases where it was based on comprehensive reforms including macroeconomic stabilization and institution building.

In sum, the international community has shown its willingness to alleviate the most pressing transition needs with special mechanisms, but, in essence, the process has so far been conducted on the basis of *trade rather than aid* or, to put in more general terms, on the basis of *market forces rather than grand institutional schemes.*

What are the implications of this sobering conclusion for the future of international economic and monetary co-operation? Does it imply that, apart from the management of crisis situations, no new initiatives are required? I will defend the opposite view by submitting:

17

1   that the integration of the transition economies in the trade and investment system reinforces the need for systematic co-operation on all aspects of economic policy (an agenda for economic co-operation);

2   that the international monetary system should better reflect the basic principles of global stability, shared responsibility, and co-operative financing, which also inspired much of Professor Triffin's work (a system based on global partnership).

An agenda for economic co-operation

Let me first turn to the agenda for economic co-operation emerging from the recent challenges, opportunities, and flows of liberalization.

The conclusion of the Uruguay Round, the conclusion of European Agreements with the Central and Eastern European countries and of Partnership Agreements with the countries of the former Soviet Union all have considerably improved the prospects for trade and investment in transition countries. They are expected to stimulate economic integration to the benefit of all. The globalization of markets, especially of the financial markets, has created new opportunities for investment in emerging market economies.

So much for the principles and expectations. In practice, the reactions are far less confident. The European industry is fearing stiff competition from low-wage countries in Central and Eastern Europe, although, globally, the European Union is accumulating growing trade surpluses on these countries. Overall, the world-wide liberalization of trade is fuelling concerns about a massive delocalization of industries to countries with low social and environmental standards, although the flows of foreign investment into the transition countries have so far remained very modest. The global markets are in the limelight due to their high volatility rather than to their contribution to a stable allocation of world savings.

How can these tensions be alleviated? *How can we achieve an international distribution of labour and investment which is consistent with the long-term interests of both, the old and the new participants in today's market system?* Let me briefly mention five principles which will, in my view, shape the economic agenda of the coming years.

1   The integration of the former command economies requires wide-ranging *structural reforms* not only in the transition countries themselves,

but *also in the industrial country markets,* especially in Europe. It would be short-sighted to found expectations of a successful integration concerning reforms which would only apply to the new participants in the system. The old ones have to adjust as well.

The European White Paper has the special merit to place the revitalization of the European economy explicitly in the context of a lasting partnership with the new market economies in Central and Eastern Europe. The members of the European Union will have to accept that the validity of their structural reforms should, from now on, also be judged in terms of their contribution to a stable association with their partners in transition.

2   Due to the globalization of the markets, structural policies have to receive, in any event, a *higher attention from the multilateral institutions.* All countries are now directly exposed to the international competition for savings and investment. Pressures for pursuing efficient economic policies have increased dramatically.

The 'quality label' from the multilateral institutions on the validity of countries' economic policies is bound to become increasingly relevant for their access to financing. This applies especially to institutions such as the IMF and the World Bank with a legal authority over the viability of countries' balance-of-payments and development policies. All countries, the transition countries in particular, are thus in need of a systematic dialogue with the Bretton Woods institutions on all aspects of their reform policies.

In this connection, I fully support Managing Director Camdessus's insistence on the Fund's central role in promoting 'high quality growth'. Progress in this direction will require the IMF to abandon its partial and purely quantitative approaches in favour of more comprehensive judgements on the viability of countries' economic policies including the qualitative aspects of their public finances and the efficiency of their social protection and employment systems. Rigid interpretations of the Fund's legal mandate have for long delayed such an evolution. In today's environment, these interpretations have become much less relevant. The problems of transition have shown that there is no alternative to IMF-programmes attacking countries' adjustment needs at their roots. Moreover, the universal acceptance of the validity of market-based solutions makes it easier to convey the Bretton Woods institutions with policy mandates, which, until recently, could have been resisted on ideological ground. Their responsibility for the orientation of world economic developments will thus rather increase than decrease in today's global environment.

3   Political bodies, such as the *Interim and Development Committee, will,* in this context, *have an increasing role to play.* It is their task to establish the broad guidelines on the basis of which their respective institutions should pursue their policy co-operation with member countries. The international spill-over effects of domestic policy choices should figure more systematically on their policy agenda.

The present efforts of the Interim Committee to launch a more direct policy dialogue amongst its members and the Committee's recent Declaration on Co-operation to Strengthen the Global Expansion respond to this objective. Moreover, by organizing a systematic follow-up of the implementation of this Declaration, the Committee will be better equipped to signal the need for corrective actions at an early stage.

A similar orientation is still needed on the side of the Development Committee. The Bank has recently come to accept the need to refocus its activities in favour of policy advice and greater selectivity in an environment characterized by the predominance of private financing flows in the international development process. While I support this orientation, it implies that the Bank must set priorities for its actions, which will at times confront it with difficult policy choices. In my view, the Bank would be better prepared to assume such responsibilities, if its management and Executive Board could rely on a policy-making body having the same status as the Interim Committee does in relation to the IMF.

4   With respect to the transition countries, the World Bank, together with the EBRD, will have the special responsibility to *promote conditions for a stable expansion of employment and investment.* Recent reports of the United Nations and of the EBRD show that the low level of wages in these countries has so far not contributed to a substantial inflow of foreign direct investments. Such inflows rather depend on the creation of an environment conducive to private initiative, on the access to local markets, and on the availability of a stable and skilled workforce.

These requirements will have to receive a higher attention in the years ahead. In this connection, I welcome the institutional reorientation of the EBRD's priorities in favour of the development of a resilient local private sector, even if this focus on transition may initially moderate the volume of its transactions. Proposals are under consideration for improving the leverage on private investment of the European assistance programmes with Central and Eastern Europe. They reflect a legitimate desire to see that available funds work more productively, to increase their impact on the transfer of expertise and technology, and to show, more generally, that the expansion of investment in the transition countries is a positive sum game to the benefit of all.

5   The *World Trade Organization*, will henceforward have the primary responsibility for managing the international trade system in a truly multilateral perspective. It will have to ensure that national trade policy instruments are used wisely, in conformity with commonly agreed principles.

The Organization would, however, fall short of becoming a strong international pillar next to the Bretton Woods institutions if its activities were to be limited to the settlement of trade disputes. Issues which have a direct bearing on the direction of international trade and investment, such as the protection of environmental standards and elementary social rights, cannot be left unsettled, even if their influence may be more limited than one would assume. The WTO will from the outset have to show leadership in discussing these issues in a truly multilateral perspective and in co-ordinating its policies actively with other institutions sharing responsibilities in shaping countries' growth and development strategies.

One of the major challenges for the coming years will be to accept that the globalization of the economy is not limited to the financial and commercial spheres; it also concerns that of labour. We would be seriously mistaken to underestimate the concerns expressed about a downward levelling of working conditions as a result of large-scale industrial dislocations. To ignore these concerns would mean compromising the new world order we seek to build by proclaiming the universal values of free trade, private initiative, and political democracy. From this point of view, I welcome the Interim Committee's recent initiatives to launch an active policy dialogue with both the World Trade Organization and the International Labour Organization.

Never before have so many institutions been involved in the management of international economic co-operation. The impressive list of institutions represented at today's conference is a case in point. The risk of overlapping, conflicting signals and frustration for unfulfilled expectations cannot be dismissed. However, I do not see any realistic alternative to this panoply of organizations each trying to promote international co-operation within their respective fields of competence. The beauty of simple solutions is probably ill-suited for the complex agenda imposed by today's global environment. Under these conditions, the system's efficiency and credibility will depend

1   on effective co-ordination, extending to *all* policy issues with cross-border effects and

2   on a sufficient discipline, especially monetary discipline, implying a fair balance of rights and obligations among all participants.

Let me turn to this second topic of my intervention, which was also at the heart of Professor Triffin's preoccupations with the international monetary system.

A monetary system based on global partnership

With the end of Soviet imperialism, the environment for monetary co-operation has radically changed. It is most doubtful whether the new members can be integrated on the basis of the prevailing structure. *Partnership rather than power relations seems the key to the future of monetary co-operation,* even more so since, on top of the emerging East-West integration, we are witnessing a wider reshuffling of vested interests and positions with world-wide implications. Europe and Japan have become prominent reserve currency centres next to the dollar zone, although the implications of such a multipolar exchange rate system have not yet been reflected in new institutional arrangements. An increasing number of developing countries have become important partners in the conduct of world economic developments; they have the legitimate desire to see their internal stabilization policies protected by a stable monetary system, in which they fully participate in accordance with their growing responsibilities in the world economy.

How can the Bretton Woods institutions be adapted to cope with the new challenge? How should we reformulate the principles of global stability, shared responsibility, and co-operative financing, so that they should respond to the new environment? Let me make a few suggestions on the requirements a future monetary system should fulfil.

1   The future system needs, first of all, to be based on *rules of the game which are sufficiently consistent and accepted by everyone.* The available arrangements fail to ensure effective currency co-operation under all circumstances. Most countries, including the transition countries, are in search of stability anchors ensuring the stable pursuit of their adjustment policies. It required the vision of someone like Robert Triffin to foresee, as early as in the 1950s, that these expectations were more likely to be fulfilled through a decentralization of monetary co-operation at the regional level. The prospects for the European Monetary Union and the anchor it will provide to our partners in transition are directly indebted to his insight and perseverance. However, the international community consistently failed to implement the other pillar of Robert Triffin's proposals on the exchange rate system, which is the concerted management of the relations between the major currency zones based on a commonly accepted discipline.

Would it not be time to move, in this field, from a world run by events to the acceptance of some minimal rules of conduct? As a first step in that direction, I would suggest the major industrial countries to reach systematic agreements on the desirable direction of their exchange rates based on an explicit recognition of the IMF's surveillance powers over all policies having an impact on the behaviour of international capital flows.

Rather than departing from the present procedures, such a step would, in my view, be the natural complement of decisions which the IMF Interim Committee has recently taken in the field of policy co-operation: the achievement of durable convergence is now universally accepted as a prior condition for the pursuit of sound growth policies; the IMF's surveillance powers have effectively been extended to cover all aspects of countries' external accounts; and the follow-up procedure adopted at the last Interim Committee meeting forebodes the possibility for the IMF to organize multilateral consultations whenever the risk of currency slippages would need to be countered with corrective measures.

The conditions for envisaging moderate steps in the direction of greater exchange rate stability seem favourable, as each of the major countries is completing a process of profound internal adjustment. Postponing such steps would expose all of us to the risk that the world-wide benefits of these adjustments would be compromised by the resurgence of fundamental exchange rate distortions. It would be difficult to accept, especially for the transition countries who still have to establish their share in the world market, if the opportunities created by the trade liberalization were to be offset by exchange rate manipulations for protectionist purposes.

2   Future monetary co-operation will have to rely on *decision-making mechanisms in which all members can participate in conformity with the responsibilities they assume in the global economy.* I can be brief on this second requirement of a more stable monetary system. For the past twenty years, the system has been managed on the basis of *ad hoc* arrangements. Informal bodies, such as the group of seven major industrial countries, may have played a useful role in offsetting acute crisis situations, but are poorly equipped to produce durable contributions to the operation of the system. Being the product of internal political compromises, their decisions are seldom relevant to the whole membership and fail to provide a basis for more systematic co-operation in the future.

The recent IMF meetings in Madrid have shown that this approach to international monetary management has probably been stretched to its limits. The failure to agree on a special SDR allocation in the context of a wider financing package for the transition countries was not the result of a new North-South division; nor did it point to a lack of solidarity from the developing countries with the exceptional needs of the transition countries. The single most important lesson to be learnt from these events is that, in the long run, the Fund's instruments for monetary co-operation can play their role only if their availability in the interest of the global membership is preserved. It required a crisis situation to demonstrate that this condition can be secured only if decisions on the operation of the monetary system are effectively shared by all members of that system. The Fund's Interim Committee is so far the only body capable of mobilizing this kind of political responsibility and solidarity on a truly multilateral basis. I will continue my efforts to strengthen the Committee's effectiveness, in accordance with the mandate which has been given to me.

3   As the third requirement for a more efficient system, I would like to
insist on the *availability of financing instruments allowing the rapid
mobilization of resources to meet the exceptional needs which countries may face in markets of a global scale.*

Thanks to the intellectual and political leadership of its consecutive
managing directors, the Fund has never hesitated to be at the service
of its members on each occasion the system was confronted with
financing needs of an exceptional nature. On each occasion, these
interventions have been subject to the creation of special facilities: the
oil facilities to offset the economic shocks of the 1970s; the contin-
gency mechanism to protect the balance-of-payments correction of
indebted countries against external shocks; the Structural Adjustment
Facility to meet the special needs of the low income countries; and
now, the Systemic Transformation Facility to assist the transition
countries during the initial stages of their reforms.

Is it desirable to rely on special mechanisms each time an exceptional
need arises? They affect the transparency of Fund operations; they
require special majorities which can often be obtained only at the cost
of protracted negotiations and political compromises; and they create
the impression that the system is functioning on exceptions rather than
on the basis of stable rules. (Over the last twenty years, we have seen
that countries are increasingly exposed to financing needs, not directly
related to the conventional variables which determine their access to
IMF resources. This appears to be the natural complement of a system
characterized by increasing integration, market volatility, and systemic
shocks.) It may be wise to take stock of this development by consoli-
dating the Fund's intervention possibilities in situations unrelated to
its members' quotas.

Belgium has long since proposed to complement the periodic quota increases with an allocation of SDRs to be rechannelled to the Fund for
onlending to countries confronted with payments needs of an exceptional
nature. I am grateful to Chairman Szabó-Pelsőczi for the support I received
from his foundation in favour of this proposal; its implementation would
be directly relevant to the transition countries, since they would be enabled
to continue their integration in the world payments system in the confidence
that the exceptional financing needs which may arise in the process will be
adequately met.

Creating confidence is the essence of monetary co-operation and the key to a successful transition process. Let me conclude by quoting one of the leading persons in this process, EBRD President Jacques de Larosière, remembering Robert Triffin as 'a man working for a world where logic and morality would reign, where international savings would be employed rationally to achieve harmonious development, for a world where the great powers would submit to discipline based on international co-operation'. This is also the world which transition countries expected to discover when they decided to join the international community; they deserve no less.

5 Comments on Minister Maystadt's Statement on the Challenge of Creating a Global Economic and Monetary Environment Conducive to a Successful Transition of the Former Centrally Planned Economies

Gusztáv Báger

Introduction

Minister Maystadt's statement is a rational and, at the same time, impassioned plea for a new agenda for global partnership. In establishing this, the Bretton Woods institutions, strengthened by the new European structures, like the European Union, the European Investment Bank, the EBRD, the PHARE programme, must play a central and ever-expanding role. They must be supported by the responsible co-operation of the transition countries. They must become increasingly responsible policy-making partners and not simple policy takers, without regard to the intrinsic value of the policy choices handed to them. So, when suggesting rational economic policy therapies, the boundaries of political feasibility should be also sufficiently considered. Unfortunately, this is not always the case. In my comments, first, I want to stress the positive contributions transition countries can bring to the needed global partnership and, second, to suggest wide-ranging structural reforms in Europe.

Positive contributions of transition countries

Most transition countries have already demonstrated their commitment to democracy and free markets. They are committed to abide by the rules of the game, seeking political and economic stability, the balancing of their internal and external accounts, and optimal factor mobility to achieve these results.

Their success in making maximum contribution to global partnership depends essentially on two elements:

1   a cool-headed, realistic evaluation of their current predicament;

2   a liberal, down-to-earth global monetary and economic system geared to promote dynamic non-inflationary growth: a system anchored in the original institutions and purposes of Bretton Woods, and not in a system which, in spite of its suboptimal successes, is burdened with a bias for economic contraction and stagflation.

As to the first element, recent economic policies in transition countries tend to be increasingly in harmony with the evaluation and suggestions of international organizations.

As to the second element, transition countries can hardly be satisfied with the too costly functioning of the international monetary system tending towards, instead of discouraging, exchange rates' volatility and misalignments, as well as towards high interest rates on capital markets. These shortcomings were widely pointed out by the participants of the IMF and World Bank Annual Meeting in Madrid this year.

The substance of the malfunctioning of the endogen forces of transition countries is well known. Actually, the surprise is not that these forces existed and in some instances are still surviving. A broad spectrum of pre-war economic thinkers from Schumpeter to Hayek and Keynes were aware of the great shortcomings of centrally planned economies. Economists and public opinion of transition countries had their bitter personal experiences with the phenomenon. Without this dearly acquired knowledge, there would have been no 1953, 1956, 1968, 1980, and 1989. The surprise is that anybody is surprised at the depth of these distortions, at the gravity of the wounds, politic and economic, inflicted on the body of the one-hundred-dred million Europeans in bondage for decades from Tallinn to Tirana, not to mention the 300 million inhabitants of the former Soviet Union. The surprise is that anybody thought the transition process will be a one-day miracle and, even under the best of circumstances, not a long, arduous process of removing the debris of the past and of building bridges to a better future. Here, in this context, I should like to express the view recently spreading in Hungary suggesting that it is more proper to identify the current crisis as both transitional and long-standing structural rather than just transitional. Utilizing this wider concept, we may say that most transition countries have built up the basic market infrastructure and, at present, they step into a second phase of transition in which, together with the tasks of stabilization, the challenging tasks of restructuring (modernization of existing capacities, development of infrastructure etc.) must be solved.

Above everything else, it is surprising that until very recently there were only few efforts made to measure the true cost of structural change. Now, after knowing the order of magnitude of the cost of German unification, we have a better idea of it. One cannot quite accept the suggestion that Germany is a special case. Of course, to a certain extent, it is. Germans joining Germans must require special considerations. But in the wider context, we are dealing with Europeans joining Europeans, and through Europe, the democratic free market economies. They also require special considerations and the sharing of the burden of transition.

I have already said that structural change is costly. Therefore, measures aiming at structural change can be successful only if they are scrupulously cost effective. One of the reasons why German unification is so expensive is that it aims at equalizing per capita output in West and East within a very short span of years. The aspirations of other transition countries are more modest. Hungary, whose per capita GDP amounted in 1938 to 21 per cent of that of the United States, would be probably quite satisfied if her 1993 per capita GDP of $3,500 (see *International Financial Statistics,* IMF, 1991, pp. 109 and 111) representing 14 per cent of the 1993 US per capita GDP of $25,000 (ibid. p. 743), would in ten years time reach again 21 per cent of the US GDP. This would imply an average yearly growth rate of 4 per cent in Hungary and none in the United States.

To finance such a modest expansion exclusively from domestic sources is almost impossible, as the country underwent since 1990 a 20 per cent GDP decline, due to the transition and structural depression. Financing from past accumulated savings is also impossible. They simply do not exist in the required amount. Private capital inflows are considerable but far from sufficient to the country's development, particularly to infrastructural needs. Export-led growth is difficult. Eastern markets do not exist at present, Western markets are difficult to approach for the known reasons. Trade liberalization has resulted in significant import increases, much of it non-essentials, and in a decline or slow growth of exports. There is no export-led growth, and existing trade agreements make it difficult to reverse the trend. In this context, I consider existing trade barriers especially important. Lending by international institutions is significant but bilateral sovereign resource transfers are limited. The limitation of domestic demand is important, but it hardly will improve the trade balance and reduce non-essential imports. The servicing of the external debt absorbs close to

5 per cent of the GDP. *Mutatis mutandis*, the Hungarian picture is not that much different concerning the position of other transition countries.

This is where the second element of the possible significant contribution of transition countries to successful global monetary and economic co-operation enters the picture. Only a liberal, non-inflationary global monetary and economic policy can solve the problems of the transition economies, those of the developing countries, and those of the industrialized countries. This requires stable global foreign exchange markets. The Maastricht Treaty, I am convinced, will eventually lead to a unified European currency, and further pioneering work on the *de jure* convergence among the DM, the ECU, the dollar and the yen could create the needed stability and progress towards a global monetary and economic partnership. In order to arrive to such a situation, there is need for a stronger will to co-operate among the main players of the international monetary system. Further strengthening of IMF surveillance linked to the gradual liberalization of endogen productive forces is needed.

Before leaving the issue of global partnership, let me express briefly my views on two widely debated financial programmes closely linked with assistance to transition countries:

1   an urgent decision is needed on the extension of the Systemic Transformation Facility;

2   also, an urgent and positive decision is needed on the allocation of Special Drawing Rights. I hope that your efforts, Minister Maystadt as the Chairman of the Interim Committee will finally be successful.

Turning to European co-operation, I am convinced that global partnership must be based on a broad European partnership. To build up an efficient European partnership, the consideration of two policies would be desirable:

1   in the perspective of future EU membership, the European structures might want to examine the possibility of increasing their assistance to the Central and Eastern European countries much beyond the current level of assistance;

2   the EU countries might find to their advantage to redeploy part of their traditional labour intensive activities to Central and Eastern European countries.

The first policy would replace habitual balance-of-payments loans by European structural adjustment loans which would better respond to the development need in transition countries now. Such a new Community facility, instead of financing individual projects, would be used for the funding of comprehensive development programmes. Such new instrument would be aimed for facilitating the process of deep-going structural adaptation preparing our joining the EU. Primarily, it should happen through the restructuring of companies, assisting of small- and medium-sized companies, and the development of infrastructure and education. Thus, one of the preconditions of preparation for EU membership – modification of the product mix and improvement of the competitiveness of our companies – would be better satisfied.

As to the second policy, the EU countries might want to shed lower-grade technologies in favour of transition countries, while they could concentrate on the deployment of higher-grade technologies in the use of their economic resources. At the same time, transition countries could use their existing capacities and properly qualified labour resources. Such a new division of labour by both groups of countries would increase the market, European trade would grow, it would be better balanced and, due to these factors, unemployment pressures would be reduced overall, at least, on the long run.

In favour of the second policy, one must develop and follow a long-term strategy helping the realization of continent-wide projects of such magnitude. The development of such a strategy could take place in the framework of a multilateral structured dialogue among the EU and the associated countries.

This suggestion is in the spirit of the intentions and of the principles of the Bretton Woods institutions. We must relight the candle of this spirit, so that in the light of it, we can enter a new age of efficient and constructive global partnership.

6 General Economic and Trade Policies of Transition Countries

Henryk Kierskowsky

An interesting question about Central Eastern Europe is that drastic liberal reforms are often blamed for bringing about economic collapse and deep recession which occurred around 1989–1990. It has been often suggested that in many countries, you should not go rapidly with transition, but rather slowly. This way, presumably, collapse could be avoided. Poland, as an example, demonstrated what happens when you start with a big bang. Indeed, the evidence was persuasive in the first three months of 1990. There was a dramatic collapse of output. In Czechoslovakia and Hungary, the decline in output was much slower. Therefore, it seemed, indeed, at that time, that if you introduce reforms very drastically on a big scale, collapse is inevitable. If you do it very gently, somehow you can muddle through. But then an incredible thing happened. Even in Czechoslovakia and in Hungary, a similar collapse occurred. When I say similar, it does not mean that it followed exactly the same output behaviour as Poland, but if you look at the picture of a period of, say, three years, and accumulate the output collapse, you come to the same numbers. So it was not the big bang that created collapse. It seemed, after the experience has been completed, that the reform period results in the economic collapse. That is a very different proposition. And then we waited for some more data. It has turned out that interestingly enough, in some countries, collapse occurred even before the reforms were introduced. If you integrate results again, you cannot make a distinction between the reformers and non-reformers.

I am referring to a joint study with Net Phelps and Ilfisoega for the EBRD looking at the sources of economic collapse in Eastern Europe. Therefore, I come to the conclusion that the mechanism of growth and collapse occurs basically throughout the whole region. In countries that did not introduce reforms, the collapse was just as great as in reform countries, if not greater.

32

The important conclusion that stems from this is that you cannot blame the events of the last three years of world policy. To be sure, you can get individual reforms wrong, you can get the timing wrong, there can be mistakes, no question about this. What we observed in Central Eastern Europe was that the structural collapse of the system started even before the reform process began.

The causes of this collapse did not start working in 1989, or in general in 1990 in Poland; or in Czechoslovakia, in January 1991. They have been at work in some of these countries for four decades. And it is important to identify why this collapse occurred, because if you identified its causes wrong, then the medicine, the policies that might be recommended, could be misleading.

Actually, it is very difficult to say what has happened. There is a famous historian who said that it is impossible to predict the future, but with a lot of luck, perhaps we can predict the past. In Eastern Europe, it is hard to say what has happened, partly because of the data problem and of possible disinformation. In spite of these difficulties, it seems that one of the important sources of the collapse that was at work right from the beginning was that the economies were geared toward channelling resources on an incredible scale, with great efficiency, an efficiency defined loosely here, into specific areas such as heavy industry.

These policies created what I would loosely call black holes in the economies. Once you put resources in there, you are a prisoner of past mistakes and you have to pour more resources and for more decades. Those black holes absorb enormous amounts of resources, including human resources. There is a strain on the economy. Energy consumption in Central Eastern Europe per unit of GNP is twice that of Western Europe. Twice, or even more. The same thing would go for steel. Russia was producing almost twice as much steel as the United States, though the GNP of the then Soviet Union was one tenth of that of the United States. This has meant an incredible waste of resources. All sectors had to be maintained on that basis. We had a situation in which there was an accumulation of inefficiencies. And the system finally collapsed on its own way.

Is this is all structural? It cannot be. There are also macroeconomic factors we must not neglect. It is important to get the macroeconomic picture right. But it is important to identify the sectors of the real economy where fundamental improvements are needed. It is not only macroeconomics but also the structural problems that have been with these countries for so many decades. And that is where reform policies have to be directed to. I find this an important lesson of our study that must be taken seriously.

Now I come to the trade issues which are very important.

The integration of Central Eastern Europe with the West is occurring at three different plains. One is the integration of trade. Second is the integration through joining the international monetary system. The third is integration through foreign direct investment.

We would like that much of this would happen without delay. But change is slow. Maybe it will accelerate. Maybe it will improve. In any case, it is very selective, as to individual countries. However, there is the danger, not universal, but its exists, that foreign investors may be becoming agents of protectionism in Eastern Europe. We want foreign investment in Eastern Europe, so that when they locate production in any Central Eastern European country, their scope of production horizon goes beyond the local market. They think in terms of the world economy. And they locate there because the supply conditions are right. Because there is technology, human capital, skills, and so on, or the technology they bring.

This process could be perverted, if they think, when they move into Eastern Europe, not in terms of the larger regional or the world market but rather in terms of the local market. And when they get that perspective, when they come in, all they want to get is protection. The protection is a price for getting in. And if they get protection, we will be in real trouble. Because we will be creating again black holes in the economy, we will have protected car producers in Bulgaria, car producers in Poland, you name it. I think we have to worry about this. It does not have to happen but the danger is there.

The last point, about asymmetry: trade is relatively important for Central Europe, and it is relatively unimportant for Western Europe. The percentages speak for themselves. If you look down the road, beyond Central Europe, you realize that the asymmetries will not stop there. As soon as Ukraine gets on with reforms – one would hope that it will happen soon – you will not be talking about marginal exporters. You are talking about major exporters. Historians called Ukraine the bread basket of Europe. When Ukraine starts producing food efficiently and starts exporting in earnest, you will not be thinking that this is just one per cent of the local consumption in Western Europe. One must think about how the problem will be solved then. Will you shut them out completely? Or will new policies be implemented then in a hurry in Western Europe to make room for that country? The time to think is now. Now it is easier. There are marginal producers from Poland and Hungary and other countries in Central Europe which are expected to join the EU when the process gets under way. But when you talk about the large countries, Ukraine and Russia in particular, that is a threat coming from the reforming countries. This threat to the system will be real and will constitute a far greater problem than the one we are facing at the present time.

7 Is the International Monerary System Fit for the Task of Eastern European Reconstruction?

Francesco Papadia*

Introduction, summary, and conclusions

The transformation of failed planned economies into modern market ones is a gigantic task whose burden and responsibility falls predominantly on the countries undergoing this historical passage. The premise on which the assigned title of the paper is based is nonetheless true: the international monetary system (IMS) can support, or hinder, this process. The paper analyses the contribution and the shortcomings of the IMS in carrying out this function.

The analysis is framed, in section 2, in terms of demand by the previously centrally planned economies (PCPE) and supply by Western industrialized countries (West) of transition technology, i.e. of the complex series of actions required for the transformation. The analysis is carried out for the three components of a broadly interpreted IMS: monetary and exchange rate policy, banking supervision, payments systems oversight.

As far as *monetary and exchange rate policy* is concerned, the comparison of demand by PCPE and supply by the West shows quite serious gaps in two areas which are at the core of the IMS: exchange rate regime and international trade. As regards the exchange rate regime, the West offered little support to PCPE's efforts to achieve exchange rate and monetary stability. As regards international trade, the West, and in particular the

* Foreign Department, Banca d'Italia. The views presented are not necessarily those of the institution to which the author belongs. I wish to thank T. Padoa-Schioppa for his contribution to define the conceptual framework of the paper, I am also grateful to D. Gros, G. Kopits, P. Praet, and C. Santini for comments and to B. Bossone, G. Godano, S. Giustiniani, C. Mastropasqua, S. Rebecchini, V. Rolli, D. Russo, and L. Zeloni for help in preparing this paper.

36

European Union (EU), failed to grant to PCPE the most important element for a successful transition: totally free access for all they could profitably export. On convertibility, another crucial issue PCPE had to deal with in the transition, there is not much evidence of a gap between what PCPE demanded and what the West supplied: the only possible reproach is that the West could not offer a precise, codified model on how to achieve convertibility. Finally, in terms of financial resources or technical assistance, it is difficult to conclude that the West, and in particular its public sector, should have offered more, given what the private sector can and should do and given PCPE absorptive capacity.

In the area of *banking supervision,* PCPE could find in the West only general expertise and support, not a precise solution, for two crucial issues in the transition: bad loans, jeopardizing the viability of the entire banking system, and the distinction between central banking and commercial banking. PCPE could, instead, find precise inspiration and, in many cases, actual model legislation in two other crucial areas: first, the regulatory set-up to foster the growth of a stable, competitive and efficient banking system; second, banking supervision. The source of legislation in these two areas were the Agreements reached in Basle by the Committee on Banking Supervision and the EU directives established to assure the European single market in the banking sector.

Both in PCPE and in industrialized countries, monetary and exchange rate policy and banking supervision are conditioned by the state of *the payments system.* The apparent similarities, however, end here: in the area of payments systems, PCPE have problems which are domestic and basic, industrialized countries have to deal with issues which are essentially international and sophisticated.

Notwithstanding the differences, PCPE did find substantial support in the West for the difficult reconstruction of their payments systems. The mature technology they need to minimize the serious problems originated by a payments system based on, poorly monitored and controlled, interbank accounts rather than central bank funds was very well present to Western central banks: they had had to deal with a similar problem in a domestic setting at the beginning of the eighties. In addition, a similar problem reappeared as soon as the work of preparing the payments system for the final phase of the European Monetary Union started since, at international level, the use of correspondent accounts is predominant. The choice of PCPE, which will probably concentrate for quite a while on net settlement systems is likely to be different from the answer at EU level, i.e. the linking of national, real-time gross settlement systems. The fact remains that it was relatively straightforward to pass on to PCPE the expertise accumulated in the field by Western, and in particular EU, central banks.

Overall, somewhat ironically, the comparison between demand of PCPE and supply by the West shows the most serious gaps right in the fields of exchange rate regime and international trade, which are at the core of the IMS and the *locus classicus* of multilateral co-operation.

The illustration of the sense, and the limits, in which the IMS is not 'fit for the task of Eastern European reconstruction', carried out in section 2 of the paper, and a comparison with the greater success of European and Japanese reconstruction after World War II, induces to look for an explanation of this phenomenon. In section 3 of the paper, three possible, non-mutually exclusive reasons are mentioned. First, the world lacks now a world leader as effective as the United States was after World War II, and, without a leader large enough to internalize the benefits of a smooth transition of PCPE, there will be underproduction of the public goods this requires. Second, in the present 'market-led' IMS which has not, however, yet achieved complete trade liberalization, it is more difficult to support fledgling market economies than it was in the government-led monetary system prevailing after the war. Third, the problem of the reconstruction and development of the European and Japanese economies after World War II imposed itself more clearly as a crucial issue to be resolved, because of the sheer economic size of the countries concerned and of the vivid memory of the misery which had followed the collapse of the IMS after World War I.

Confronted with a shortcoming, the obvious instinct is to look for a solution but, unfortunately, there is not one springing to the eye. What seems feasible is working at the margin to enhance the role the IMS can play in favouring the transition. Additional moves to liberalize imports from PCPE; financial help in setting exchange rate stabilization funds within economic programmes approved by international financial institutions (IFIs) and, particularly, the IMF; continuous efforts to provide technical assistance and training are useful, but not decisive, steps to help PCPE.

The technology of transition: demand by the PCPE and supply by industrialized countries

When the PCPE were liberated, they expressed a great demand for *transition technology* to transform planned economies into modern, market ones. This immediately raised the issue about the ability of the West to match this demand with adequate supply.

This paper concentrates on the role of the IMS in contributing to this supply. This emphasis, however, is only the result of the assigned boundary of the paper, it does not deny that at the single country level a successful transition from plan to market depends predominantly on what every single country will be able to do domestically.[1] The substantial differentiation of performances of the various PCPE of Central Europe, of the Balkans, and of the former Soviet Union (FSU) that at the turn of the decade started their transition towards the market is a powerful reminder that the fate of each country predominantly lies in its hands.

Still, many of the issues with which PCPE have to deal in their transition have a connection, sometimes obvious, sometimes more subtle, with the IMS. Following Padoa-Schioppa and Saccomanni (1994), an IMS is considered to be made up of three components: monetary conditions, banking and finance, payments services. Each component has its policy counterpart: monetary and foreign exchange rate policy, banking supervision, payments oversight. These three areas will be examined to ascertain what kind of demand PCPE expressed and what kind of supply the West was able to deliver.

Monetary and foreign exchange rate policy

In the area of monetary and exchange rate policy, PCPE had to deal with *five main problems,* to be examined in turn. The *first problem* to confront PCPE countries as soon as they started their transition towards the market was that of *convertibility*.

It is well known that in a command economy the degree of 'moneyness' of money was very limited (Catte and Mastropasqua 1994). Indeed, money, or more precisely cash, was used nearly exclusively by households and was, under any possible definition, inconvertible. One necessary step to transform the monopoly money of command economy into the real money of a market economy was *convertibility*. However, as soon as the discussion on convertibility started, the complex nature of the concept manifested itself (Williamson 1991b).

The first difficulty is that the definition of convertibility, i.e. the ability to exchange one currency into another, is only apparently precise. Indeed, if the 'ability to convert' is interpreted broadly, practically all currencies are convertible, and the concept thus loses any discriminating power: there is always some kind of market in which a currency can be exchanged for another at some exchange rate. The idea, then, must be that the market where the exchange takes place is not too obstructed by regulations and controls. Thus, the problem becomes one of degree: what is the *minimum* of freedom of the foreign exchange markets to speak of convertibility?

The second difficulty is that it is not clear whether convertibility can be defined independently of the stability of the price at which it can be exercised. As noted by Greene and Isard (1991), before the 1930s, a currency was convertible if it could be exchanged into gold at a pre-set price. More recently, the requirement of a constant price has given way to the softer one of the 'prevailing market rate'; still, the idea lingers that if there is too much uncertainty about the price at which a currency can be exchanged for another, convertibility is impaired.

The final difficulty is that convertibility can be defined according to many dimensions (Williamson 1991b; Greene and Isard 1991; Kenen 1991; Borensztein and Masson 1993): first, the kind of transactions for which it is assured (current account or capital transactions); second, the currencies in which a currency can be converted (according to Kenen the term transferability is used if a currency can be converted only into a subset of other currencies, convertibility if there are no such limits); third, the agent which can exercise convertibility (convertibility is defined internal if it can only be exercised by residents as opposed to non-residents).[2]

Confronted with this manifold phenomenon, PCPE countries had to decide which kind of convertibility to achieve, in what sequence with other measures and over what time period.

Closely connected to the problem of convertibility is the *second one*, that of *trade liberalization*. The link is obvious since conversion of one currency into another is the payment counterpart of an international trade. As the 'moneyness' of money in command economies was severely limited so was the 'internationality' of international trade, as this was kept bilaterally balanced. Also trade liberalization required complex choices: should liberalization be *erga omnes* or should, at least initially, follow regional lines?

should it treat differently quantitative restrictions from tariffs? what tariff level should be established? should full liberalization be achieved immediately or in a progressive way? in what sequencing should it be carried out with respect to the process of internal price liberalization and to the introduction of competitive forces into the monopoly-dominated domestic market?

Convertibility and trade cannot, in their turn, be considered in isolation from the *third issue*, the *exchange rate regime*: the exchange rate is the price at which a currency is converted into another to settle a trade or any other international transaction.[3] But the exchange rate is also one of the hinges between the real and the monetary side of the economy and thus the question of the exchange rate regime immediately introduces that of monetary policy.

In theory, PCPE could choose any of the exchange rate regimes: from fixed to purely floating. Analogously, in theory they had all the options available to consolidated market economies for the conduct of monetary policy: use as intermediate objective a money aggregate, the exchange rate, interest rates, a final objective as the general price level, or follow an eclectic approach.

The *fourth*, related problem in the area of monetary and foreign exchange policy was that of the *availability of international reserves*: the amount of available reserves constrains convertibility and exchange rate choices. The availability of international reserves is, indeed, one aspect of the more general *need of external resources*. Notwithstanding the contrary arguments of Collignon (1994), it is difficult to see how the enormous capital accumulation required by PCPE to catch-up towards income levels of the West can be financed exclusively with domestic resources. Attempts to estimate the capital import requirements of PCPE produce very large amounts (see Giustiniani *et al.* 1992). However, as important as the issue of the *quantity* of external resources is that of its *quality* (Goldstein and Mussa 1993). Ascertaining the quality of capital inflows is difficult, but some examples can be made: direct investment, which brings with it technical and managerial competencies, or IFIs' loans, to which economic conditionality is attached, are of high quality; tied help, which forces the recipient to buy goods in the donor country, is of poor quality. Also timing matters for ascertaining the quality of capital flows: money early in the transformation process can be more useful than in a more advanced stage.

For many of the PCPE countries, the problem of external resources had as an integral component that of external debt: on one side, external resources could be provided by rescheduling, or in other ways changing, the terms of, existing debt; on the other side, the sustainability of the overall external situation had to be taken into account in bringing about new capital inflows.

In addition to the four, fundamental issues listed above (convertibility, trade liberalization, exchange rate regime, international reserves and external resources) the PCPE had a *fifth problem* given by the *lack of technical competencies*. CEPR (1990) and Giustiniani *et al.* (1992) argue that PCPE have an endowment of human capital which, in general terms, does not compare too unfavourably with that of Western Europe. However, they have a dearth of skills in those fields which are typical of a market economy: accountants, managers, financial market specialists, macroeconomists, lawyers, and so on. A pressing demand PCPE countries brought to the Western world was therefore for *technical assistance and training in these fields.*

The judgement about the fitness, in the area of monetary and exchange rate policy, of the IMS for the task of Eastern European reconstruction is a judgement about the supply the West could put up against the demand by PCPE in the five areas mentioned above. Elements for this judgement are presented below, following the same order used to examine PCPE's demand.

The issue of *convertibility* has been, from the start, subject to intense study and controversy, with entire books examining it (Williamson 1991a; Fleming and Rollo 1992). The case for extending immediately convertibility to capital transactions was never really made: even if most authors admitted that any distinction between capital and current transactions could not be waterproof (Greene and Isard 1991), the consensus (EBRD Transition Report 1994) was that the liberalization of the current account transactions should come first, followed by that of long-term capital, with short-term capital liberalized at the very end of the process. On the timing and scope of current account convertibility, however, views were split. The argument in favour (Williamson 1991b) was that this was a very powerful instrument to instantly import two fundamental components of a market economy: prices consistent with relative scarcities and a degree of competition on the goods market. The arguments against were, first of all, that the exchange rate may undergo an excessive devaluation; more generally, there was the idea (Lencik 1991) that too much of a good thing administered all in one dose may kill more than corroborate. It was feared, in particular, that firms would be wiped out from the market before they could carry out the reorganization necessary to produce value added.

In the face of the variety of suggestions by economists, what was lacking was a consensus, maybe enshrined in a legal international text. Of course Article VIII of the Articles of Agreements of the International Monetary Fund (IMF) prescribes, as a norm, current account convertibility but so many exceptions to this principle are made (as witnessed by the number of cases listed in the annual Report on Exchange Arrangements and Exchange Restrictions, published by the IMF) that it cannot really be taken as a hard and fast rule, nor has the IMF established, through its action, a custom in this area to complement the imprecision of the written law.

The interconnection between convertibility and trade has been recognized by all the economists, which proposed to set up an arrangement, modelled on the European Payments Union created after World War II, either among all PCPE countries (e.g. Brabant,1991a, b and c) or only among the countries of the FSU (Bofinger and Gros 1992). The idea was to move to transferability (in Kenen's definition) before convertibility and to achieve in a regional setting a more liberalized trade regime. Several authors (e.g. Kenen 1991 and Bofinger 1990) have, however, forcefully made the point that the economics, and the politics, of a payments union including the countries of Central Europe and the Balkans were not favourable, while it may have made more sense among the countries of the FSU, at least on a temporary basis.[4]

As regards specifically *trade arrangements*, multilateral trade liberalization was, generally, preferred to regional, intra-PCPE integration, since the purpose of the whole process of reform was to reverse the isolation of PCPE from the world economy; in the case of the FSU, however, it was often conceded that a preferential intra-regional trade regime could be justified. In addition, many economists argued that PCPE should eliminate all quantitative restrictions from the start but proposed to match an immediate move towards current account convertibility with the maintenance of a limited, uniform tariff on imports, to be reduced on a scaling basis (Kruger and Teuteman, 1994; Greene and Isard 1991). Other economists favoured, instead, a more rapid liberalization on the part of PCPE also as regards tariffs. One unanimous view was, in any case, that Western countries should immediately liberalize all imports from PCPE and that this would be the most powerful instrument for helping the transition.

The variety of arrangements proposed for the trade of PCPE is a symptom of the uncertain characteristics of the world trade system, with the unresolved tensions between regional and global agreements, between the reduction of tariffs and the erection of non-tariff barriers, between the larger and larger number of countries participating in the world trade system and the still numerous, hard to eliminate, sectoral exceptions to free trade (e.g. textiles, agriculture, services).

Against this contradictory background, PCPE countries have not obtained from the West and, in particular, from their largest trading partner, the EU, the one element everybody agreed was crucial: totally free trade. Notwithstanding the great efforts of the Commission of the EU, the Europe Agreements with the Czech and the Slovak Republics, Poland, Hungary, Romania and Bulgaria and the Free Trade Agreement with the Baltic States (see the Annual Report of the Banca d'Italia for the years 1992 and 1993, the EBRD Transition Report for 1994 and Lemoine 1994) do not achieve complete liberalization of exports from Central European and Balkan countries. The two main drawbacks of the Europe Agreements, which overall enacted a broad trade liberalization on the part of the EU, are the limited liberalization of some sectors, protected in the EU, in which PCPE have a comparative advantage and the 'contingent protectionism' implicit in anti-dumping safeguards, the possibility of imposing countervailing duties and, more generally, the room left to discretionary changes in trade arrangements. This last factor must have a 'chilling effect' on exports and investment decisions in PCPE (Faini and Portes 1995) as it can be seen as a possible 'tax on success', to be levied if PCPE exports made inroads on the EU. The discretion implicit in the Europe Agreements has been used very sparingly so far and exports from the associated countries to the EU have grown fast in the first half of the '90s, at an annual average rate of around 18 per cent. The uncertainty effect associated with possible discretionary changes in trade arrangements must have, nonetheless, negatively affected trade flows and, hence, investment and growth in PCPE.

The resistance to complete opening to PCPE exports is not easy to understand, since, in principle, granting free access to the EU should cost little to its members: Central European and Balkan countries are economic pigmies in relation to the EU giant (the combined exports of PCPE represented, in 1992, about 2 per cent of the total imports of the EU) and whatever increase in their exports could not have any significant macroeconomic impact. The point often made is that, since the sectors in which the Central

44

European and Balkan countries have a comparative advantage (agriculture, textiles and clothing, steel and ferrous metals, basic chemicals) are also the most heavily protected ones in the EU, the members states had to limit 'concessions', even if, also in these sectors, the exports of PCPE are small with respect to the overall European market (3.7 per cent of the total EU imports). The point is vigorously and convincingly rebutted by Faini and Portes (1995) who summarize their conclusions, based on sectoral and regional studies, as follows:

> We conclude that the process of trade and economic opening with CEECs (Central and Eastern European Countries) could proceed at a faster pace than envisaged in the Europe Agreements. This would ease the transition in the EAS and would not inflict substantial costs even in the short run on EU producers (p. 7).

In the internal debate between the Commission of the EU, which supported a more liberal approach to trade with PCPE, in particular with Central Europe and the Balkans, and member states, which were more protectionist, Faini and Portes (1995) side firmly with the Commission. In May 1995, the need for a more forthcoming approach towards Central European and Balkan countries, going beyond the trade area, was embodied by the Commission in a White Paper on 'Preparation of the Associated countries of Central and Eastern Europe for integration into the internal market of the Union' which sets the general framework for the approaching between the EU and the associated countries in view of their future accession to the Union.

As regards the countries of the FSU and, in particular, Russia there are, of course, fewer problems in granting free access to the EU market, given the concentration of Russian exports on raw materials. However, the fact that the process of market reforms in the FSU lags seriously behind that in Central European and Balkan countries makes it more difficult to establish free trade;[5] in addition the FSU has a comparative advantage in certain energy intensive sectors, such as iron and steel, non-ferrous metals and some chemicals which are heavily protected in the EU.

Also regarding the *exchange rate regime* there has been no dearth of analyses of what would suit PCPE best. Economic literature has clearly identified all the pros and cons of fixed versus flexible rates for PCPE and both lists are long.[6] A widespread, but not uncontroversial, conclusion is that, if at all possible, some form of stability of exchange rates is preferable, in particular in the initial stages of the transition. One negative reason for this choice is at least as important as all the positive ones: all conceivable options for the conduct of monetary policy look distinctly worse than the one based on exchange rate stability.[7] A money supply target is out of the question in countries characterized by an extremely unstable demand for money because of the financial shocks implicit in the transition process; an interest rate target is even less suitable for PCPE than for any other country: with widespread uncertainty about inflation, the nominal rate of interest is a dangerously ambiguous monetary indicator; the direct targeting of a final objective, such as price stability, is, given the lags and noise affecting the link between monetary policy and inflation, too sophisticated an approach for the novel central banks of PCPE;[8] an eclectic approach is too risky for institutions which have not yet had a chance to establish their credibility. In conclusion, an exchange rate target for monetary policy is, *faute de mieux*, a solution with a strong appeal. The case for a stable exchange rate is so strong that even its most extreme form, achieved through a currency board, can, in certain cases, be desirable, as the experience of Estonia and, more recently, Lithuania shows. The absolute precondition to pursue an exchange-oriented monetary policy is that money creation should not be dictated by the existence of a large budget deficit: if that was the case, the only possibility would be floating or, rather, sinking. Indeed, in many cases adjustment programmes failed, and it was impossible to adopt or maintain an exchange rate peg because of a lack of fiscal discipline which could be attributed, at least in part, to the drastic fall of output and to soft budget constraints in state-owned enterprises and banks. In some other cases it was the inordinate behaviour of wages which made it impossible to adopt an exchange-oriented monetary policy. More generally, aiming macropolicies at a stable exchange rate is one particular way to shape strong adjustment policies, not a contrivance to do without them.

The only opportunity the West has offered to PCPE countries to import monetary discipline through some form of exchange rate stability has been the possibility to establish a unilateral peg towards some stable currency. Proposals have been made to expand, in modified form, the European Monetary System (EMS) Eastwards in order to provide a handle PCPE countries could grasp (Bofinger 1991; Collignon 1993); the fact is that, after the crisis of 1992 and 1993, the EMS is certainly in no mood to expand. At world level, the exchange rate system lacks structure (Kenen *et. al.* 1994)

46

and there is not much PCPE can find in it in their quest for stability. In conclusion, one is led to agree with Mundell's (1993) sharp statement:

> In my judgement, the new countries today are less well served by the IMS than was the case for countries in the post war period. If there existed now a system of fixed exchange rates to which the major countries adhered, as was the case in the post war period, it would be a comparatively simple matter for the countries of eastern Europe and the new countries of the FSU to frame their monetary and exchange rate goals in terms of the international standard (p. 12).

One possible way in which the West could help is in the supply of *international reserves* to be used in exchange rate stabilization funds. Even if a PCPE country states that it will subjugate its monetary and budgetary policy (and wage developments) to an exchange rate target, the statement does not carry much credibility until this is earned the hard way. But the measurable credibility offered by a stabilization fund could make the difference between a hard and an impossible way. In addition, it is very difficult to see how the private sector could provide the resources for a stabilization fund: to be effective, and not too risky, this instrument must be accompanied by strong macroeconomic conditionality which only the public sector, in particular the IMF, has the technology to establish and monitor. The importance of a stabilization fund was clearly illustrated by the experience of Poland where, although never used, it underpinned the stability of the zloty which contributed so much, in the initial stage, to the overall success of the reform programme (on the Polish reform programme see Berg and Sachs 1992).[9] Recently (September 1995) the IMF has concluded that these reasons were strong enough for it to be prepared to support, with its financial resources, the use of the exchange rate as an anchor to restablish monetary stability. The Fund's contribution to stabilization Funds depends on the adoption of strong adjustment programmes, whose implementation is to be carefully monitored.

One other instrument proposed to provide PCPE countries with international liquidity is the creation of additional SDRs (Special Drawing Rights), as part either of a general or of a selective allocation. But, at the time of writing, no agreement was reached either for one or the other. In any case, SDR allocations have, for the purpose examined here, the basic drawback of not being conditional, thus being unable to tilt the balance towards sound macropolicies.

If the provision of international liquidity has been so far insufficient, the same cannot be said for *general financial resources*.[10] First of all, the bulk of financing for the catch-up process should come from domestic savings, in order to ensure an efficient allocation of resources. Second, capital mobility is now so high that private capital flows, and in particular foreign direct investment, should take the predominant role in the financing of the reconstruction and development of PCPE. Indeed, global and free capital markets provide a potentially large prize, in terms of financial resources, to countries with credible, stability-oriented and market-friendly policies. For these two reasons, any comparison with the post-World War II period, and particularly with the Marshall Plan, is misleading in this area.[11] Even overlooking this fundamental difference, however, the financial help provided by Western countries to PCPE does not compare unfavourably with what the US disbursed under the Marshall Plan. From 1991 to 1993 official, gross flows to PCPE (grants, bilateral and guaranteed credits, multilateral credits) amounted to about 20 billion of dollars per year, equivalent to around 3 per cent of these countries 1992 GDP, an amount similar in terms of recipient countries GDP, to what was disbursed under the Marshall Plan between 1948 and 1951. Several sources contributed to this overall result: the financial help extended by IFIs (in particular the IMF and the World Bank), for a total of 13 billion dollars between 1991 and 1993, special multilateral help organized by the EU (Group of 24 donor countries), bilateral help. Among the countries of the Group of Seven (G-7), Germany has shouldered a larger burden than its sheer economic size would have implied: in the case of Russia, for instance, it has provided about 65 per cent of all official bilateral assistance granted by the G-7 countries.

For some countries, an important part of the package of financial help consisted of debt rescheduling, renegotiation on more favourable terms or even outright cancellation, either from private or from public lenders. Official creditors granted relief on over 60 billion dollars of debt for Poland, Bulgaria, and Russia since 1990. Commercial banks agreed debt and debt service reduction for Bulgaria, on over 6 billion dollars of debt, and for Poland, concerning over 9 billion dollars of debt. Overall, 'special finance' to PCPE amounted to nearly 20 billion dollars per year in the 1991–1993 period.

The preoccupation of the West to provide PCPE with financial resources has also had institutional consequences: a new institution, the European Bank for Reconstruction and Development (EBRD), has been created, and the IMF has set up a new facility, the Systemic Transformation Facility, to cater for the special needs of the countries in transition.

On top of these official financial flows, in those cases where investment opportunities were more brilliant (particularly Hungary and the Czech and Slovak Republics but also, relative to the small size of the country, Estonia and Slovenia), direct investment and, more generally, private capital has already started to flow in significant amounts: overall, private gross financial flows increased from 5 to nearly 12 billion dollars between 1990 and 1993, with an average over the period of more than 6 billion.[12]

As private financial flows come normally together with business competencies, so IFIs' loans come with economic competencies, more macro in the case of the Fund, more micro in the case of the World Bank and the EBRD. This is answering the demand from PCPE for the abilities necessary to run a market economy. The conditionality accompanying IFIs' loans is the strongest instrument to pass on *technical assistance* in the economic field to the PCPE countries, but is not the only one. Indeed, the Western countries have done much to supply as much technical assistance and training as PCPE countries could absorb: on top of the technical assistance provided directly by the IMF and the World Bank and bilaterally by individual countries (Zecchini 1994), six international institutions – IMF, World Bank, Organisation for Economic Co-operation and Development (OECD), Bank for International Settlements (BIS), EBRD and EU – have created the Joint Vienna Institute; the EU Commission has organized and financed the Technical Assistance to the Confederation of Independent States (TACIS) programme; the OECD has created a Centre for Cooperation with the Countries in Transition.

In conclusion, a comparison between what the PCPE countries have been demanding in the field of monetary and foreign exchange policy and what the Western countries have so far been able to offer shows two serious gaps: first, Western countries lent little support for a stability-oriented monetary and foreign exchange policy; second, they were unable to offer fully liberalized access for PCPE exports. The gap between demand and supply is less apparent regarding the issue of convertibility: what can be reproached to Western countries is a wavering approach, lacking a precise model PCPE countries could follow. It is, instead, difficult to see a clear gap in the fields of financial help or technical assistance from Western countries, and specifically from their public sectors, taking into account the PCPE's absorptive capacity and what the private sector can and should do.

Banking supervision and oversight of payments systems

Banks and, more generally, financial systems have a fundamental role in the transition from a command to a market economy (Calvo and Kumar 1993): much of the allocation previously done by the plan has now to be done by the financial system. The allocative role is fundamental both for domestically generated funds and for those flowing from abroad. Thus, the reform of the banking system soon appeared as one of the crucial steps in the transition.

In the area of *banking*, PCPE have had to deal basically with *four problems*: 1) *bad loans*; 2) the creation of a *two-tier banking system* (central versus commercial banking); 3) the setting of a *legal and regulatory framework*; 4) the establishment of an *adequate supervision of the banking system*.

The *first problem* originates from the fact that banks financed firms which are now unable, and in many cases were never really expected, to repay. Unfortunately, *bad loans* are not a prerogative of PCPE, and Western countries also suffer from them. In Western countries, however, the problem never took a systemic dimension as in PCPE: beyond the difficult measurement problem (Czech National Bank 1994; Calvo and Kumar 1993), it is clear that the viability of the entire banking system, which makes up the dominating part of the financial system in PCPE, depends on the resolution of this problem.

The *distinction between central banking and commercial banking* activities was not accepted in command economies and the central bank carried out all the rudimentary, commercial banking operations available in PCPE, generally in monopolistic conditions. The issue was, therefore, that of separating, once and for all, the tasks, the powers, the personnel, the balance sheet belonging to the central bank from those involved in commercial banking activities; this was a precondition for the incorporation of commercial banks and their privatization.

The setting up of a *legal and regulatory framework* to allow the development of a competitive, stable, and efficient banking system (Padoa-Schioppa 1994) required, first of all, a broad decision: what kind of financial and banking system to constitute. The choice was between a 'Glass-Steagall' model, based on specialized banking intermediaries, other financial intermediaries and institutional investors and a strong market component, on one side, and, on the other side, a German system, where the universal bank is the dominant player. Beyond this very fundamental choice, a whole series of regulations had to be prepared answering crucial questions: what is a bank? how can it be set up and liquidated? what kind of rules should regulate its actions?

Once the banking system is no longer totally controlled by the state, as in PCPE, and competitive pressures begin to influence banks behaviour, the *regulatory set-up* must include *bank supervision* and two difficult questions arise here as well: which institution should supervise banks? with what instruments?

The four issues just illustrated made up the demand PCPE brought to the West. Which supply did the West make available to match this demand?

As far as the problem of *bad loans* is concerned, the West could offer general expertise for: 1) their identification and measurement; 2) a provisioning and reserve regime to safeguard the stability of intermediaries. This it did through many channels, including the IMF and contacts with the Basle Committee on Banking Supervision. One could not, however, expect the West to offer a neat, hard and fast solution: first, because, as argued above, the problem had in PCPE a systemic dimension, different from that generally known in the West; second, because there is no internationally agreed solution to deal with bad loans but only many national ones.

Also as regards the *separation of central from commercial banking*, quite obviously, the West could offer more general ideas and expertise, including information about the institutional set-up and organization of central banks, than a specific model. In the West, the process whereby central banks have lost their commercial activity lasted centuries, while in PCPE it had to be achieved in months rather than years. The dramatically different time dimension and the monopolistic condition initially prevailing in PCPE made, in many ways, the separation of a proper central bank from the commercial banking system a task without precedents.

For the two remaining problems, *the regulatory set-up* and *banking supervision*, PCPE could draw fully-fledged models from two sources in the West: the Group of Ten (G-10) supervisors meeting in Basle and the EU.[13] Of course, neither the Basle recommendations nor the EU directives were established to create a model for the PCPE to copy: the Basle Agreements were set-up to promote the soundness of banks involved in international business; the EU directives to support the creation of the single market in banking and other financial services. However, PCPE supervisors, with active Western encouragement, are explicitly adopting the elements of regulation and banking supervision established in these two *fora* to create their own regulatory and supervision framework. V. Tesar (1992), of the Czech National Bank, made a very clear remark in this respect: 'Attempting to establish an optimum framework for banking supervision would be risky and even impossible without the support and assistance of our counterparts in countries with long-standing supervisory tradition' (p. 3). Indeed, some of those responsible for supervision in PCPE countries go as far as stating that it is an advantage to start from scratch so that the G-10 and EU models can be more easily followed.

The two sources (G-10 and EU) are broadly consistent in the issues they both cover: 1) capital/own funds; 2) solvency ratio; 3) large exposures; 4) supervision on consolidated basis; 5) instruments used for prudential supervision.[14]

The EU directives, however, cover a larger set of issues relating to other three main areas: 1) definitions; 2) basic conditions for authorization of credit institutions; 3) other issues.[15] Overall, they define a broad model of banking system which is not one of specialized institutions: banks are given substantial freedom to decide in which sectors of business to engage.[16] The model does not prescribe a universal banking system of German tradition, but it allows market forces to move in that direction. One advantage of the EU directives, with respect to the Basle Agreements, is that they can be easily translated into domestic legal provisions since they are drafted from the start as legally binding acts.

Also in the area of banking, a new dimension in the relationship between the EU and the associated countries in Central and Eastern Europe was achieved with the White Paper on the 'Preparation of the Associated countries of Central and Eastern Europe for integration into the internal market of the Union', prepared by the EU Commission in May of 1995. With this document the necessary steps required for associated countries to participate in the single market, including its financial sector, were clarified and a blueprint was established to align the banking and financial set-up in associated countries with that in the EU. The White Paper stresses not only legislative measures but also implementation issues, since, in many cases, PCPE have a long way to go before making even basic regulations completely operational.

In conclusion, it is not surprising that PCPE supervisors have extensively used G-10 and EU components to design their prudential frameworks (Table 1); indeed, the only issues for which they have not followed this model is for market risks, supervision on a consolidated basis and supervision of international banking groups, i.e. the problems characteristic of Western sophisticated banking systems more than of the fledgling ones prevailing in PCPE.

Drawing concepts, models, and actual regulations from the work done by the G-10 Committee and by the EU is not the only support PCPE supervisors found in the West. As is well known, the Basle Committee on banking supervision was set up by the G-10 countries to regulate banks active in the international market but soon the rules for international banks were extended also to banks without large international operations. As part of this broadening of the scope of the agreements reached within the Basle Committee, a series of regional groups were created to establish *fora* where supervisors from a given world region could meet and discuss issues of common interest. One particularly active gathering has been the group of banking supervisors from Central and Eastern European countries. This group holds regular meetings, with the participation of both PCPE and Western supervisors, and has also been active in promoting training assistance.

In conclusion, in the area of banking supervision there seem to be much smaller gaps between what PCPE countries have been demanding and what the West has so far been able to offer. Of course, this better balance could be, to a certain extent, the result of lower demand: the amount of help PCPE countries can expect in a field, like banking, which is domestic in nature, is necessarily smaller than what they could expect in the fields of exchange rates or trade, which are intrinsically international. The fact remains that PCPE countries have found in the West a complete model, resulting from a very long experience. In addition, they found as many contacts, exchanges, technical assistance and training as they could absorb.

In the field of *payments systems*, more than in the area of monetary policy and banking supervision, the world of PCPE is *prima facie* apart from that of industrial countries.

In the industrial countries, payments systems have been rediscovered as a policy issue in the last 15 years. The rediscovery started with a group of 'computer experts who were asked to study the problems related to physical circulation of different payment instruments and systems for electronic fund transfer' (Padoa-Schioppa and Saccomanni 1994 p. 256) and eventually led to the wide-ranging Angell Report (1989) and Lamfalussy Report (1990). Payments systems had always been the untold foundation of monetary and exchange rate policy and of banking but, for a long period, it seemed that all the interesting action had moved away from the lower to the upper, more exciting floors. The gradual, but eventually overwhelming, factor which brought payments systems back to the forefront was that, as recalled by Padoa-Schioppa and Saccomanni (1994), G-10 countries 'increasingly perceived the systematic implications of a rapidly growing network of international payments in a vacuum of public monitoring and control' (p. 256). These developments created sizeable risks which, analysis soon showed, the private sector would be unable to deal with and would therefore inevitably fall onto the central banks shoulders. The intense activity in the area, first within the G-10, subsequently also at EU level, was a recognition of these risks.

Also for PCPE a sound, efficient, and fair payments system is a precondition for achieving a satisfactory monetary and exchange rate policy and banking system, as well as a fundamental component of an efficient monetary system where users are not subject to unnecessary costs, delays, and risks. This is, however, the only evident thing the two groups of countries have in common in the area of payments systems. From this general, common characteristic onwards, the problems take very different shapes: they are domestic and basic in PCPE, they are international and sophisticated in industrialized countries.

The analyses of payments systems in the FSU by Gros (1993) and in Central European and Balkan countries by Hook (1992), and by Baliño, Sundararajan and Dhawam (1994) provide clear examples of the needs of PCPE and lead to three fundamental conclusions:

1   a poorly functioning payments system may jeopardize the efforts of PCPE to achieve a stability-oriented monetary and foreign exchange policy as well as make it very difficult to conduct effective banking supervision;

2   a thorough reform of the payments systems prevailing in PCPE is a long-term affair, but some substantial improvements can be achieved very quickly, even with unsophisticated instruments;

3   the central bank must take a leading role in PCPE in the restructuring first and in the running, afterwards, of payments systems; commercial banks co-operation is, in any case, indispensable.

The problems PCPE have to deal with in the area of payments systems are well within the technology frontier on which industrialized countries are now concentrating their effort. They are very close, however, to those with which Western central banks have dealt with domestically over the last fifteen years. In particular, PCPE have to cope with the problems associated with the use of bilateral, poorly monitored and controlled interbank accounts for settlement of transactions instead of central banks accounts. This creates relevant problems in terms of soundness and efficiency. As for soundness, systemic risks are likely to emerge, due to the delays in settlement finality and to the existence of correspondent risk. This risk can be amplified by the fact that the central bank has no possibility to monitor and prevent them since it has no timely information (and often not even untimely one) on settlements effected via correspondent accounts. Moreover, different velocity of settlements (depending on different bilateral arrangements) may create liquidity risk and complicate the transmission of monetary policy impulses. As far as efficiency is concerned, the use of correspondent relationship may entail higher costs and higher time-lags for funds availability, and this can create a competitive disadvantage for smaller banks.

The problems created by the use of interbank accounts for the settlements of transactions have re-emerged, under an international guise, for EU central banks preparing the final stage of Economic and Monetary Union. To answer these problems, the EU central banks have decided that payments arrangements for the final stage of EMU will be based on the interlinking of national, real-time gross settlement systems (see the Target Report by the European Monetary Institute [EMI] and the 1994 EMI Annual Report). It is, instead, likely that PCPE will concentrate their efforts for quite some time on net settlement systems.

Overall, Western countries, and in particular their central banks, have exploited their past and present experience in the reforming of payments systems to help implant in PCPE the mature technology they urgently need. In addition, the IMF, the BIS, the EU, and some central banks have provided technical assistance and training, including at the Joint Vienna Institute. Furthermore, some central banks have provided concrete support in the design of interbank transfer systems, while three Western clearing banks have co-operated in creating and are now running with 12 PCPE banks, within a Clearing Bank Association, an ECU-linked clearing system whose aim is to facilitate payments between participating PCPE and, by this means, favour intra-area trade and the build-up of closer relationships between PCPE banks.

1945 and 1989: the US and the Western industrialized countries

To shed some light on the transformation of PCPE, economists have been looking at the experience after World War II in Europe: imperfect as they are, the analogies between the war-hit economies of Western Europe and the communism-hit economies of Eastern Europe and the explicit action of the US to build, essentially by institutional measures, an international environment leading to a rich and free Europe and world have attracted a lot of attention.

There was, of course, not a pre-set, rational blueprint the US followed after 1945; however, looking with hindsight, the final result was impressive. The Bretton Woods system, the Marshall Plan, the European Payments Union, trade liberalization, eventually embodied in General Agreement on Tariffs and Trade (GATT), the Organization for European Economic Co-operation (OEEC), then transformed into the Organization for Economic Co-operation and Development (OECD), even the impulse given to European integration all contributed to create an international environment which goes a long way in explaining the golden age which followed World War II.

The role of the various components in helping Western Europe and Japan, and indeed the whole world, to enter into a period of sustained, non-inflationary growth, never achieved before and not repeated since (Maddison 1989), is still disputed and even when a specific component is attributed the merit, the channels through which it worked out its effects are a subject for debates.

A prominent role is often ascribed to the Marshall Plan, even though, according to Eichengreen (1993a) and De Long and Eichengreen (1993) it was not the actual amount of financial assistance which helped European countries get on their growth path but rather its effects on attitudes and expectations. As far as attitudes are concerned, the Plan worked at the margin to convince social partners to concentrate on increasing the pie rather than quarrelling on its distribution. On the expectations side, the Plan gave a 'go' signal to the whole world, thus co-ordinating expectations towards a high activity equilibrium rather than towards a low activity one.

Mundell (1993) forcefully makes the point that, even if in a not entirely satisfactory way, the system which eventually came out of the Bretton Woods[17] negotiations helped the post-World War II reconstruction assuring three important functions:

1   'provide an international money to serve as a unit of account, a standard of value and a means of international settlement' (p. 10);

2   'recognise the mutual interdependence of exchange rates and provide for a multilateral solution to the management of this interdependence and avoid monetary bilateralism' (p. 11);

3   'provide a mechanism for monetary discipline' (p. 12).

Several authors (Kenen 1991; Carli and Peluffo 1994) have emphasised the contribution of the European Payments Union (described in Kaplan *et al.* 1989) to the recovery in the '50s, favouring trade liberalization and lessening the problems of balance-of-payments financing.

   The importance of the recovery of trade within Western Europe, stimulated in particular by liberalization, is one element unanimously recognized as decisive in initiating and supporting the golden age of growth after World War II.

   The existence of differences in evaluating the contribution of each component of the post-World War II international economic environment does not shake the broad agreement that it favoured the era of growth and stability which lasted until the beginning of the '70s, through the promotion of high exports, high investment and wage moderation in a framework of domestic and international monetary stability. Thanks to such favourable environment, the social cost of stabilization was presumably lower than it would have been otherwise; with favourable external conditions, stabilization became an integral part of a growth-oriented strategy. Bossone and Papadia (1993) go as far as arguing that the international environment was the single most important explanation of the fact that the reform and stabilization programme of Italy in 1947 (similarly to what happened in Germany and Japan) was close to being an instant success (Charts 1 and 2), both in terms of growth and inflation, while the transition in PCPE after 1989 has proved so far to be much more difficult and costly, with large and sustained income losses and difficulties in controlling inflation.

When the fall of the Berlin Wall threw on the West the responsibility of helping PCPE to 'reconstruct and develop' the conditions were very different from those prevailing at the end of World War II; a comparison between the two episodes is thus not entirely fair.[18] It is difficult, nonetheless, not to conclude that while the US led Western Europe and Japan, and the whole world, through institution building, to a period of growth and stability, the West has not managed, so far, to do as much for PCPE. The precise sense in which the West fell short, after 1989, of what the US did after 1945 was made clear in the previous section. Here it may be useful to explore the possible causes of this shortcoming.

The first possible cause of difference, vividly recollected by Volcker (in Gyohten and Volcker 1992), is that in 1945 the US was a natural leader: it was economically, militarily and politically large enough to establish the political and economic conditions for the rehabilitation of a capitalist West and to internalize the benefits of a thriving world economy. The account of the Bretton Woods negotiations by Mikesel (1994) clearly shows that, notwithstanding the much greater intellectual stature and broader ideas of J.M. Keynes with respect to those of Harry D. White, it was more often the US delegation that took a world view, while the United Kingdom one, the only other delegation with significant clout at the negotiations, was more often 'obliged' to defend parochial interests. This is entirely consistent with the idea that relative size induced the UK to behave as a free rider and the US as a leader.

Fifty years later, there is no longer a leader as 'natural' as the US was in 1945: European countries and Japan, but increasingly also some emerging countries, have greatly grown in relative size with respect to the US, so much that free rider temptations have begun affecting the US as well; in any case they no longer have the force to lead the world where they think it should be led.

Special factors, such as geographical position and history, made Germany acutely aware of the need to help PCPE's transition. Thus it contributed more than its share to this task. Obviously the greatest effort in this respect was what it did for the former East Germany, but this did not exhaust, as seen in more detail above, its contribution. However, Germany is neither economically or politically large enough to act as a leader, and its contribution, useful as it was, could not be decisive.

The desirability of an international system based on a natural leader should not be exaggerated, however. The history of the Bretton Woods system and of the EMS seems to provide ample evidence in favour of the thesis of McKinnon (1993) that leadership-based systems are inherently fragile, being exposed to the possibility that the interests of the leader no longer coincide with those of the followers.[19] If this is true, one has to choose between a pessimistic and an optimistic alternative. The pessimistic alternative is that since leadership systems, which can bring about a good set-up for the world economy, cannot be sustained for very long, we have to accept, normally, a sub-optimal IMS. The optimistic alternative is that to have a system which is both performing and stable one must have recourse to international co-operation. The problem with this alternative is that international organizations, such as the IMF or the World Bank, not to mention GATT/WTO (World Trade Organization), are not strong enough to allow the full internalization of the benefits of a smooth and rapid transition of PCPE to growth and stability, and that it is not clear that they will become much stronger in the future. The G-7, as well as the G-10, on their side, are too informal gatherings to carry out effectively any joint leadership action.

In a way, the institution which came closest to performing the function of 'specialized leader' for supporting the transition of PCPE was the EU. If the US finds it difficult to behave as a global leader, this role is even more difficult for the EU, but, given the European slant of the PCPE problem, one could have imagined that it could have taken up a limited leadership role in this area. As seen above, particularly under the impulse of the Commission and Germany, the EU went close to taking this role, even with the encouragement of the US and Japan, as witnessed for example by its leading role in the PHARE project.[20] Its leadership, however, was neither strong nor broad enough. The objective reasons for this are not difficult to find. A strong leadership role would have required the ability to offset costs in one sector, or geographical area, with advantages in another: say an opening to PCPE agricultural products against a lower immigration pressure from these countries, or generous help in achieving macroeconomic stability against the advantages of economically and socially stable partners. However, these offsets are extremely difficult to achieve in a set-up in which the EU institutions have very heterogeneous responsibilities and powers in the various sectors and a limited capacity to favour side-payments, or other forms of compensation, between member countries. In a way, the EU was, and still is, not united enough to carry out its leadership function towards PCPE's transition. The experience with association agreements with Central and Eastern European countries, described above, is significant in this respect: the Commission of the EU insisted for a more liberal approach while most member states pressed for maintaining some degree of protection for EU producers.

The second reason of difference between the situation in 1945 and that in 1989 is that while the government-led IMS (Padoa-Schioppa and Saccomanni 1994) prevailing after World War II intrinsically required management, the market-led IMS now prevailing counts much more on an invisible hand co-ordinating individual actions. Still, in the international scene, no less than in the domestic one, there are plenty of externalities which have to be dealt with by some form of public organization. A gap has emerged between the increasingly international attitude and mode of operations of private operators and the predominantly domestic one of public bodies, and in particular of central banks.

The institutional gap in the world economy has manifested itself in a particularly worrying way, as regards the PCPE's transition, as an asymmetry in the degree of internationalization and liberalization of financial versus real goods markets, compounded by the weakness of international organizations in addressing this asymmetry. The power of the invisible hand is weaker, and the need of a leader more acute, the less competitive are markets, say because of the hindrances of protectionist measures. In a way, the half-way house between a market-led IMS and a world trade system still riddled by protectionist tendencies has proved inhospital for PCPE as the co-ordinating function was carried out neither by a leader nor by a free and competitive market. After World War II, the US reconstructed the conditions for world trade and put stability in the fledgling world financial system through the Bretton Woods instruments and, in particular, through the parity regime for exchange rates. In 1989, PCPE found a world of floating exchange rates, very high capital mobility and not fully liberalized international trade that nobody was in a position to adapt to their specific needs.

The third reason of difference is that the need to support, through international action, the reconstruction and development of Western Europe and Japan was so obvious, and the memory of the misery which had followed the inability to do so after World War I so vivid, that all the minds and souls were fixed on that objective in 1945. The large economic and political size of Europe and Japan was an additional, powerful factor which induced to create an IMS instrumental to their reconstruction and development. The responsibility for the task of helping PCPE is not now so strongly felt in Western public opinion which is, after all, the master of governments. The possibility of a long-drawn and painful transition of PCPE, seen as a somewhat peripheral area of the world, has not created enough concern in Western countries to oblige them to act more forcefully.

Notes

1. On the integration of PCPE in the international monetary system, see Portes, 1993.
2. For a short but comprehensive analysis of the convertibility problem of PCPE, see Portes, 1991.
3. Article XV.4 of GATT provides that one cannot frustrate by trade actions the content of the provisions of the Articles of Agreement of IMF and vice versa.
4. On the usefulness of a payments union for PCPE, see also Eichengreen, 1993b and Rosati, 1991.
5. On the reform process in Russia, see Giustiniani and Rebecchini, 1994.
6. Exhaustive and perceptive analysis of the issue are in Bofinger (1991), in Williamson (1991b), in Borensztein and Masson (1993), in Villanueva (1993), in Kroger and Teuteman (1994); the general issue of an exchange rate anchor in disinflation programmes is illustrated in Ades *et al.*, (1994).
7. The argument is very close to that developed by Kenen (1994) whereby stable exchange rates may be desirable not because they are the best instrument for adjustment but because they allow importing a better monetary policy.
8. Witness the care and effort exercised by the Bank of England to make its price-stability-oriented monetary policy concrete, credible, and precise.
9. On the Hungarian experience, see Kopits, 1995.
10. A comprehensive illustration of the financial inflows into PCPE is in Economic Commission for Europe (1994), which is the source for the figures quoted below.
11. See Eichengreen and Uzan, 1992.
12. For a comprehensive illustration of foreign direct investment, see the EBRD Transition Report for 1994 which notices that, with the improvement in economic conditions in a larger number of countries than achieved so far, foreign direct investment to the area could increase considerably.
13. See Basle Committee on Banking Supervision, 1992.
14. The sources for the regulations in the various area are the following: 1) '1988 Basle Capital Accord' and Dir. 89/299/EEC; 2.) '1988 Basle Capital Accord' and Dir. 89/647/EEC; 3.) 'Measuring and controlling large credit exposures' – Basle, March 1990 and Dir. 92/121/EEC; 4) 'Concordat' – Basle, May 1983; 'Minimum standard for the supervision of international banking groups and their cross border establishments', April 1992 and Dir. 92/30/EEC; 5) Market risks – 'The supervisory treatment of market risks' – Basle April 1993 and Dir. 93/6/EEC; Holdings in Commercial undertakings – Dir. 89/646/EEC; Quality of the structural organization and internal control mechanisms – 'Risk management guidelines for derivatives' – Basle, July 1994; Dir.s 77/780/EEC; 89/646/EEC and 92/30/EEC.
15. The sources for the regulations in the various area are the following: 1) Definition of 'credit institution' – Dir. 77/780/EEC; Definition of 'banking business' – Dir. 89/646/EEC; Restriction of banking business to credit institutions – Dir. 89/646/EEC;

2) Authorization shall be granted only when a specific list of conditions is complied with – Dir. 77/780/EEC and 89/646/EEC; Authorization may soon be subjected to further prudential criteria – Common Position CE 24/94; 3) Deposit Protection – Dir. 94/19/EC; Money laundering – Dir. 91/308/EEC.

16. The model characterized by low specialization between intermediaries seems to be prevalent at world level: of the 114 countries answering a questionnaire prepared before the eighth International Conference on Bank Supervisors (Vienna, October 1994) 75 per cent imposed no regulatory barriers between commercial and investment banking, 43 per cent imposed no barriers between banking and securities activity.
17. On the Bretton Woods system, see Bergsten *et al.* (1993) and the other papers in the book edited by Bordo and Eichengreen (1993).
18. Dornbusch *et al.*, 1993 and Eichengreen, 1993c.
19. A historical confirmation of this thesis can be found in the breakdown of the Austro-Hungarian monetary system after World War 1 (Dornbusch 1992 and Garber and Spencer 1994).
20. The PHARE programme (Poland-Hungary Assistance for Reconstruction of the Economy) was initially set up by the EU to provide financial assistance to Poland and Hungary and then extended to cover the other economies in transition with the participation of the other industrialized countries.

References

Alberto F. Ades, Miguel A. Kiguel and Nissan Liviatan, *Disinflation without Output Decline. Tales of Exchange Rate Based Stabilizations*, paper presented at a IIASA conference on 'Output Decline in Eastern Europe: Prospects for Recovery?', June, 1994.

Tomas Baliño, V. Sundararajan and Juhi Dhawan, *Features Payments System and Price Reforms in Transition Economies*, IMF Staff Papers, September, 1994.

Basle Committee on Banking Supervision, *Report on International Developments in Banking Supervision*, Report No. 8, Bank for International Settlements, Basle, September, 1992.

Andrew Berg and Jeffrey Sachs, *Structural adjustment and international trade in Eastern Europe: the case of Poland*, in 'Economic Policy: a European Forum', No. 14 April, pp. 118–173, Press Syndicate of the University of Cambridge, Cambridge, 1992.

C. Fred Bergsten, Martin Feldstein, Stanley Fischer, Ronald McKinnon and Robert Mundell, *Implications for International Monetary Reform*, in M.D. Bordo and B. Eichengreen (eds.), 'A Retrospective on the Bretton Woods System', The University of Chicago Press, Chicago, 1993.

Peter Bofinger, *A Multilateral Payments Union for Eastern Europe?*, CEPR Discussion Paper No. 458, London, 1990.

——, *The Transition to Convertibility in Eastern Europe: A Monetary View*, in J. Williamson (ed.), 'Currency Convertibility in Eastern Europe', Institute for International Economics, Washington DC, 1991.

Peter Bofinger and Daniel Gros, *A post-Soviet payments union: why and how*, in J. Fleming and J.M.C. Rollo (eds.), 'Trade, Payments and adjustment in Central and Eastern Europe', RIIA and EBRD, 1992.

Michael D. Bordo and Barry Eichengreen (eds.), *A Retrospective on the Bretton Woods System*, The University of Chicago Press, Chicago, 1993.

Edoardo Borensztein and Paul R. Masson, *Exchange rate arrangements of PCPEs*, in 'Financial sector reforms and exchange arrangements in Eastern Europe', IMF Occasional Paper 102, February, 1993.

Biagio Bossone and Francesco Papadia, *Stability and Credibility in the Transition Process of the Previously Centrally Planned Economies: a Comparison with the Postwar Italian Experience*, in H. Herr, S. Tober and A. Westphal (eds.), 'Macroeconomic Problems of Transformation', E. Elgar, England, 1993.

J. M. von Brabant, *Convertibility in Eastern Europe Through a Payments Union*, in J. Williamson (ed.), 'Currency Convertibility in Eastern Europe', Institute for International Economics, Washington DC, 1991a.

——, *A Central European Payments Union: Technical Aspects*, Institute for East-West Security Studies, New York-Prague, 1991b.

——, *Integrating Eastern Europe into the Global Economy: Convertibility through a Payments Union*, Kluwer Academic Publishers, Dordrecht-Boston-London, 1991c.

Guillermo A. Calvo and Manmohan S. Kumar, *Financial markets and intermediation*, in 'Financial sector reforms and exchange arrangements in Eastern Europe', IMF Occasional Paper 102, February, 1993.

Centre for Economic Policy Research, *The impact of Eastern Europe*, in 'Monitoring European Integration', CEPR, October, 1990.

Stephan Collignon, *Economic Transformation and the Integration of Central and Eastern Europe in the European Community*, in W. Gebauer (ed.), 'Foundations of European Central Bank Policy', Physica-Verlag, Germany, 1993.

——, *From stabilization to growth: reconsidering trade and foreign investment*, in H. Herr, S. Tober and A. Westphal (eds.), 'Macroeconomic problems of transition', E. Elgar, London, 1994.

Czech National Bank, *The Transformation of the Czech Banking Sector, Recapitalisation, the Issue of Bad Credits*, mimeo, 1994.

Bradford J. De Long and Barry Eichengreen, *The Marshall Plan: history's most successful structural adjustment program*, in R. Dornbusch, *et al* (eds.), 'Postwar Economic Reconstruction and Lessons for the East Today', The MIT Press, Cambridge, Mass., 1993.

Rudiger Dornbusch, *Monetary problems of post-communism: Lessons from the end of the Austro-Hungarian Empire*, Weltwirtschaftliches Arkiv, pp. 391-424, vol.128, No.3, 1992.

Rudiger Dornbusch, Peter R.G. Layard, and Wilhelm Nölling (eds.), *Postwar Economic Reconstruction and Lessons for the East Today*, The MIT Press, Cambridge, Mass., 1993.

Barry Eichengreen, *Institutions and Economic Growth: Europe after World War II*, paper presented at a CEPR conference 'The Economic Performance of Europe After the Second World War', Oxford, December, 1993a.

——, *A Payments Mechanism for the Former Soviet Union: Is the EPU a Relevant Precedent?*, CEPR Discussion Paper No. 824, 1993b.

——, *A Marshall plan for the East: options for 1993*, Working Paper No. C93-010, Center for International and Development Economics Research, University of California at Berkeley, February, 1993c.

Barry Eichengreen and Marc Uzan, *The Marshall Plan: economic effects and implications for Eastern Europe and the former USSR*, in ' Economic Policy: a European Forum', No. 14 April, Press Syndicate of the University of Cambridge, Cambridge, 1992.

European Bank for Reconstruction and Development, *Transition Report*, London, October 1994.

European Monetary Institute, 'Report on the TARGET System', Frankfurt, 1995.

——, 'Annual Report', Frankfurt, April, 1995.

Riccardo Faini and Richard Portes, *European Union Trade with Eastern Europe: Adjustment and Opportunities*, CEPR, London, 1995.

John Fleming and J.M.C. Rollo (eds.), *Trade, Payments and adjustment in Central and Eastern Europe*, RIIA and EBRD, 1992.

Peter M. Garber and Michael G. Spencer, *The Dissolution of the Austro-Hungarian Empire: Lessons for Currency Reform*, in Essays in International Finance, Princeton University, Princeton, No. 191, February, 1994.

Alessandro Giustiniani and Salvatore Rebecchini, *Riflessioni sulle riforme economiche in Russia*, Banca d'Italia, mimeo, 1994.

Alessandro Giustiniani, Francesco Papadia and Daniela Porciani, *Growth and Catch-up in Central and Eastern Europe: Macroeconomic Effects on Western Countries*, Essays in International Finance, Princeton University, No. 186, April, 1992.

Morris Goldstein and Michael Mussa, 'The integration of World Capital Markets', IMF Working Paper, No. 93-95, December, 1993.

Joshua E. Greene and Peter Isard, *Currency convertibility and the transformation of Centrally Planned Economies*, IMF Occasional Paper, No. 81, June, 1991.

Daniel Gros, *Mettre un terme à la désintégration monétaire dans la CEI*, in Économie Internationale, La Revue du CEPII, No. 54, II trim., 1993.

Group of Ten, *Report on Netting Schemes*, (Angell Report), Bank for International Settlements, Basle, February, 1989.

Group of Ten, *Report on the Committee on interbank netting schemes of the Central Banks of the Group of Ten countries*, (Lamfalussy Report), Bank for International Settlements, Basle, November, 1990.

Toyoo Gyohten and Paul Volcker, *Changing Fortunes: the World's Money and the Threat to American Leadership*, Times Books, New York, 1992.

Andrew T. Hook, *Managing Payment System Risk During the Transition from a Centrally Planned to a Market Economy*, IMF Working Paper, November, 1992.

Jacob Julius Kaplan, Alexandre Lamfalussy and Guenther Schleiminger, *The European Payments Union: Financial Diplomacy in the 1950's*, Clarendon Press, Oxford, 1989.

Peter B. Kenen, *Transitional Arrangements for Trade and Payments Among the CMEA Countries*, in IMF Staff Papers, pp. 235-267, vol. 38, No. 2, June, 1991.

——, *Floating Exchange Rates Reconsidered: The Influence of New Ideas, Priorities, and Problems,* in P.B. Kenen, et. al (eds.), 'The International Monetary System', Cambridge University Press, Cambridge, 1994.

Peter B. Kenen, Francesco Papadia and Fabrizio Saccomanni, *The International Monetary System*, Cambridge University Press, Cambridge, 1994.

George Kopits, *Midway in the transition*, forthcoming in Acta Oeconomica and Eastern European Economies.

Jurgen Kroger and Manfred Teuteman, *The EMS and development strategies for countries in central an Eastern Europe*, in H. Herr, S. Tober and A. Westphal (eds.), 'Macroeconomic problems of transition', E. Elgar, London, 1994.

Françoise Lemoine, L'*Europe centre-orientale et l'union européenne: du commerce à l'intégration*, in La lettre du CEPII, No. 127, September, 1994.

Friedrich Lencik, *The place of convertibility in the transformation process*, in J. Williamson (ed.), 'Currency Convertibility in Eastern Europe', Institute for International Economics, Washington DC, September, 1991.

Angus Maddison, *The World Economy in the 20th Century*, OECD, Paris, 1989.

Ronald McKinnon, *The Rules of the Game: International Money in Historical Perspective*, in Journal of Economic Literature, vol. xxxi, pp. 1-44, March, 1993.

Raymond F. Mikesel, *The Bretton Woods Debates: a Memoir*, in Essays in International Finance, Princeton University, Princeton, No. 192, March, 1994.

Robert Mundell, *Prospects for the International Monetary System and its Institutions*, paper presented at the ICMBS conference on 'The Future of the International Monetary System and its Institutions', Geneva, September, 1993.

Tommaso Padoa-Schioppa, *Welcome Address* to the 'Sixth Conference of the Group of Banking Supervisors from Central and Eastern European Countries', Sinaia, Romania, February, 1994.

Tommaso Padoa-Schioppa and Fabrizio Saccomanni, *Managing a Market-Led Global Financial System*, in P.B. Kenen (ed.), 'Managing the World Economy. Fifty Years after Bretton Woods', Institute for International Economics, Washington DC, 1994.

Richard Portes, *The transition to convertibility for Eastern Europe and the USSR*, CEPR Discussion Paper, No. 500, January, 1991.

——, *Integrating the Central and East European Countries into the International Monetary System*, paper presented at the ICMBS conference on 'The Future of the International Monetary System and its Institutions', Geneva, September, 1993.

Dariusz K. Rosati, *After the CMEA Collapse: Is the Central European Payments Union Really Necessary?*, Foreign Trade Research Institute, Discussion Paper, No. 18 Warsaw, 1991.

Vlastimil Tesar, *Report on Banking Supervision in Central and Eastern European Countries*, September, 1992.

United Nations Economic Commission for Europe, *Economic Survey of Europe in 1993–1994*, UNECE, New York, 1994.

Delano Villanueva, *Options for monetary and exchange arrangements in transition economies*, IMF Papers on Policy Analysis and Assessment, 1993.

John Williamson (ed.), *Currency Convertibility in Eastern Europe*, Institute for International Economics, Washington DC, September, 1991a.

Convertibility, in P. Marer and S. Zecchini (eds.), 'The transition to a Market Economy', pp.252, OECD, Paris, 1991b.

Salvatore Zecchini, *The Role of International Financial Institutions in the Transition Process*, mimeo, OECD, Paris, 1994.

Table 7.1 Use of basic international principles and instruments for prudential supervision by Central and Eastern European banking supervisors

	ALBANIA	BULGARIA	CZECH R.	HUNGARY	LATVIA	LITHUANIA	MACEDONIA
Definition of 'credit institution'	Y	Y	Y	Y	(Y)	(Y)	(Y)
Definition of 'banking business'	Y	Y	Y	Y			
Restriction of banking business to credit institutions				Y			
Basic conditions for authorization of credit institutions	Y	Y	Y	Y	(Y)	(Y)	
Capital/Own funds	Y	Y	Y	Y	Y	Y	
Solvency ratio	Y	Y	Y	Y	Y	Y	
Large exposures	Y	(1)	Y	Y	Y	Y	
Market risks	N	N	Y	(1)	N	N	N
Holdings in commercial undertakings	N		Y	N			
Quality of the structural organization and internal control mechanism	N			Y			
Supervision on a consolidated basis	N	N	(1)	N	N	N	N
Provisioning	Y	Y	Y	Y	Y	Y	
Prudential reporting	Y	Y	Y	Y	(Y)	(Y)	N
On-site inspections	Y	Y	Y	Y	Y	Y	N
Interventions and sanctions	Y	Y	Y	Y		N	
Supervision of international banking groups	N	N	N	N	N	N	N
Deposit protection	N	N	(1)	Y	Y	N	N
Money laundering			Y	Y			N

Blank space means lack of information.
(1) in preparation

A number of reservations have to be made. In many cases:
- *there are only draft regulations, not agreed by parliament and/or government.*
- *existing regulations are not applied or enforced.*
- *no English translations are available.*

66

Use of basic international principles and instruments for prudential supervision by Central and Eastern European banking supervisors

Table 7.1 (continued)

	MOLDOVA	POLAND	ROMANIA	RUSSIA	SLOVAKIA	UKRAINE
Definition of 'credit institution'		Y	Y	Y	Y	(1)
Definition of 'banking business'						
Restriction of banking business to credit institutions						
Basic conditions for authorization of credit institutions	Y	Y	Y	Y	(1)	Y
Capital/Own funds	Y	Y	Y	Y	Y	(1)
Solvency ratio		Y	Y	Y	Y	
Large exposures	Y	(1)	(1)	(Y)	Y	
Market risks		(1)	N	N	N	
Holdings in commercial undertakings						
Quality of the structural organization and internal control mechanism						
Supervision on a consolidated basis		N	N	N	N	
Provisioning		Y	(1)	(1)	(1)	
Prudential reporting	Y	Y	Y	Y	Y	(Y)
On-site inspections	Y	Y	Y	Y	Y	Y
Interventions and sanctions				Y	Y	(1)
Supervision of international banking groups			N			
Deposit protection		N	N	(1)	N	N
Money laundering		Y				

Blank space means lack of information.
(1) in preparation

A number of reservations have to be made. In many cases: — *there are only draft regulations, not agreed by parliament and/or government.*
- existing regulations are not applied or enforced.
- no English translations are available.

67

Percentage change over previous year

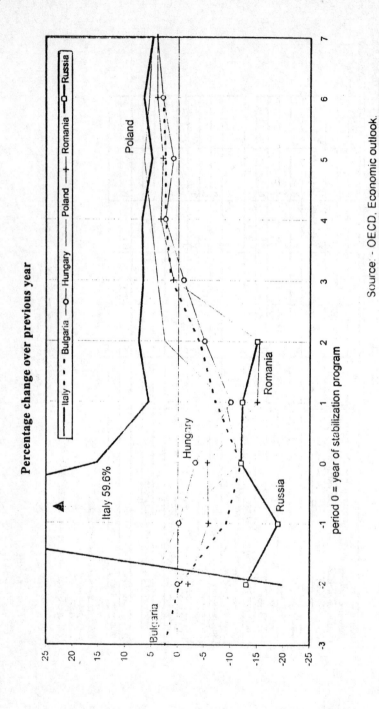

period 0 = year of stabilization program

Source: - OECD. Economic outlook.
- IMF. World Economic outlook.
- ISTAT, Annuario di Contabilità Nazionale.

Figure 7.1 GDP before and after stabilization

68

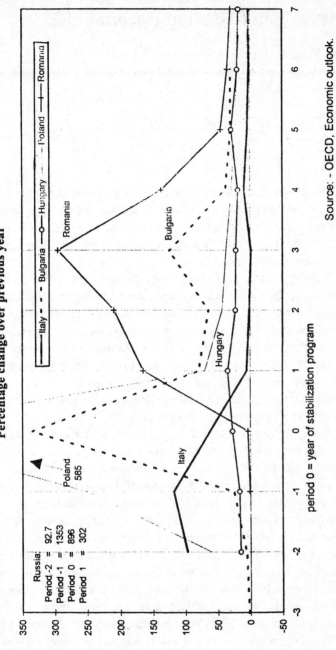

Percentage change over previous year

Legend: Italy —— Bulgaria —○— Hungary ····· Poland --+-- Romania

Russia:
Period -2 = 92.7
Period -1 = 1353
Period 0 = 896
Period 1 = 302

Poland 585

Italy

Hungary

Bulgaria

Romania

period 0 = year of stabilization program

Source: - OECD, Economic outlook.
- ISTAT, Annuario Statistico Italiano.
- IMF, World Economic outlook
* Italy: Cost of living index, average period.

Figure 7.2 Inflation before and after stabilization

8 International Financial Institutions: Their Role in Reducing Uncertainties

Peter Praet

If we want to make an assessment of the efficiency of international organizations in handling this problem, we have to ask the following question: have these organizations contributed in a significant way to reduce uncertainties both in the East and West on the successful and harmonious completion of the transition process?

We know there is often an analytical confusion between risk and uncertainty. Markets can deal with risk but not with uncertainty. Risk can be priced but uncertainty leads agents to follow 'play-it-safe' strategies and conservative behaviour which often lead to vicious circles. In capital markets, we know what 'flight to quality' means. Reducing uncertainty concerning the transition process should be a main objective of international organizations. To what extent have they been successful?

My overall perception is that they did not fare well; but at the same time, I do not know what else could have been done.

In this context, the economics of 'supply and demand for transition technology' permits a well-organized discussion on e.g. how to create a legal-institutional frame which reduces uncertainty on the integrity of (private and public) contracts etc. Discussions of this nature are somewhat misleading because they tend to ignore the obvious fact that there is also a problem of supply and demand for solidarity, for cheap money. A clear public commitment in terms of financial aid would reduce uncertainties.

It is also easier to examine desired demands than to understand how a mutually benefical equilibrium can be realized, minimizing problems of moral hazard and of fairness vis-à-vis other lesser developed economies. We have heard that it was very unfortunate that most West European countries were in a recession when the liberalization process started in the Central and East European countries. I would add that we were very lucky that growth was strong in major lesser developed regions of the world, and that a substitution between official capital movements in favour of private flows was at hand. Fortunately, debates within international organizations on fair treatment have been minimal.

Now, coming back to my main question: have international organizations contributed in a significant way to the reduction of uncertainties? The Marshall Plan was above all successful because it has influenced attitudes and expectations. This is exactly what we should look at. Considering capital markets, we know that open markets can be very successful as an engine of growth when uncertainty on the direction of policy is small. When uncertainty is very large, open capital markets tend to destabilize the economy. This is what we should address when we talk about private capital movements.

But the issue also concerns labour movements: East European countries could specialize either in labour intensive activities or in more human capital intensive activities, which obviously leads to different long-run equilibria. All depends on people's expectations. If the qualified labour force expects stabilization to be successful, then, it is likely to stay in the country. In the opposite case, there will be an export of human capital to other countries. The long-term equilibrium is determined, to a major extent, by people's perceptions. How can they be successfully be influenced?

Comparisons with World War II should not be exaggerated: technically, politically, and culturally, the present situation is much more complex. A process of 'tâtonnement' is unavoidable. What strikes analyists above all is the lack of strong leadership with a clear vision and good communication skills.

For the present, negative expectations prevail. In the West also, most workers do not see the opportunities of the transition to a market economy on the major part of the Planet.

Ten years ago, however, we had only about one billion people on the Planet which was producing under a system of market economy. In the next ten years, there will be four to five billion. That is a tremendous positive change if markets can be organized. But expectations are negative. What exacerbates the problem is that Western European countries are also in a process of liberalizing their economies and of diffusion of technology. This process is in itself difficult to manage: politicians have lost credibility, public debts continue to rise, an increasing part of the labour force is idle, numbers of distortions have still to be wiped-out. The persistence of structural imbalances in the West is not conducive to a positive climate.

71

International co-operation on exchange rates can be very useful. We tend to underestimate the capacity of major countries to co-operate in an environment of acute crisis. What markets really need, however, is a reduction of uncertainty when news are difficult to interpret by market agents. Then is when the authorities have to intervene. But there is a difference between acute crisis intervention which is *ad hoc*, and designing (*ex ante*) a mechanism of intervention in a crisis situation. At present, interventions are improvised, as during the stock exchange crash in October 1987, or in any currency crisis since then. The globalization of private capital markets requires well-designed procedures of action and money. In such a context, stabilization funds are useful in specific circumstances, but should not be designed for constant interventions. Newly created SDRs (liquidity) can be useful in such schemes.

9 Public Policies and Private Intermediation*

Nicolas Krul

General equilibrum, state of expectations, and indeterminacy

Few subjects have attracted as much attention among specialists in international relations as the problems of world economic management. Since Robert Triffin reopened the debate, the number of scholarly publications runs into the thousands, and a complete survey of contributions would require literally millions of entries. Yet, for all the intellectual energy expanded and the huge capital invested, there is no trace of a self-sustaining, cumulative process of theoretical innovation, or even a common agenda to tackle the basic issues. The proliferation of methodological and theoretical controversies, the confusion of terminology, and the successive failures of prediction, in reality, have come to resemble a case of medieval disputation at its worst.

This rather depressing picture reflects primarily the interaction of three intellectual failures. The post-war economic profession has invested too much in vulgarized Keynesianism, barely reconstructed monetarism, econometric abstractions and the corporatist manipulations of *a-priori* assumptions derived from conventional introspection or casual empirical observation, and not enough in the main puzzle bequeathed by Keynes, Hayek, and their contemporaries: the fact that in a world of pervasive uncertainty the very notion of adjustment to equilibrium is meaningless

---

* *Mr Krul, a participant at the Conference, submitted this paper during 1995. In view of Hayek's importance on contemporary professional thinking, the inclusion of this paper at this juncture is more than justified. If global monetary and economic partnership is ever to be realized, not only macroeconomic aggregates must converge but theoretical structures as well. –* Ed.

because the state of expectations on which any equilibrium depends has itself no rational basis. Neo-Keynesians inherited an analytical framework but rejected the doubts which, one year after the publication of the *General Theory* and the restatements of Townshend and Hicks, led Keynes to the introduction of a new central theme in terms of uncertainty of knowledge and foresight. Neo-Hayekians, similarly, disregarded that Hayek, after a last attempt to reconstruct the business cycle theory, turned to the division of knowledge as 'the really central problem of economics as a social science' (Hayek 1937, p. 50). The great majority of economists thus continued to lean on concepts of general equilibrium, perfect competition, and comparative statics and carefully avoided the problems of indeterminacy in favour of a theoretical framework which '... is of little relevance to the real world' (Polak 1994, p. 15).

That bias towards mechanistic abstraction, more often than not marked by a high degree of political and market naivety, coexists with an equally sterile proclivity in political science. Mainstream economics tends to introduce politico-social considerations as a mere static constraint on economic activity or policy, and remains singularly unable to address questions such as how rules or conventions are established, how social dynamics interact with economics, or how institutional structures strengthen or undermine different configurations of economic activity over time. In principle, such questions ought to provide the essence of political science. All too often, however, its practitioners are alien to economic reasoning and, when the real world nevertheless forces its way in, the economic constraints are minimized or converted into subordinate hypotheses. Modern economics, today's society, and current policies are inextricably intertwined, but their relations cannot be captured in a meaningful common framework, or even discussed in a common language.

Finally, the confluence of theoretical degenerations, mediocre performance, and bureaucratic overexpansion has led to a collusive international superstructure composed of civil servants, academics, policy makers, and market participants whose status and stature is a function of the world's management failures rather than the disinterested search for causes and remedies. It is no coincidence that Popper's exception to best-practice science in the 1930s – the proclivity of scientists to evade falsification of their theories through the introduction of suitable qualifications to their argument – became a central issue in Kuhn's explanation of scientific behaviour in the 1970s and neither is it fortuitous that the new type of

74

disequilibrium corporatism emerged when a large part of academics embraced floating exchange rates, turned to financial modelling, and the guerilla between markets and policy makers became another opportunity to create a fair-sized cottage industry or an opportunity for profitable job switches.

Until the middle to late 1980s, these developments raised awkward questions but remained, on the whole, a relatively innocuous set of phenomena. The cold war provided for an overriding security foundation of trans-Atlantic and trans-Pacific co-ordination, US policy options and US dominated international institutions provided for an evident fulcrum, and the relative weight of the US economy essentially shaped world economic and monetary trends. The oil-shock and the ensuring recession revealed a sudden break with the past. But mainstream economics and political science still could focus on the narrowly defined puzzles of their respective disciplines, oblivious to, and without any apology for, the costly sterility of their contribution. National economic policies, meanwhile, merely shifted from national demand management to a process of relative adjustment paced by an increasingly permissive US policy and implemented by means of exchange rate adaptations, liquidity and credit creations, and public debt accumulation. Theoretical sterility and policy irresponsibility thus started to interact at precisely the moment uncertainty started to critically pervade public and private calculations. As Skidelsky notes: 'The uncertainty which imposed mediocre performance on unmanaged market economies applied equally to the effects of government policy. Keynes's disciples, the policy makers of the 1960s and 1970s, could not hold this balance in their minds. They actually did start to act as though they believed that the power of economists over economies was virtually unlimited. This is because they inherited Keynes's machinery but not the philosophy which sets limits to the scope and effectiveness of that machinery. Their hubris was inevitably succeeded by Nemesis' (Skidelsky 1992, p. 410).

The cumulative decay of the domestic economies and national policies triggered a series of minor reactions in the early 1980s. The main impulses for change, however, surfaced only at the end of the decade. For one, the end of the cold war radically altered the security foundations of the international economic order. Suddenly, there was neither a compelling need for nor an evident advantage in the subordination of economic objectives to the preservations of alliance solidarity, to spend energy and capital on the promotion of a particular economic philosophy, or to view global multilateralism as an indispensable underpinning of geopolitics. The shift from cohesive geopolitics to divisive geoeconomics not only exposed most of past analysis as a mix of correlations rather than causations, it also induced a gradual transformation of mentalities which, ramifying well beyond the conventional East-West division, set an entirely new agenda for analysis and conflict resolution. For another, the material foundations entered into a process of mutation. Suddenly, the world economy once again entered a phase of global income, output, and employment recomposition along the lines of highly differentiated projects and potentials but carried by the identical forces of transportable technology, mobile capital, integrated production, sales systems, and the accelerating progress of telecommunications. This recomposition of the real world, furthermore, coincided with the globalization of finance, more and more dominated by a virulent category of instantly transmitted expectations. Unfettered global financial market dynamics started to largely determine national economic policies and the pattern of adjustment. But this dominance was shaped by uncapturable and volatile expectations, moved through constantly mutating channels, and opened on a wide spectrum of futures ranging from functional integration and spreading prosperity to conflictual disintegration and demand destruction.

The current majority view is that the resulting near-total unpredictability can be met through the consolidation and extension of the 'Washington consensus', i.e. through the gradual adjustment of existing policy models and collective management systems on the one hand, and the spread of market mechanisms as an automatic, self-regulating force of 'conjectural realism', on the other. This extrapolative, self-interested concept of change seems at best naive.

First of all, the 'Washington consensus' fails to deal with the now confirmed simple but destructive thesis which Townshend was the first to distil from the economic history of the 1930s and the *General Theory:* '...the mechanical analogy breaks down, as it surely must, if prices are influenced, through liquidity premium, by mere expectations. There is no position of equilibrium. The foundation of theory has disappeared. The future is not merely unknown to the economic man; it is also undermined' (Townshend 1937). The patent failure to provide policy with Archimedean points relevant to the times hence transformed policy making into a knife's edge on which the private sector totters in alternating spasms of acute agony and anxious hope. Private behaviour, in turn, has acquired a defensive bias which greatly strengthens the staying power of deflationary relative to expansionary policies, and generally weakens growth, favours parochialism, and forms a source of deformative tensions in and among the industrial countries.

Second, the main tool of consolidation – preventative monetary policy – is a far from sufficient response. By definition, the preventative effort is a Sisyphean enterprise, any gain of credibility vis-f-vis the congenital anxiety of capital or the disbelief of business and labour immediately raising new sustainability worries, and thence setting a new, more demanding equilibrium target for policy. Moreover, it is a mutually destructive policy. Indeed, while isolated prevention in minor countries may reduce national risks and risk premia at a low collective cost, a collective credibility strategy would obviously end in a deflationary policy competition sharpening both the decreasing returns dilemma and the potential for conflict.

Third, the 'Washington consensus' fails to take account of the widening gap between the tools and resources of the existing institutional set-up on the one hand, and the scope for financial distortions, systemic accidents, and perverse chain reactions inherent in private market growth, on the other. The G-7, the G-10, the International Monetary Fund and the Bank for International Settlements may aggregate impressive monetary means. But that force is dwarfed by the dimensions of the international financial market and notably by net daily currency tradings now averaging $13,000 billion a day, and still growing at a rate of 47 per cent per year (since 1992). Similarly, policy co-ordinations may use more of the modern techniques of control. Even so, its narrowly defined, mostly asset-based interventions – still largely geared to conventional intermediation and burdened by divergent current account targets – are no match for risk-based, leveraged international finance converging with electronic speed on the single objective of short-term profit maximization.

Search for monetary stability in an increasingly fragmented world

There is little doubt that the assumption of evolutionary adjustment under conditions of adequate growth and efficient structural change will ultimately succumb to the realities of the spontaneous forces now active, and singularly to the growing capacity of private finance to exploit the externalities generated by co-ordination failures and outdated structures. Already, it is obvious that the recovery of the industrialized world is more anaemic than assumed under the 'Washington consensus', with long-term projections declining well under the politically desirable and fiscally restorative rate of 3 per cent to 3.5 per cent. Meanwhile, exchange and interest rate volatility remains extraordinarily high, and international liquidity is again rising beyond the pace consistent with sustained price stability. The call for liberal institutionalism, finally, has turned into a policy of vague but costly commitments to existing bureaucracies or into wishful statements that substitute for actual accord.

None of the predictive efforts which combine the information from economic theory, comparative strength analysis, and underlying fundamental trends, however, yield a plausible alternative scenario. On the one end of the spectrum, one thus finds the prospect of global crisis, under which the process of decay generates growing tensions, leading at some stage to a vicious circle, unsustainable inequalities, systemic shocks, and ultimately to a cumulative contraction when price-signalling and price-coordination failures totally destroy confidence. This is the well-known Hayekian view of cumulative disorder formulated in the 1970s: 'Unless we succeed in the reasonably near future in restoring monetary stability, the market order is doomed and with it not only our wealth but peace and civilization, with the most frightful effects on the lives of a large part of the world population' (Hayek, 1979, p. 1). On the other side of the spectrum, we find an extensive collection of frictional shift scenario characterized by the strong dynamics of technological and socio-political change, disfunctional regionalism and private alliances, more creative destruction and partial price-signalling failures, in sum a fragmented world economy constantly exposed to tensions which periodically erupt in local adjustment crises transmitted to an expectational world economy. In our view, this latter type of evolution is the most representative of today's fundamental trends and compatible with the information from theory. It heralds a typically Townshendian future over the remaining years of the century.

There is, furthermore, little doubt that international finance will remain the main dynamic source of actual and potential disturbances. That identification is unsurprising insofar as the exploitation of imperfect integration, information, differences in national conditions and preferences, and of divergent trends in regulations, tax laws, and supervision, has generated an international financial sector of staggering dimensions. We have already mentioned the daily volume of currency transactions. The latter, moreover, are intertwined with a derivatives market whose notional value has risen to between $15,000 and $20,000 billion in the second half of 1994, and the accelerated internationalization of bond and equity markets worth an estimated $40,000 billion. Numbers alone, however, do not convey all the implications. Financial innovation means that risks formerly attached to a single asset (credit, exchange rate, and interest rate risks) are now unbundled, repackaged, and traded separately, on usually highly leveraged markets, out of off-balance positions, and merely backed by on-balance net worth. Ongoing product innovation, furthermore, has been accompanied by a diversification of market participation as deregulation, cheapening data processing and competition blurred the formerly rigid functional border lines in the financial sector. Non-bank intermediaries compete for funds, credits, and assets which previously were the near-exclusive franchise of banking. And as banks found their traditional business base eroded, they responded by diversifying their asset and liability management. Market growth and product diversification thus form a dynamic process which increasingly involves eccentric regions and unconventional participants.

The financial history of the last few years confirms that the risk of domestic and global price-signalling with macroeconomic repercussions have multiplied, and that these can originate outside the banking sector, indeed outside the conventionally defined financial intermediation sector altogether. It also confirms that the power of markets to determine key macroeconomic prices – notably interest and exchange rates – has vastly increased relative to the capacity of policy makers. After all 'lock-in' effects have vanished, interest-rate risks can be transferred or covered, and the markets' capacity to unbundle means that relative price distortions can critically affect official trade-off options. It finally confirms that the cost of balancing adjustment and of the risk distribution in national economies has shifted to a large extent from the financial to the business sector and labour. In summary, the growth of Townshendian uncertainty is aggravated by a significant weakening of the policy capacity to steer and supervise the economy.

The fatal mix of lower potential growth, growing risks, and weakening policy capabilities imposes, in my view, a revision of our basic approach to international economic management. My proposal, in that context, is directly related to my work in the 1970s when I noted that the developments in the Euromarkets had led to '...substantially increased (international) substitutability and transferability' (Krul 1978-1980). It was subsequently

79

first formulated when the market expansion and product diversification process started to affect the relationships between market pricing power and policy, and I proposed to introduce 'co-ordinated policy controls over the volume and use of credit, international as well as domestic, through variable reserve requirements on both bank assets and liabilities' (Krul 1981, 1983, 1984). As from then, indeed, it became evident that as long as markets will not reform and cannot guarantee that '...somewhere in the system a fundamental element of consistency sets limits to its spontaneous, inherent instability', common institutional constraints on credit use for the purpose of malign intermediation should provisionally provide for a second best solution. As such, it represented a variation on a proposal to levy an international uniform tax on spot currency transactions advanced by James Tobin in 1978.

Balance between market forces and policy

The proposal raised – and still raises – questions concerning the balance between market forces and policy, i.e. about the philosophical underpinning, and with regard to operational feasibility. In many respects, these questions are analogical to the ones which stood at the centre of the Hayek–Fisher controversy in the 1930s.

As is well known, both Hayek and Fisher explained the 1929 crisis and its aftermath with reference to inadequate liquidity and credit control and the subsequent emergence of an over-indebtedness crisis (Fisher) in response to relative price misalignments. Hayek and Fisher, however, differed profoundly as to the policy lessons to be drawn. Fisher – and the Chicago school – advocated the '100 per cent solution', that is the abolition of fractional reserve banking by separating pure deposit banking, covered by 100 per cent reserves, from investment banking, i.e. pure savings-investment intermediation, so as to 'divorce the process of creating and destroying money from the business of banking'. Hayek, following the 19th century banking school, argued in favour of a competitive money and credit supply system and price-led self-regulation. For Hayek, there was no reason to assume that governments are able to make superior discretionary management decisions under conditions of volatile and indeterminate expectations, and that any effort to control existing structures and flows would merely drive them '...into other and less controllable forms' (Hayek 1937, p. 82).

Since then, the debate has followed a twisting road and was extended to such issues as the regulatory impact on steady-state wealth creation, the institutional structure, maturity, and risk preferences etc. The basic controversy, though, remains intact, and its arguments are abundantly mobilized against both active monetary policies and the current proposals to extend them to the international scene. The opposition against activism, however, is ideological rather than analytical.

First, advocates of a Hayekian free market financial order tend to present the *process* of competition as a *theory* of optimum price determination, even though competition will merely establish 'a set of prices' and a 'set of structures, allocations and compatibilities'. Hayek himself was careful to note the limits of the relativist assumption: '...all we can hope to find out is that, on the whole, societies which rely for this purpose on competition have achieved their aims more successfully than others' (Hayek 1978, p. 180), which cannot be tested empirically '...because if we do not know the facts we hope to discover by means of competition, we can never ascertain how effective it has been in discovering those facts that might be discovered' (ibid, p. 180). In reality, there is no proof that competition inevitably leads to optimum economic welfare and the most efficient intermediation structure, just as there is no proof that market corrective policy inevitably leads to a loss of welfare and inefficient intermediation.

Second, the 'completion of markets' argument neglects the transition problems, or otherwise stated, claims the perfection of competititon as a cumulative process yielding increasing returns. As Kenneth Arrow pointed out, however, 'perfect competition can prevail only at equilibrium', hence that 'out-of-equilibrium behaviour is necessarily imperfectly competitive', and that thus neither the returns of the process as such nor its final result can be presumed (Arrow 1959, p. 41). The 'completion of markets' argument against policy activism thus simply rests on another misuse of Walras's fictitious models as representative of the free market economy.

Third, the operational arguments against constraints on foreign lending in addition to monetary management with respect to domestic credit expansion are manifestly exaggerated. Clearly, leakages will occur, as they always do, even in the most sophisticated management systems. Even so, common or co-ordinated reserve requirements which discriminate, on liquidity grounds, between covered and uncovered currency lending in the G-10 sphere, would constrain well over 90 per cent of the international leverage pool used for malign intermediation, without exerting an unwanted influ-

81

ence on domestic interest rates or long-term portfolio adjustments. The very existence of a discretionary reserve requirement tool, moreover, would constitute a powerful deterrent to speculative behaviour.

Reserve requirements, stability, and predictability of the foreign exchange markets

Since exchange rates form the Archimedean point of the international management system, reserve requirements should primarily aim at greater stability and predictability of the foreign exchange market. Furthermore, the proposal should at least be compatible with, and if possible supportive of, the policy targets with regard to international payments services and supervision. The tool thus has to be analysed in terms of its potential contributions to exchange rate management and the systemic development of the market-led monetary-financial order.

In that sense, we believe that the proposal fits in the present debate as marked by a disappointing experience with the managed float, the revealed preference for a more orderly exchange rate arrangement, and the persistent uncertainty which surrounds the longer-term economic outlook.

That the floating rate experience has been disappointing, and markets are unlikely to ever behave in the way textbooks used to postulate, is by now a largely shared and extensively documented conclusion notably discussed by Marris, Williamson, Krugman, and Rose. The empiric evidence of recurrent miscalculations and constant manipulation, with evident adverse macroeconomic and microeconomic repercussions, indeed, is overwhelming. That furthermore *de facto* target zones do exist is uncontroversial insofar as G-7 practice is clearly led by negotiated ranges and the current European arrangements are explicitly based on precise fluctuation margins. Finally, it is obvious that a fundamental global reform will be resisted as long as the outlook remains uncertain, even though experience proves that present target zones are too wide to prevent cumulative misalignments, their limits are insufficiently credible, and rules to shift zones or to organize crisis management remain absent.

Common or co-ordinated reserve requirements on international lending, in that context, would serve two main permanent policy goals. On the one hand, it would tend to reverse the trend in international liquidity creation which shifted due to the 1974 decision to let the markets handle the recycling of petro-dollars, and the subsequent failures to regulate the creation of Special Drawing Rights or to agree on a 'substitution account' from intergovernmental management to the vagaries of private demand. This would greatly reduce uncertainty and hence strengthen the credibility of international and domestic monetary policies. On the other hand, it would reinforce the positive interaction between exchange rate and domestic stabilization policies insofar as the implied interest premium required to keep the exchange rate stable in nascent but still inadequate credibility situations would be reduced by the constraining effects of reserve requirements, thereby lowering the cost of adjustment in terms of lost output and employment (inversely, the gains in the still low credibility countries would alleviate the pressures on exchange and monetary management in the high credibility countries). The main contribution, however, would surface in times of unfounded speculative attacks. Experience shows that the use of a parity peg or a target zone invites 'bets' from the markets when these are able to mobilize virtually unlimited resources for that purpose, and that few countries are able or willing to push interest rates to the punitive levels needed to blunt short-term speculation. Reserve requirements represent, in such a situation, a cost-effective tool to prevent cumulative dislocations.

The Tobin proposal to levy an international uniform tax on spot transactions in foreign exchange targeted essentially a similar protection of long-range objectives relative to speculation, and of national monetary policy autonomy. In comparison, though, minimum reserve requirements represent a rather more familiar and flexible tool, liable to be finely adjusted to structural developments and short-term circumstances. Furthermore, whereas taxes imply a cumbersome legislative process and cannot easily be terminated or adjusted, minimum reserve requirements are part of central banking and can be made dormant when reform becomes finally a fact.

International payments services, in an evolution akin to domestic structural development, have generated a complex netting practice within a string of clearing institutions. But whereas national clearing systems function under central bank regulated rules and procedures, and within a homogenous financial and legal environment, international schemes are mainly based on bilateral or multilateral agreements whose enforceability is uncertain, supervision precarious, and lender-of-last-resort support totally absent. The international payments system, therefore, is vulnerable to potential risks which extend well beyond the conventional unfulfilled contract. First, disturbances in one national structure can be transmitted to others under conditions of rising vulnerability to individual and policy failures. Second, multilateral netting schemes in which individual participants retain responsibility for gross transactions are exposed to microeconomic domino effects when a participant fails to settle its obligations at the end of the netting process.

All of this means a rise in systemic risks to the extent that the total amount of gross transactions to be settled is rising relative to central bank money balances and the net capital of the participants (Padoa-Schioppa 1994). More recently, when systemic risk overtook individual risk, netting systems have, in addition, started to rely on implicit public guarantees under which participants reap the benefits, while central banks, and ultimately tax payers, bear the costs in case of trouble.

Central banks have responded through an intensification of co-operation and co-ordination which, from the establishment of the G-10 Group of Experts in 1980, to the constitution of the permanent Committee on Payment and Settlement Services in the Bank for International Settlements, has radically yielded minimum standards for clearing systems and common principles for oversight. By general consent, however, this institutional configuration is neither wholly efficient nor able to guarantee a degree of sustained stability (Crocket 1995). An operational minimum reserve agreement to control international private liquidity creation, stabilize exchange rates, and contain speculative bubbles, therefore, would make for a more secure underpinning until global real time gross settlement procedures become technologically and economically feasible.

Basically the same argument applies to the related field of prudential supervision, where cautious consensus building around common principles and techniques started in 1974 (after the Herstatt crisis) and was deepened in the wake of the Ambrosiano and BCCI affairs. The Capital Accord of 1988 set out the details of a framework for measuring capital adequacy in terms of credit risk. Lately, other proposals aim at the supervision of interest rate and investment risks, and at the extension of prudential rules to internationally active non-banks, notably security firms and insurance institutions.

Hitherto, supervisory arrangements place strong emphasis on capital asset ratios so as to provide cushions to absorb capital losses, incentives to monitor risk and more time to detect anomalies and enforce remedial action before failures occur and spread. However, both the numerator and the denominator in the ratios rely on conventional book value accounting which may understate the effective risks of exposure to price volatility or of malign intermediation ventures. As the 1994 US General Accounting Office report shows – and the experiences of Orange County, Metallgesellschaft or Barings confirm – these risks are not only highly leveraged and opaque, but alien to most management assessment systems and relatively untested under unfavourable cyclical conditions. Moreover, the extension of non-G-10 countries has increased the systems vulnerability to regulatory competition while the market participation of non-banks leaves wide gaps and risks of information hoarding which indirectly affect banks. As in the case of the international payments arrangements, the reserve requirement instrument would help to create a more secure environment until a more comprehensive approach to prudential supervision can become effective.

I have refrained from presenting a detailed model of reserve requirements. Obviously, the road ahead is long and raises organizational and operational issues which can only be answered through a succession of adjustments, first among a small group of major countries, then by a process of widening and deepening. By way of conclusion, however, three issues deserve to be stressed.

First, the growth of the market-led international monetary and financial systems will increasingly expose the inadequacy of the intragovernmental policy focus and the need to adjust monetary management to relations between governance and markets. In that context, reserve requirements are part of a pragmatic, undogmatic approach toward the actual problem of malign intermediation which should cover both domestic and non-resident funding, be guided only by deviations from normal lending patterns, and combined with flexible reporting rules so as to leave markets more uncertain of reserve policy moves (or positively stated, to convey information and to prevent misinformation from taking hold).

Second, the implementation of common or co-ordinated reserve require- ments will gradually shift the institutional balance of policy making from intergovernmental action to the independent central bank and the Bank for International Settlements. This is a welcome and necessary development. For one, it sets international monetary management apart from the other instruments which affect either the distribution of income or the pattern of expenditure. Indeed, 'It is monetary policy alone that is interested only in the level of income and expenditure, and not in its composition' (Holtrop 1963, p. 18). For another, the Bretton Woods institutions – built on fixed exchange rates, official liquidity creation, restrictions, and government-to- government relations – have clearly become redundant, while the substitute

Gs to G-10 groups tend to reflect the political economy of corporatism rather than the imperatives of market-led evolutionary reform.

In reality, the shift to reserve requirements would fit in an already well-established trend. In the areas of international payments and settlements and of prudential supervision, central banks and the BIS have pragmatically moved from data collection and *ad hoc* co-operation to rule production and implementation. They furthermore form the hard core of permanent policy co-ordination and the emerging international lender-of-last-resort function. Since the protection of such essential public goods as systemic stability and the internalization of payments externalities is now largely centred on the BIS and central banks, it is logical to complete and consolidate the network by a means to prevent co-ordination failures and harmful relative price misalignments.

Finally, the BIS is ideally equipped to perform global monetary and financial policy functions. It belongs to the central bank community and has a fast expanding, multicultural market experience by virtue of its agent operations and payments and supervisory functions. The extension of its rule-making and operational co-ordination capacities would thus benefit from an existing base and credibility. In the same vein, the BIS is traditionally sensitive to structural variables, and able to exploit the ample room for informal multilateral or bilateral arrangements when leakages occur, malign intermediations persists in non-G-10 locations, or regulatory competition threatens. The BIS as experience shows, is not an institution to curb market development but a policy maker which should be able to prevent misinformation from taking hold as a compliment to private risk management and domestic policy making.

References

Arrow, Kenneth: 'Toward a Theory of Price Adjustment', in *The Allocation of Economic Resources*, Stanford, 1959.

Bisignano, Joseph: 'The Internalisation of Financial Markets: Measurements, Benefits and Unexpected Interdependence', XIIIth Colloque Banque de France – Universite, Paris, 1993.

Eichengreen, Barry and Kenen, Peter B.: 'Managing the World Economy under the Bretton Woods System: An Overview', in *Managing the World Economy*, Washington, 1994.

Crocket, Andrew: 'Challenges to International Financial Stability', I.C.M.B.S. Geneva, 1995.

Hayek, F.A. von: 'Competition as a Discovery Procedure', in *New Studies in Philosophy*, London, 1978.

Holtrop, Marius W.: 'Monetary Policy in an Open Economy: its Objectives, Instruments, Limitations and Dilemmas', *Essays in International Finance,* Princeton, 1963.

Krul, Nicolas: 'Financial Markets and Economic Nationalism', in *The New Economic Nationalism*, London, 1980.

——, 'Some Remarks on Monetarism and Monetary Policy', in *Coherence on Monetarist Experiences*, Aix-en-Provence, Paris, 1981.

——, *The Debt Problem: A Search for New Financial Balance,* Geneva, 1983.

——, 'The International Debt Situation', in *International Debt, Financial Stability and Growth*, Atlantic Institute for International Affairs, Paris, 1983.

——, 'Exchange Rates and the International Financial System', *Aspen Institute for Humanistic Studies,* Aspen, 1984.

——, 'Apply Reserve Ratios to Control Flows', *International Herald Tribune,* 7-3-1985.

Padoa–Schioppa, T.: *Central Banking and Payments Systems in the European Community,* Washington, 1994.

Polak, J.J.: 'Repairing the International Monetary System: An Unfinished Task', in *The International Monetary System*, Berlin, 1994.

Skidelsky, Robert: *John Maynard Keynes: The Economist as Saviour 1920–1937,* London, 1992.

Townshend, Hugh: 'Comment', *Economic Journal*, Vol. XLVII, 1937, pp. 321-326.

Part II

Are the Current Approaches of
International Financial Institutions
to the Transition Problem the Right Ones?

10 The Witteveen Years*

Ferdinand Chaffart

Five years after the start of the transition in Central and Eastern Europe, it seems essential to step back and assess the progress made thus far. The debate on the adequacy of the approaches currently followed by the international community to support the transition in this region and the need for more partnership initiatives are the two of the major challenges now facing us.

I am very honoured to introduce our guest speaker Mr Witteveen, who is very familiar with the subject. I will try to put his professional career in a nutshell.

After fifteen years as Professor of Economics at the Rotterdam School of Economics, Johannes Witteveen was in politics from 1963 to 1971. In this period, he was Minister of Finance and Deputy Prime Minister of the Netherlands. In September 1973, at the age of 52, Mr Witteveen became the fifth Managing Director of the IMF.

During the five 'Witteveen years', he was plunged into difficult international monetary problems. He expressed his preference for the management of floating exchange rates and for renewed consultations between the Fund and its members. He also gained support for the creation of a number of new facilities (including an oil facility) and for the introduction of new borrowing arrangements.

After the IMF years, Professor Witteveen kept busy with positions at Amro-bank and ING and is still very much the mainstay of things as advisor to various institutions.

That is why, today, we will all appreciate listening to his ideas on international monetary problems.

* *Introducing H.J. Witteveen at the luncheon of November 17, 1994*

11 The Determination and Consequences of International Liquidity*

H.J. Witteveen

It is a pleasure and an honour for me to address the Robert Triffin–Szirák Foundation. I have always admired Triffin for his crystal-clear and courageous analysis of the flaws of the present international monetary system – or non-system, as he would say. I continue to share his central concern about the creation and development of international reserves, although the problem seems to have shifted somewhat out of focus in the international monetary discussions in later years.

The last time I met professor Triffin was in the beginning of 1974 when I was giving a talk at the Council of Foreign Relations in New York. I spoke about the critical economic situation caused by the enormous increase in oil prices that had just been carried through and about the proposals for international monetary reform. Triffin reacted very positively to my talk and agreed with me that some 'management' of floating exchange rates was desirable, and that the International Monetary Fund could play an important role in this. He also pointed up the importance of a solution to the gold-problem.

The international monetary system has two main functions, which are related but still different: the determination of exchange rates and the regulation of international liquidity. Exchange rates are important for the competitive position of different countries and for equilibrium in their balance of payments. International liquidity is important, because it can cause inflationary or deflationary developments in the world economy. Both functions were central to the monetary reform discussions in 1972–1973. But these reform efforts have failed.

* Keynote speech for the Foundation Robert Triffin–Szirák, November 17, 1994.
© 1995 Kluwer Academic Publishers. Reprinted by permission of Kluwer Academic Publishers. In: De Economist. No.4. 143, 1-13, 1995.

Exchange rates, to a large extent, are managed by most countries. But there are no agreed guidelines for it, and the role of the International Monetary Fund with respect to exchange rates of the industrial countries is minimal. With respect to controlling international liquidity, the international community has given up its previous efforts almost completely. The gold-problem has not been solved. With respect to international liquidity in general, the amended Articles of Agreement of the IMF state that allocation or cancellation of Special Drawing Rights should 'meet the long-term global need, as and when it arises, to supplement existing reserve assets in such manner as will promote the attainment of its purposes and will avoid economic stagnation and deflation as well as excess demand and inflation in the world' (Art. XVIII. 1). But this aim has not been met at all.

On the contrary, the dollar standard that developed after 1971 has brought about very large increases in international reserves that seem to be far in excess of any long-term global need. This development was the core of Triffin's concerns. In one of his last papers on 'The International Monetary System: 1949–1989', he gave a table incorporated in Table 1, setting out the different sources of reserve increases over these years. From 1969 to 1979, this table shows that reserves in the IMF have increased only moderately. But there has been an enormous jump in total reserves from 79 billion dollars in 1969 to 845 billion in 1979, an increase of almost a 1,000 per cent! The largest part of this was caused by the increase in gold prices; but foreign exchange reserves – the most liquid component of reserves – also increased by more than 700 per cent. It is clear that once the system was cut off from the gold-anchor in 1971, there was an explosion of liquidity. In the next period from 1979 to 1989, the total increase was only 36 per cent because gold prices diminished somewhat; but foreign exchange reserves continued to increase by 138 per cent – strongly, but not as excessively as in the previous ten-year period. Continuing this table to 1993, we find that the increase in the foreign exchange component was still sizeable from 1989–1991: 34 per cent over two years. In the period of 1991–1993, the increase moderates to only 8.3 per cent (only 4 per cent per year). But in the first quarter of 1994, it accelerates strongly again to 5.6 per cent, that is more than 20 per cent at an annual rate. It is interesting that this recent increase is larger for developing countries than for industrial countries.

These increases in foreign exchange reserves have not all taken the form of dollars. Other important currencies, especially the DM and the Japanese yen have also begun to play a reserve currency role. The share of the dollar in reserves has gradually declined to 61.4 per cent in 1993; against this, the DM share increased to 16.1 per cent and that of the yen to 9 per cent (IMF 1994, p. 158). Fund reserves have remained only a modest proportion of the total over this whole period.

In all these periods, foreign exchange reserves increased more than the growth of world trade values. This is a *prima facie* indication that the increases were larger than the growth of reserve needs. This has probably been an inflationary element in the world economy. Such an inflationary influence is, of course, very undesirable. The root cause is that the dollar system makes it very tempting for the United States to increase its international payments because they can so easily be financed in its own currency. In addition, it is clear that this process leads to very unfair and illogical financing flows, as the rich United States economy is financed by increasing dollar holdings of the rest of the world, including especially the much poorer developing countries. Triffin shows in his table that from 1979 to 1989, net claims of the central banks of industrial countries (mainly United States) decreased by 227 billion dollars; the claims of non-oil developing countries increased by 176.5 billion dollars (Table 1).

Nevertheless, this aspect of the international monetary system has not received much attention in recent years. International discussions about the system have focused almost exclusively on the problem of exchange rates. This is understandable: changes in exchange rates have an immediate impact on real economies; their management has become extremely difficult, so that serious exchange crises have humiliated some governments and caused shocks to the financial system. In this context, changes in foreign exchange reserves were seen as a corollary of exchange rate management; and their function in providing international liquidity remained in the shadows.

But I believe, with Triffin, that the regulation of international liquidity should be an important function of the system. I will, therefore, try to explain the consequences of the present monetary system for international liquidity and for the world economy in somewhat greater detail. For this purpose, we need to see clearly that the development of international liquidity during the last 20 years is part of a process of phenomenal growth in international financial flows. This process started when capital movements were more and more liberated from the beginning of the 1970s. It was strongly stimulated by improvements in financial technology. Advances in telecommunication and computers, giving instant access to worldwide information and risk management programmes have made international investments easier. Institutional investors which have increased their role in the management of savings tend more and more to diversify their portfolios internationally. At the same time, the markets have become more sophisticated, using new financial instruments as options, swaps, and derivatives.

In this rapidly growing financial world, the Euromarket or, more generally, the off-shore markets have begun to play a crucial role. Triffin mentions this very briefly in passing, but he has not shown the critical role it can play in the process of liquidity creation.

The Eurodollar market is a banking market that comprises lending and deposit-taking in dollars outside the United States. This started when commercial banks wanted to avoid American regulations limiting foreign lending. It continued after these restrictions were abolished, because banking activities in the United Sates remained subject to reserve requirements with the Federal Reserve System, which restrains and increases the cost of these banking activities. Because the Euromarket was free of these restrictions, it has grown into a highly efficient and high-yielding wholesale international banking market. It has become an attractive market for keeping international monetary reserves, both for private corporations and institutions and for official holders: central banks and governments. On the other hand, both private and official institutions can easily borrow in this market. Thus the Eurocurrency market has become an important centre of the world's international financial markets. And this market has developed outside the control of any monetary authority. Indeed, the lack of such controls is its foundation, its *raison d'être*. The quantity of lending and deposit-taking in this market is not subject to any direct central bank influence, although the rate of interest in this market (the London Inter-Bank Offer Rate, LIBOR) is, of course, very closely related to American short-term interest rates. It is always somewhat higher because of the cost of required reserves on deposits held in the United States.

The Euromarket, or better, the off-shore currency markets which started as dollar markets have now begun to develop a multicurrency character. Other important currencies: the DM, yen, pound, and French francs, in particular, are also being used for deposit-taking and lending outside their respective countries. The US dollar still forms approximately one-half of total assets and liabilities in these off-shore markets. Dollars still play a dominant role; my next argument will, therefore, be focused on the Eurodollar market. Similar relationships can hold in the markets in other reserve currencies. As Germany and Japan have generally maintained balance-of-payments surpluses, the use of their currencies has not created the same problems as the widespread use of the dollar as international money. In the last few years, however, Germany's balance of payments, on the current account has moved into deficit because of the cost of unification with East Germany. In the previous year, this deficit was financed to a substantial extent by increasing foreign exchange reserves in DM.

The Euromarket plays a very special and crucial role in the present monetary system, which, in a sense, has become market-based. Its freedom from regulation gives it a large growth potential. To understand the mechanism of this market, we can compare it to national banking systems. As we know, lending in such a banking system can lead to money or liquidity creation, because the borrowed amounts will, for a large part, directly or indirectly, be deposited in bank accounts. The limits on this process are determined by the 'leakages' from the banking circuit because a proportion of the borrowed money is taken up in the form of currency or flows to the central bank. Commercial banks, therefore, need to guard their liquidity position; and by controlling this, the central bank can have a certain influence on the process of money and liquidity creation.

The Eurodollar market shows a similar mechanism in the sense that additional loans extended in this market will also, for a certain part, be re-deposited in it. The money borrowed in this market will have to be put into bank accounts – either by the borrowers themselves or by subsequent recipients – and these re-deposits can either flow into the Euromarket again or back into the United States banking system. The latter constitutes the 'leakages' from the Eurodollar circuit. The proportion of these leakages has often been seen as determining a multiplier process, where an initial deposit in the market causes a larger total increase in deposits. This multiplier is probably not very large, however, and it may also be unstable as the extent of the leakages may depend on the spending pattern of the borrowers.

But what is more important, in my view, is that additional lending in this market can very easily be financed by attracting the funds, which are not coming in automatically by re-depositing, i. e. back from the United States into the Euromarket. A minimal increase in interest rates can already do this; the two markets are very close substitutes. And the crucial factor is that the American money supply will then remain unchanged, because the deposits drawn back into the Euromarket must be exactly equal to the deposits which have 'leaked' into the American banking system. In this way, the Eurodollar circuit will always be closed, so that additional lending in this market will not influence the American monetary situation or withdraw savings from the American capital market. This lending then does not form a capital movement out of the United States into other countries, but results in *international credit and liquidity creation*. This implies a very high elasticity of supply in the Eurodollar market (Wallich 1979). In the short term, capital asset ratios probably remain the main limiting element in the growth of this market. Central bank regulations had some limiting effect here in 1991 (BIS 1992, p. 158). The need for Eurodollar banks to maintain some working balances with banks in the United States against their deposits could be another limiting factor; but these cash balances are probably only a quite small and flexible proportion of Eurodeposits.

This is one side of the story. The other is that there can also be an impulse, a push from the supply side in this market. A shift of deposits from the United States into he Eurodollar market can create pressures in this market to expand lending. This can lead to a lowering of the spread between lending rates and LIBOR, to longer maturities and/or a greater willingness to take risks. The causes of such a shift of dollar deposits could be a change in preferences in favour of the Euromarket, for example, by some changes in regulations – or a United States balance-of-payments deficit, which could cause central banks, commercial banks, or business corporations to deposit some of the outflowing dollars in the Eurocurrency market. M.G. Dealtry gives an example when the Euromarket became a 'borrowers' market' in 1977 and 1978 (BIS 1988, p. 11). This was caused by US payments deficits, a reduction of payments deficits of other oil-consuming countries, and relatively slow growth in the world economy. As a consequence, the average spread in the Eurocurrency market decreased from 1 7/8 per cent in 1976 to 1 1/8 per cent in 1977 and 7/8 per cent in 1978. At the same time, the average maturity went up from 5 years and 9 months in 1976 to 7 years and 7 months in 1977 and 9 years and 5 months in 1978. This had important consequences for the development of international reserves and liquidity and for world inflation. We will come back to this later.

The amount of Euromarket lending is difficult to trace accurately. It is the main part of the figures of the Bank for International Settlements (BIS) on net international bank lending (BIS 1993). These figures show increases which have been as large or even larger than those of official reserves, going up from approximately 60 billion in 1969 to 3,600 billion dollars in 1991. In this last year, there was a reduction in this figure, while its growth in the last two years up to 1993 has slowed down considerably (see Table 1). The reason for this was that in 1991, commercial banks became more conscious of credit risks and wanted to increase their capital asset ratios, in line with the work of the BIS to strengthen its guidelines in this respect.[1]

In these later years, a larger proportion of international financing has, therefore, been conducted through the securities market. A part of these securities was bought by commercial banks for their own account, creating a large overlap between the credit and securities markets (BIS 1993, p. 95).

Consequences of the present system

We have already seen that the dollar standard (or more accurately the dominant role of the dollar in the multicurrency system) makes it easy for the United States to finance payments deficits in its own currency. We can now add some further implications of the system as it has developed and trace the consequences of it for the world economy.

1   Central banks of all countries can easily borrow reserves in the off-shore market; and this need not cause any tightening of monetary conditions. A precondition for this is, of course, that they are believed to be credit-worthy. But this credit-worthiness can show large fluctuations because of a kind of mass-psychology among bankers. The debt crisis of 1982 was a drastic turning point when a period of overlending to middle-income developing countries – in the view that 'sovereign risk did not exist' – changed to an almost complete cessation of lending. In this way, commercial bank lending to countries has been a dangerous and harmful element of instability in the world economy. Apart from this factor of credit-worthiness, official reserves then become, to a certain extent, *demand-determined*. They are not a limiting factor on payments deficits any more as they have been under the gold standard.

2   The ease with which payments deficits can be financed *tempts many countries to overspend* either through higher budget deficits, lower savings rates, or larger investments. We can see this in the development of payments balances on the current account (see Table 2). In 1973, the situation was still what one should normally expect: a reasonable surplus on the current account for all industrial countries of approximately 10 billion dollars. But in successive periods, these balances have been negative, sometimes by large amounts. Instead of making part of their savings available for developing countries, industrial countries have themselves been drawing on the pool of world savings.

This was for a large part caused by enormous United States deficits of over 80 billions dollars per year in the 1980s and in the last two years. Against this, there have been sizeable surpluses for Japan and Germany, countries that have not given in to the temptation of overspending (except for the last few years in Germany). But all other industrial countries – apart from these three largest mentioned – have together remained consistently in deficit. This means, of course, that fewer savings are available for developing countries and now for the countries in transition in Eastern Europe, which need large amounts of capital for rebuilding their economies. For these countries, which are not yet sufficiently credit-worthy to borrow in the Euromarket, this is a serious handicap.

3   The existence of such a large pool of international liquidity can be a source of *exchange rate instability*. These funds can move very quickly and in large amounts from one currency into another. Such speculative movements can create currency unrest. This can, in some cases, be an element of discipline when policies are unbalanced and unsustainable. But they also make it very difficult and sometimes impossible for the monetary authorities to manage their exchange rates. Sizeable funds can also move in and out of a certain country, disturbing the internal monetary situation. Thus the massive development of international liquidity in the 1970s and 1980s can now even undermine the power of central banks over their national money supply.

4   The possibility to finance payments deficits in dollars, in other reserve currencies or through liquidity creation in the Euromarket, can have serious *inflationary consequences*. Additional imports or capital exports by the United States, or alternatively by another reserve currency country, or by other countries borrowing in the Euromarket, will in a managed exchange rate system create more international reserves. This will not create pressure in the United States – or in the other reserve currency countries – to reduce effective demand. But in other countries, effective demand and the money supply will increase: so, in the world as a whole, there will be an inflationary effect. If the increased reserves will then not be completely matched by the demand for such reserves, which will have gone up to some extent with total spending and imports, the resulting *reserve ease* can further augment spending tendencies.

How this relationship between reserve increases and inflation works out will depend on the reaction of the monetary authorities. Central banks can sterilize the effect of reserve increases on the money supply by a compensating open market policy, withdrawing liquidity from the credit market. But this will only partially compensate the direct spending effect of a balance-of-payments surplus. The greater reserve ease can then still have an influence on government spending. But as far as reserves are demand-determined – as we have just seen – any excess in reserves can also be eliminated by repayment of loans in the Euromarket. In this way, reserve changes caused by balance-of-payments disequilibria will generally have a clear influence on world money and prices; but reserve changes can also be caused by a shift in demand for reserves, for example, because of greater uncertainty created by volatile capital movements. Reserves could then be adjusted by borrowing or repaying in the Euromarket, without an appreciable influence on the real economy. We can conclude from this that international reserves will not completely determine inflation as the international monetarist approach would suggest. There can be different situations and different influences on world inflation. But besides other factors, changes in international reserves will generally have an important effect.

This corresponds with what has been found in econometric investigations, which have shown a clear relationship between changes in international reserves, changes in the world money supply, and the rate of inflation, although this relationship leaves some room for other influences. It shows a time-lag of approximately three years. This relationship also holds separately for developing countries and industrial countries, but the time-lag was found to be much shorter for developing countries (Heller 1976, 1979; Khan 1979; Robin–Pratt 1981). We can also trace this relationship for specific periods as was done by Professor Ronald I. McKinnon (McKinnon 1982). McKinnon takes two periods in which there was heavy intervention by central banks to brake a fall in the dollar because of US payments deficits: 1971–1972 and 1977–1978. Then:

1   Taking as a measure of international reserves the annual increases of liabilities of the US government to central banks of Western Europe, Canada, and Japan, he shows very large increases of these reserves from very low or even negative figures in earlier years to 75 per cent and 142 per cent in 1970–1971 and 48 per cent and 34 per cent in 1977–1978.

2 As an indicator of the world money supply, he takes the weighted percentage increase of the money stock *(M1)* in ten industrial countries. In these two periods, this money supply then rises by 10 per cent to 13 per cent per year, much more than in intervening years. The US money supply, however, did not increase significantly more than in other years; but also did not diminish as should have been the case under the gold standard.

3 This monetary expansion is then followed by an inflationary explosion in 1973–1974 and 1979–1980, showing a similar time-lag as in Heller's econometric calculation. Among the other factors that played a role in these inflationary episodes were large oil-price increases. But the oil crisis of 1973 caused such concern for the world economy because its upward price impulse came exactly on top of an inflationary movement that was already going on.

Against all this, one could argue that the inflationary effects of lending through off-shore markets should still remain limited because the rate of interest in this market depends on the American short-term interest rate, which is determined by the Federal Reserve with and eye on preventing inflation. But this need not work because:

(a) the American money supply need not increase in parallel with the world money supply, so that a larger increase in the latter does not trigger an increase in interest rates by the Federal Reserve System;

(b) as world prices then begin to increase, the real interest rate for borrowing countries can become negative, while it would will be around zero or slightly positive for domestic prices in the United States. Thus from 1977 to 1980, increases in the unit value of world trade were substantially higher than LIBOR:

	1977	1978	1979	1980
Percentage increase of world trade prices	8.5	10	18.5	19.1
6 months LIBOR	5.3	7.2	10.1	14
US GDP deflator	5.8	7.3	8.5	9

These figures show that real interest rates were clearly negative with respect to world trade prices while they were still approximately zero or clearly positive with respect to domestic prices in the United States. The difficulty is that American short-term interest rates can have a major effect on the world economy; but interest rates considered good for the American economy need not be appropriate for the world economy.

To what extent are these inflationary tendencies of the dollar – or multicurrency system – still a danger at the present time? We have seen that increases in official international reserves have been moderating in recent years. There has also been an important reduction in international bank lending in the last two years. As was mentioned earlier, this was partly caused by more stringent capital asset ratios that were prescribed by central banks. Commercial banks have also become more cautious about balance-of-payments lending after their experience in the debt crisis of the 1980s. Financing of balance-of-payments deficits have, therefore, shifted for a large part to the capital market: bond issues and portfolio investment. This is a healthy development.

Nevertheless, the structure of the Euromarket remains in place. As soon as a need would arise for larger financing than the world's savings can provide, an excess demand for funds may be accommodated in the Euro-market through its credit-creating mechanism. This remains a potential danger. And the US payments deficit again plays an inflationary role as in earlier periods of dollar weakness. The serious and persistent weakness of the dollar since the beginning of 1994 is causing large reserve increases. In addition – as we have seen – just in the last year, the German balance-of-payments deficit was also partly financed through accumulation of DMs in world reserves. Of the reserve increase of 62 billion SDRs in 1993, an amount of 21 billion SDRs was in DM against 35 billion in US dollars (IMF 1994, p. 159). Reserve increases were accelerating rapidly in 1994. This was especially the case in many developing countries. The rapid growth of emerging developing countries is bringing about bottle-necks. Consumer prices in many of these countries are already increasing sharply.

For most industrial countries with high unemployment which are subject to very strong international competition, inflation seems rather far away. But in view of the strong inflationary pressure in developing countries, we should not underestimate the inflationary potential in our monetary system. It seems to me, therefore, that it would be wise to give some careful attention again to developments in international liquidity.

Remedies

Can anything be done about these undesirable aspects of the present monetary system? This will not be easy. The dollar and other reserve currencies offer great practical advantages in satisfying the growing needs for international liquidity. We cannot return to gold as international money. Special Drawing Rights are still less attractive than reserve currencies; and as long as international reserves grow and can grow as fast as they have done, it is, in my view, impossible to see a 'long-term global need' for their creation. This remains true whatever the advantage of an SDR allocation would be for certain groups of developing countries or countries in transition.

But it would be possible for the world's monetary authorities to work together in order to manage the development of international liquidity. The exclusive focus of central banks on their own money supplies can no longer be sufficient in our financially integrated world. It is time for central banks, together with the IMF and the BIS, to set up a *more systematic surveillance system* for international liquidity. In regular meetings of central bankers of countries that play a significant role in the monetary system[2] with IMF and BIS top officials, developments in the system could be monitored and policies could be adjusted in a co-ordinated way to maintain a balanced situation.

What monetary instruments could be used for this purpose?

1   With respect to the growth of official reserves as a consequence of US payments deficits, the most logical measure could be for the US authorities to finance their deficits in foreign currencies in world capital markets. Then these deficits would directly be financed from world savings as they should be, and no increase in international reserves and liquidity would be caused. If this is not done, intervening central banks in other countries can still try to sterilize their internal monetary effect if this is desirable in their national context. With respect to the world monetary situation, there is a choice between investing the increasing reserves either in off-shore markets or with the US government, which has a sterilizing effect.

2   If the growth of the Euromarket would again tend to accelerate, a specific instrument for influencing this market would be needed. As the strong growth of this market originated in its freedom from regula-

tions – especially reserve requirements and deposit insurance in the United States – it would be logical to also apply such an instrument to the Euromarket. Reserve requirements now play a more modest role in American monetary policy than in the past. But it would probably only need a very modest reserve requirement in the Euromarket to take away its advantages compared to the US market, so that its growth would be reduced. This would introduce a new element in central bank co-operation, which is now based on the geographical location of the main office of banks. Close co-operation between central banks would, of course, be needed for this. And off-shore markets in other currencies than dollars would similarly have to be brought under the influence of the monetary instruments of their central banks.

In this way, the systematic co-operation of the world's monetary authorities could lead to a better management of the international monetary system avoiding or limiting inflationary influences. Such monetary co-operation would also be needed to pave the way to the more fundamental monetary reform that was discussed in the beginning of the 1970s. For only in this context can SDR allocations, that would indeed meet a long-term global need for reserves, become one of the instruments in managing international liquidity. Following this path, we could, in the course of time, also come closer to the agreed goal of the world community of 'making the Special Drawing Right the principal reserve asset in the international monetary system' (IMF Art.). When international reserves are properly managed, the role of SDRs could be further enhanced by a substitution account which would enable the exchange of certain amounts of dollars in reserves for SDRs and/or an agreement to settle at least a certain proportion of payments deficits in SDRs (Witteveen 1975). In this way, we could develop a less inflationary, healthier, and fairer world monetary system.

Notes

1. However these figures also include foreign lending in domestic currencies, which is not part of the Euromarket. That category of foreign lending was approximately 20 per cent of total gross international lending in 1991. Euromarket lending would thus be about 80 per cent of these figures for net international bank lending.
2. Besides the Group of 10, this could also include some off-shore centres and large reserve holders among the Newly Industrializing Countries.

References

BIS (1988), 'Reserves and International Liquidity', *BIS Economic Papers,* 22, Basle.

BIS (1992), Annual Report of the Bank for International Settlements, 1992, Basle.

BIS (1993), Annual Report of the Bank for International Settlements, 1993, Basle.

Heller, Robert H. (1979): 'Further Evidence on the Relationship between International Reserves and World Inflation,' in: N.J. Boskin, *Economics and Human Welfare,* Academic Press.

Heller, Robert H. (1976): 'International Reserves and World-wide Inflation,' *IMF Staff Papers,* 23, pp. 61-87.

IMF (1994), *Annual Report,* Washington, D.C.

IMF, *Articles of Agreement of the IMF, Article XII,* Washington, D.C.

Khan, Mohsin S. (1979): 'Inflation and International Reserves: A Time-series Analysis,' *IMF Staff Papers,* 26, pp. 699-724.

McKinnon, R.I. (1982): 'Currency Substitution and Instability in the World Dollar Market', *American Economic Review,* 72. pp. 230-233.

Rabin, A. and Leila J. Pratt (1981): 'A Note on Heller's Use of Regression Analyses' [International Reserves and Inflation] *IMF Staff Papers,* 20, pp. 225-229.

Wallich, Henry (1979): 'Why the Euromarket Needs Restraint,' *Columbia Journal of World Business,* Fall, 1979, pp. 17-24.

Witteveen, H.J. (1975): 'Speech to the Conference Board in Frankfurt,' *IMF Survey,* 28 October 1975.

Table 11.1 Official international reserves and private international liquidity (billions of US dollars)

End of year	1949	1959	1969	1979	1989	1991	1993	end of June 1994
Official international reserves[1]								
Gold at $35/ounce	33.0	37.7	38.5	36.4	36.4	32.9	32.0	
Gold premium	-0.3	0.1	0.2	495.6	380.3	299.1	365.1	
Foreign exchange	10.9	16.2	33.5	281.2	669.7	898.3[2]	973.2*	1081.9
Reserve position IMF	1.7	3.3	6.7	15.5	33.5	37	45.1	
SDR holdings				16.4	26.9	29.4	20.1	
Total reserves	45.3	57.2	79	845.1	1146.8	1296.7	1435.5	
Percentage increase between periods								
of total reserves		26%	38%	970%	36%	13%	10.7%	
of foreign exchange		49%	107%	739%	138%	34%	8.3%	11%
Private international liquidity								
Net international bank liabilities=net international bank lending[3]			59	615	3060	3610	3780	4125
Percentage increase between periods				942%	398%	18%	5%	9.1%
Percentage increase of world trade value[4]				449%	93.6%	14.8%	4.7%	

Methodology according to Robert Triffin.

Sources: Robert Triffin, 'The International Monetary System 1949-1989'; figures for 1991 and 1993 – *Annual Reports* of the Bank for International Settlements.

[2] Including official ECUs.

[3] Tables on international banking activity in the *Annual Reports* of the Bank for International Settlements: net international bank lending, which is equal to total gross international bank liabilities minus interbank re-deposits.

[4] Figures taken from successive issues of the *World Economic Outlook* of the IMF.

Table 11.2 Current account balance-of-payments (including official transfers) average over indicated periods (billions of US dollars)

	1973	1974/79	1980/89	1990/92	1992/93
All industrial countries	+10	-11.4	-48.7	-71.1	-15.6
of which: United States	+7.1	-0.3	-81	-50.1	-87.8
Japan	-0.1	+3	+41.6	+53.3	+125
Germany	+4.7	+4.2	+18.3	+13.7	-23.6
All remaining industrial countries	-1.7	-18.3	-27.6	-88	-29.2

12 An Introduction to Appraise the International Financial Institutions' Role

Salvatore Zecchini

Whether the current approaches of the international financial institutions (IFIs) to the transition problem are the right ones is a highly controversial question which has already aroused opposing views and a wide debate among policy makers, academics, lenders, and investors in both reforming and donor countries. At this moment, I will confine my views to an essay that I wrote recently and is already in the process of publication.[1]

I start by exploring the notion of what is to be considered the 'right approach'. Rightness evokes different dimensions and can lend itself to different interpretations. I believe that rightness should be interpreted here in terms of the appropriateness and effectiveness of IFIs' approaches with respect to a given set of economic and social objectives. As the countries and institutions that have an interest in supporting the transition are different – namely the reforming countries, the IFIs, and the major donor countries – differences might exist among the objectives they wish to attain.

In the face of such diversity, questions should be raised as to what have been the objectives pursued by each of these parties and whether there has been enough coherence between the goals of the reforming countries and those of the IFIs. These questions should be considered not in the generic terms of the objective, common to all, of transforming these economies into market-based economic systems but in the specific terms of the economic policy priorities as well as financing priorities of each party throughout the transition process and the ordering of these priorities at various times in the past four years.

Once the transition began, the IFIs did not immediately adjust their operational objectives to the particular conditions of the post-communist countries. Instead, they approached these countries' economic problems along policy lines similar to those applied to any country in need of balance-of-payments financing or of investment financing, and within the constraints of the borrowing country's ability and commitment to repay these loans at maturity. Still, the transformation of centrally planned economies involves a rather unique set of problems that cannot be assimilated to any significant extent to the problems on which the IFIs have accumulated a large wealth of experience. Yes, China, Hungary, Poland, and Romania were members of the Bretton Woods institutions before 1990, the year in which the transition process began for a number of countries. However, these institutions did not aim in their operations at transforming these countries' economic systems. The IMF, for instance, did not challenge the way in which their economic system was operating; rather, it spurred and supported these countries to achieve and maintain macroeconomic balance.

Thus, when the IFIs started addressing the problems of the transition, they had to go through a learning process and to build experience from scratch. Not that these institutions knew nothing about what could be the appropriate policies for the transition but what they knew was not enough to provide borrowing countries with adequate policy guidance. In spite of their precarious state of knowledge, the IFIs took the responsibility of leading the international community in orienting the reforming countries in their efforts to restructure their economies. To this end, the IFIs have made sizeable investments in terms of human and financial resources in order to bring themselves up to the new task.

The international community of advanced industrial countries called upon the IFIs to perform several roles with respect to the transition. These can be aggregated under three main headings: financing, policy guidance, and technical assistance.

The IFIs' first responsibility has been to make it possible for the transition countries *to obtain the financing* needed to sustain a continuing flow of necessary imports and to renovate their production base. This has been accomplished through two channels. First, the IFIs have directly provided new financing to fill the gap left by the reduction of external private capital flows. Second, they have acted as catalysts to mobilize additional official financing and, to some extent, to reduce the degree of uncertainty that has been discouraging foreign investors.

Policy guidance has generally been effective in shaping reforming countries' policies to the extent that it has constituted a form of policy conditionality which the borrowing country has had to accept in exchange for financial support. Such guidance has been oriented mainly in two directions: the management of aggregate domestic demand expansion and the restructuring of individual sectors, while it has been less pervasive with respect to systemic changes in areas other than price liberalization and central banking. Technical assistance has been crucial to ensure proper implementation of reform policies and has been provided, to a large extent, independently from lending activities.

More than *technical assistance*, IFIs' financing and policy conditionality have given rise to controversy. In these two respects, several issues have been raised, and I will mention a few. As to the policy approaches, to what extent have the policy targets been in line with the final reform objectives and have been achievable given the specific conditions of each economy? Have the policy instruments been adequate to pursue the chosen policy targets? Was a critical mass of measures enacted early enough in the transition process to ensure, first, the construction of the minimum structure of a market system, and second, a self-sustained output recovery after the initial production scale-down? What balance has been struck between policy discipline and policy flexibility? The former is required in order to shorten the most painful phases of economic reform and restructuring, while the latter is necessary to allow for errors in policy design, unforeseen developments, or difficulties in policy implementation.

As regards financing issues, the question that is often raised concerns whether enough external resources have been supplied to ensure the sustainability of macroeconomic stabilization together with structural changes. Reforming countries and some observers have often reiterated their view that foreign financial flows have been inadequate to the tasks of the transition and that a financial assistance plan, of a size comparable to that of the Marshall Plan launched after World War II, is still needed. Of course, in the reiteration of such requests it is often overlooked that far-reaching economic policy conditions were attached to the use of those resources provided by the USA for the reconstruction of Western Europe's economy. The USA requested that beneficiary countries pursue forcefully macroeconomic stability and external balance, open their markets, and co-operate among themselves in managing the funds received from the Marshall Plan, thereby achieving a certain degree of economic policy co-ordination. From this experience sprang the first initiatives of international economic co-operation in Europe in the 1950s, such as the OEEC, the first European common policies in the coal and steel industries, and later the European Payments Union.

Can we expect that countries coming from four decades of central planning can duplicate the success of that experience? In other words, assuming that a new Marshall Plan (in terms of size and type of assistance) were to materialize, what is the likelihood that these countries would make an appropriate utilization of the funds and deeply restructure their economies? The experience of the past four years indicates considerable problems on both sides, that of the countries requesting financial resources as well as those that could potentially supply them.

On the demand side, the reforming economies have shown limited capacity to absorb large capital inflows, regardless whether they are from official sources or private ones. For instance, they have attracted an amount of foreign direct investment that is generally far below potential. Furthermore, the history of economic development in the OECD area in the post-world war period teaches us that economic development and investment are financed to a major extent by domestic savings. These reforming countries have not yet made enough progress in mobilizing their domestic savings to support the most viable investment opportunities. They should promote and better utilize domestic savings before calling upon foreign savings. On the supply side, the effectiveness of financial assistance has been hampered by both the difficulties in co-ordinating the various official donors and the conditions that they have attached to their resources, including non-economic conditions.

These are some of the main issues that have to be addressed but it is not wise to expect final answers to these questions. The jury is still out: it is too early to judge the results of the transition. Even the most successful reforming countries have not yet completed the construction of the structures of a market economy, including laws, institutions, infrastructures, and markets. Yet, at the end of 1994, a general improvement in the economic climate in Central and Eastern Europe (much less in Russia) can be detected, although its durability is not clear. This improvement is signalled by a gradual diffusion of the output recovery, by a continuing deceleration of inflation, although it is still relatively high, and by the emergence of a competitive and expanding private enterprise sector.

***

In closing, I would draw a few brief conclusions. First, the transition process is a task that is mainly in the hands of the reforming countries themselves. This is not a joint venture with advanced industrial countries. It is rather the responsibility of the reforming countries to transform their economies by relying on their own skills and resources, with whatever external assistance is made available. To fulfil this task, these countries have to show commitment and determination not just at the top economic management level but also at the grass roots level. This aspect of responsibility for the transition is often neglected when requests for assistance are made.

Second, there are some differences of views and perspectives among the international institutions involved in the transition process, but these differences are not as surprising as they reflect the different mandates and experiences of these institutions. There is no clear evidence of contradiction in these institutions' approaches; rather, a fair amount of complementarity among their interventions has been evident. The existence of a degree of complementarity does not diminish the need for continuing end even strengthening co-ordination among their operations.

Third, it is the general impression of IFIs that economic recovery has begun in Central and Eastern Europe. However, it is also recognized that institutional and structural changes are slow to take root and will require a long period of time.

Finally, I wish to express the hope that the rapid expansion and vitality of the emerging private enterprise sector will be the determinant factors for overcoming the current economic difficulties and bringing about fundamental improvements in these economies.

Note

1. Zecchini, Salvatore: 'The Role of International Financial Institutions in the Transition Process', in *Journal of Comparative Economics,* 20, 1995, pp.116-138.

13 The IMF's Approach to Economies in Transition

John Odling-Smee

Introduction

Since the late 1980s, a number of centrally planned economies in Central and Eastern Europe, Russia, the Transcaucasus, and Asia have become 'economies in transition', with their governments beginning a process to transform their command economies into market-based systems. At the outset of this dramatic development in 1989, some of these countries were already members of the International Monetary Fund (IMF); others sought and were granted membership in a rapid manner, with seventeen joining in 1992 alone. The IMF has been deeply involved from an early stage in advising and assisting these member states in their transformation efforts. The staff of the IMF has conducted intensive and continuous policy dialogues with virtually all transition economies, provided them with substantial technical assistance in various areas, and in many of them, the IMF has provided financial resources in support of their reform and stabilization programmes.

This paper aims at highlighting specific features of the IMF's approach to economies in transition, which distinguish it from its approaches to other economies, and assessing in broad terms the effectiveness of the approach in light of the achievements so far. In doing so, it focuses on the Baltics, Russia, and other former Soviet Union (FSU) states, although much of the discussion and conclusions apply to other transition economies as well.

Distinctive features of transition economies

As the management and staff of the IMF have repeatedly emphasized, the specific nature of policy measures designed to correct macroeconomic imbalances and balance-of-payments disequilibria will need to depend on the particular circumstances in individual countries. Against this background, the question arises for the countries in transition: what is it that makes them different from the rest, and how should the IMF's policy approach take any such differences into account? Among the main distinguishing features of these economies are the following.

First, trade and output were sharply disrupted by the collapse of the old planning system. Indeed, attempts to enhance performance and modernize under central planning failed during the 1980s, as centralized controls were ceased but market signals and discipline were not established. In addition, the increase in prices of goods traded between member countries of the Council for Mutual Economic Assistance (CMEA) (with settlement in hard currencies) in early 1991, the disintegration of the FSU, and the disruption of trade and financing arrangements between the former republics created further difficulties, as did the sharp upward revision of energy prices in intra-FSU trade.

The second distinguishing feature is the comprehensiveness of the structural reforms that were needed to reverse the stagnation and inefficiencies of these economies. Specifically, with a view to facilitating the needed changes to the industrial structure and instilling market-oriented behaviour among enterprises and other economic agents, property rights had to be defined and enforced, a sound financial system established, prices liberalized, trade policies reformed, and state-owned enterprises commercialized. A particular problem in this area was the need to deal with soft budget constraints on enterprises, which were manifested in the inter-enterprise arrears problem in the early years of transition in many countries.

A third distinction is the period of 'extraordinary politics' at the onset of transition, when public preparedness for taking radical steps has enabled reformers in several countries to quickly implement strong reform and stabilization measures.

A fourth distinguishing feature is the large decline in measured output during the initial years of transformation. Apart from the collapse of the old system and its trade and financing arrangements mentioned above, both frictional adjustment costs related to the disruption of trade, payments, and credit networks, and the sudden obsolescence of much of the stock of physical, institutional, and human capital have led to declines in measured output. Moreover, at the level of perception, statistical systems have not adequately captured the activities of the fast growing private sector, resulting in an overstatement of the decline in 'measured' output or GDP.[1]

Fifth is the risk to price stability emanating from the necessary liberalization of prices in the initial stages of transition. Price liberalization (accompanied by the removal of restrictions on the withdrawal of bank deposits) has led to jumps in the price level – often on the order of several hundred percentage points on impact. Such price adjustments feed inflationary expectations and increase the risk that inflation will spiral to hyperinflationary levels.

The sixth distinct feature is the serious erosion in government revenues during the first few years of transition, owing to problems in quickly establishing a fully effective new tax system. (For example, between 1991 and 1993, revenues as a proportion of GDP declined by 13 percentage points in the Kirghiz Republic and by 15 percentage points in Lithuania.) The magnitude of the drop in revenues typically strains the ability to cut spending, thereby adding to fiscal deficits and inflationary pressures.

Specific aspects of the IMF's approach to economic policy

The IMF's approach to economic policy in economies in transition has attempted to take account of these characteristic features. It has:

(i) aimed at introducing market-determined prices as early as possible by liberalizing prices and integrating these economies into the world economy through the introduction of liberal trade and exchange regimes;

(ii) prioritized other domestic structural reforms including enactment of suitable laws, building of institutions essential for the operation of a market economy, privatization of land, enterprises, and banks;

(iii) sought to contain inflation pressures (due to price liberalization and other factors) through the pursuit of tight fiscal and monetary policies;

(iv) encouraged the establishment of social safety nets to protect vulnerable social groups during the transitional period of output decline as well as the promotion of vibrant private sector activities;

(v) emphasized the need to build effective and market-oriented external trade and payments arrangements between the states that previously operated within the old central planning network; and

(vi) argued in favour of front-loading the policy content of reform programmes to take advantage of strong pro-reform sentiments at the outset.

While stressing the fundamental need for rapid adjustment, the IMF has also argued that it be supported by substantial external financial resources. The need for external financial assistance in any individual country will depend on the size and nature of the initial shocks as well as the transition path being followed. In particular, the more rapid the structural transformation that is taking place, the larger the amount of official external finance required initially though not over a period of years. Once macroeconomic stabilization and the basic institutions of a market economy are in place, private foreign investment can take over, especially to support the heavy investment needs of the economy.

The key distinctive features of the IMF's policy approach may be discussed in some more details as follows.

Structural reform

While macroeconomic issues remain the core of the IMF's work, we have recognized that successful transformation entails the liberalization of prices and foreign trade, and the building of new institutions, legal arrangements, work practices, economic structures, and attitudes.[2] Moreover, it has been increasingly recognized that there is a symbiotic relationship between structural reform and macroeconomic stabilization; and the sustainability of macroeconomic balance in any transition economy depends on the speed and comprehensive nature of the economic reform. For example, in the absence of financial sector reform, accumulation of bad loans in the portfolios of commercial banks by posing a systemic risk can overwhelm many stabilization programmes. Thus, the IMF has emphasized the speedy removal, at an early stage of the reform, of all price controls, trade restrictions, and administered exchange and interest rates. The 'extraordinary politics' of the initial period have facilitated such rapid liberalization in several countries. For example, in the three Baltic countries of Estonia, Latvia, and Lithuania, the governments capitalized on the popular support for radical policies in the initial years of transition, and moved to liberalize more quickly and with more determination than many observers had expected.

Macroeconomic policies

The IMF has emphasized the pursuit of tight macroeconomic policies aimed at the rapid reduction of inflation, because there is no example as yet of a country sustaining growth of national income over the longer term under conditions of chronic high inflation and large macroeconomic imbalances. In particular, conditions of high inflation and exchange rate instability lead to massive variability in, and confusion about, relative prices, and inefficiencies in resource allocation that discourage investment in activities that will support growth over the longer term. They have also led to capital flight, which deprives countries of the domestic savings that could otherwise be available for investments at home.

Framing and implementing macroeconomic policies in a market economy are completely different from running a centrally planned economy. On the fiscal side, the size of government must be reduced, and enterprises allowed to retain more of their own income to finance investments. Subsidies need to be abolished, and the social safety net based on targeted income support. The tax system should be transparent and non-distortionary, with very few exemptions, unlike taxation under central planning, which discriminated between sectors, regions, and even enterprises.[3]

On the monetary side, central banks have to operate monetary policy with a view to maintaining price stability, rather than merely to ensure an adequate supply of money and credit to allow the Plan to achieve its real goals. They also have to oversee the financial sector, which will become increasingly complex as economies move toward the market.[4]

The IMF has been active in giving policy advice in all these areas. While the macroeconomic policies to be followed, when the transition process is completed, are well known to the IMF, it has been necessary to develop knowledge and experience of the best way at handling the transition itself. An example of this is the shift from reliance on direct monetary instruments – whereby the central bank imposes simultaneous and direct controls on both interest rates and magnitudes of one or more types of loanable funds – to indirect market-based instruments, whereby the central bank determines either the rate or the quantity of a type of loanable fund, but never both, and leaves the other to be determined indirectly by the market. Initially, the transition economies often lack well-functioning interbank markets, adequate risk management, including the use of collateral and effective banking supervision. In such circumstances, the use of market-based instruments, such as central bank credit auctions, may lead to problems of adverse selection of borrowers, moral hazard, and collusion among participating banks.[5] Nevertheless, the maintenance of direct controls risks the costly continuation of administrative methods of credit allocation, with all its inefficiencies, and it is not clear that the problems noted above would necessarily be avoided. Accordingly, the IMF has favoured the early introduction of market-based monetary instruments, together with the establishment of effective supervision and prudential regulation of banks.[6] It is in the same vein that, while IMF-supported programmes in some countries initially chose to use bank-by-bank credit ceilings to help control overall credit expansion, direct approach was regarded to be temporary, to be replaced with a reliance on indirect instruments as soon as a functioning banking system emerged.

Interstate relations

With the demise of traditional trade and payments arrangements, the establishment of a new market-oriented framework to conduct trade and financial transactions between themselves has been an important task for the countries in transition. The design and co-ordination of policies and institutions in this area has been complicated by the different speeds at which these countries have pursued reforms. In the trade area, the IMF has in general stressed an outward-oriented strategy free of government intervention that exposes domestic producers to external competition as being more conducive to long-term growth. Accordingly, it is important that new bilateral trading agreements as well as proposals for 'economic union' (for example, among the CIS states) – while justified as a means of providing transitional protection and to take advantage of existing trade relationships – do not work to maintain an interventionist and inward-looking approach with all its inefficiencies and distortions. In the payments area, the modernization of payments systems, the decentralization of payments, and the establishment of mutual convertibility among newly established currencies would facilitate the development of efficient and market-oriented trade.

For the Baltics, Russia, and the other FSU states, as well as parts of Eastern Europe, the transition has involved questions regarding the future of common currency areas. For example, the newly independent republics of Russia and the other FSU states continued to use Soviet and Russian roubles during much of 1992 and 1993. The initial preference in many non-Russian states for staying in the rouble area appears to have been motivated by the objective of maintaining intra-FSU trade and payments relations, and an expectation that remaining in the rouble area would result in access to more financing and cheaper energy from Russia. It became increasingly clear, however, that the problems of trade and payments, and the prospects for obtaining assistance from Russia, were not closely linked with the rouble area issue. At the same time, many policy makers realized that the level of policy co-ordination among member states, required for the effective functioning of a common currency area, might not be consistent with the desire to maintain political and economic independence.

On its part, the IMF made it clear to all newly independent states that the decision as to whether or not to introduce a national currency was a sovereign prerogative. But, it also pointed out (i) that monetary union would entail certain economic consequences, particularly the loss of independence in financial policy making; and (ii) that the introduction of a national currency would not improve macroeconomic performance unless it was backed by appropriately prudent fiscal and monetary policies – as the Ukrainian experience with the karbovanets would attest. In the event, all states, except Tadzhikistan, have now introduced their own independent currencies.

A distinguishing characteristic of the IMF's work in transition countries has been the considerable effort that has been devoted to interstate relations. Thus, the IMF worked with the Baltics, Russia, and other FSU states on setting up new monetary arrangements. The IMF has provided substantial technical assistance on the introduction of new currencies, foreign exchange markets, and payments systems, as well as general macroeconomic policy advice and financial support in connection with the introduction of new currencies. Further, the IMF staff has helped to clarify the conditions for the establishment of an effective monetary union, and also participated extensively in the preparatory work for the establishment of the '*Interstate Bank*' as a multilateral clearing house to expedite interstate payments among CIS countries. Outside the purely monetary area, the staff prepared several papers for the authorities and the Executive Board of the IMF on interstate trade, payments, debt and arrears issues.[7] The substance of the analysis and advice has been discussed with the authorities in both regular bilateral contacts and specially arranged multilateral meetings.

Institution-building and financial support to transition economies

The IMF has augmented its policy advice to transition economies with technical assistance to build institutions and train officials, and with balance-of-payments financing.

Institution building and training

Countries attempting to carry out the process of transformation frequently face deep resistance when trying to implement policy changes, with the problem often starting at the conceptual level itself with key policy makers. Indeed, after working within the closed confines of the old system for decades, the national officials often lack the basic understanding of the interrelationships between key macroeconomic variables as well as the impact of these variables on aggregate demand and supply, and inflation. This has meant that IMF staff providing policy advice to countries in transition have needed to devote considerably more time and attention than in other member countries to raising the level of understanding of key senior officials.

More generally, however, and often in co-operation with other multilateral and bilateral agencies, the IMF has devoted considerable resources to technical assistance and training on a large scale to help build the capacity to design and effectively implement market-oriented economic and financial policies in transition countries. With a focus on the central banking, foreign exchange market, fiscal, and statistics areas, the IMF has sent about 700 technical assistance missions to all countries in transition since 1991.[8] Moreover, this effort has represented the substantial share of total technical assistance activities in the Fund. For example, in the latest financial year, half or more of technical assistance activities in the money, banking, and statistics areas were devoted to the transition economies in Central and Eastern Europe, the Baltic countries, Russia, and other countries of the FSU.

A special emphasis has also been placed on training through the work of the IMF Institute. The Institute conducts courses both in Washington as well as in other country and regional locations including at the Joint Vienna Institute in Austria, which was established in early 1992 (in collaboration with several other multilateral agencies) for the exclusive purpose of providing training to officials of transition economies.

IMF financial support

The IMF has stood ready to make its own resources available and play a catalytic role in mobilizing financing packages in support of bold reform and stabilization programmes in transition economies. Between 1990-93, the IMF supported thirty-eight programmes in transition countries with $10 billion of its own resources. Moreover, in April 1993, in special recognition of the balance-of-payments problems caused by disruptions in the traditional trade and payments arrangements of the transition economies, the IMF set up a new special facility, called the Systemic Transformation Facility (STF). The use of this facility aimed at providing early support for a member's efforts leading toward the eventual adoption of a comprehensive economic adjustment and reform programme.[9] So far sixteen countries in transition have availed themselves of the STF, and over SDR (Special Drawing Right) 3 billion has been disbursed under the facility. At this time, the STF is due to expire at the end of 1994, although discussions continue about extending it, together with a new allocation of SDRs.

The financial support from the IMF to the transition countries has been commensurate with the leadership role that the Institution has been mandated to play by its members. Indeed, the IMF is already assuming, or has expressed its readiness to assume, an unusual amount of risk in connection with financing transformation in transition economies. While the prospective financing needs of the transition countries in the period ahead are hard to predict with any precision, the recently agreed increase in annual maximum lending limits under stand-by and extended arrangements (from 68 per cent to 100 per cent of quota) is likely to be well utilized by transition countries. The IMF's portfolio has been shifting, and is likely to continue to shift, toward these countries. In response to the increased risk, it would be important for the borrowing members to adopt strong adjustment programmes that would both correct payments imbalances and preserve the revolving nature of IMF resources.

Assessment of the IMF's approach

In this section, we look at a few specific issues, and ask whether experience suggests that the IMF's approach was correct. First, we consider overall progress and the speed of stabilization, then the role of the exchange rate, and finally, external financial assistance.

Overall progress and the speed of stabilization

Progress in achieving success in stabilization and reform has been mixed, with popular hopes of a quick turn-around to a golden age of economic resurgence unfulfilled in many countries. However, some countries – including the Czech Republic, Hungary, Poland, Estonia, Latvia, and Lithuania – have gone a long way towards stabilization and have implemented major reforms. The achievement of macroeconomic stabilization has required the persistent implementation of strong policies in these countries, and the IMF has extended its financial support in all such cases. Indeed, in a number of these countries, there are now clear and encouraging indications of economic recovery. In other countries, however, inflation remains excessively high, and in many, structural transformation has hardly begun. And in these latter countries, economic activity has continued to decline significantly.

All of the more successful countries have implemented economic programmes which the IMF supported. All the countries which did not attempt such programmes have achieved little or no progress toward stabilization or reform. However, there is a small group of countries in which economic conditions have continued to deteriorate, which did embark upon IMF-supported programmes. Without attempting a detailed analysis of the reasons for this, we would note that failures usually resulted from the inability, if not unwillingness, of governments to do what had been agreed under the IMF-supported programmes. Slippages in budgetary and credit policies and delays in structural reform often took place to accommodate sectoral interests. Reviews of failed programmes are replete with cases of excessive credit expansion beyond programme limits, in response to pressures from special interest groups, such as the agricultural sector, or the granting of tax exemptions to state-owned enterprises.

That said, the question that continues to be asked is whether the programme were inherently too ambitious, and whether a slower speed of stabilization might have mitigated short-term output losses and led to greater public support and momentum for reform.

It is doubtful whether such a 'fine tuning' of stabilization and reform measures is realistic in a transition economy. International experience shows the difficulties of bringing down inflation from very high levels in incremental steps of a few percentage points per year because of the lack of credibility of the government's forward commitment to low inflation. Furthermore, as noted earlier, the economies in transition that have succeeded in bringing inflation down quickly are now experiencing a relatively early resumption of growth. In any case, even if easier financial policies were to have increased aggregate demand, it is far from clear how much output would have increased, whether the higher output would have been sustainable, and whether this would have implied a higher standard of living for the population. To the extent that consumers would not have wished to purchase much of the additional output, living standards (and consumer welfare) would not have been higher. Slower reforms and stabilization would thus only have postponed the process of shifting resources to more efficient sectors. And as Sachs and Woo point out, small reforms would likely have produced a political backlash, without much economic benefit.[10]

Nevertheless, one may still ask, would the transition countries in Europe and the FSU have been better off by following the Chinese approach, which has been described as a more gradual 'two-track approach' that has allowed the private sector to grow side-by-side with the state sector, and has been accompanied by rapid economic growth?

For a number of reasons, it is unlikely that the Chinese approach could be successfully applied in these other countries. First, a few of these countries did follow the two-track approach through the 1980s without much success.[11] Second, there were special circumstances in China which contributed to the relative success of its strategy. China's labour-intensive subsistence agriculture, which was self-financing and never strictly subject to central control, and which employed the large majority of the workforce, was able to register rapid productivity gains in response to decollectivization of agriculture and market-oriented reforms in prices and procurement of agricultural produce. Furthermore, China withdraw early from CMEA trade arrangements, was free during the initial period of reform from intractable political problems, and had access to a large pool of investable funds and human capital in neighbouring economies (Hong Kong and Taiwan).[12]

Meanwhile the question has been raised as to whether the IMF could have persuaded countries to have reformed faster. Many of the transition countries are newly emerging democracies, and reformers in these countries need parliamentary support to carry out strong reforms. There have been several instances, for example, the programme proposed by Mr Yegor Gaidar, the then deputy prime minister of Russia, in March 1992 when bold reform plans have floundered for lack of such support. Thus, while economists can analyse the economic effects of pursuing reforms at alternative speeds, the choice of speed of reform ultimately is a political decision that will rest with the leadership of these countries. In any case, reform has the greatest chance of success when it is home-grown, with a broad political commitment underpinning it.

The role of the exchange rate

Economies in transition which previously had a heavily controlled external sector with an artificial exchange rate had to choose what type of exchange rate arrangement to adopt. Given the right circumstances, the IMF has recognized the helpful role of a fixed exchange rate as a nominal anchor in stabilization. Particularly in highly open and indexed economies, the announcement of a fixed peg can signal the end of a price-exchange rate spiral and put an early stop to inflation inertia. Indeed, the IMF has supported programmes with fixed exchange rates in a number of transition countries, for example, Poland, the Czech and Slovak Republic, Estonia, and Lithuania. Further, the currency board arrangement – under which money creation by the central bank is strictly on the basis of hard currency inflows – has been supported so far in two cases as a useful means of enhancing the credibility of a fixed exchange rate regime.[13]

Fixed exchange rate regimes, however, have only been supported when there has been a reasonable assurance that adequate policies, particularly in the fiscal and monetary areas, would be in place to maintain price stability and international competitiveness, and hence sustain the peg for a reasonable period of time. Without appropriate supporting policies, the introduction of a fixed peg in a high inflation environment rapidly leads to an overvalued currency, loss of international competitiveness for the emerging private sector, a run on central bank reserves, which forces the government either to change the peg and lose credibility or to introduce exchange restrictions that lead to market distortions.[14] Moreover, in a situation where economies are undergoing rapid structural change and may be subjected to significant external shocks, the level of the 'equilibrium' real exchange rate may change considerably over time. Thus, the IMF has also supported programmes with flexible exchange rates – most notably in Albania, Hungary, Latvia, Russia, and several other FSU states.

Experience has shown that a fixed exchange rate regime is not a necessary condition for stabilization. In Latvia, for example, the tenacity of the government's policies quickly enhanced its credibility, and stability was achieved under a managed float with the central bank intervening only to maintain orderly conditions in the foreign exchange market.[15] It is noteworthy, indeed, that the successful reduction in inflation in Latvia has led to a stable nominal exchange rate, i.e. exchange rate stability has emerged as a by-product of macroeconomic stability.

External financial assistance

Should the IMF have taken more of a leadership role in co-ordinating and generating external financing for the countries in transition? And could more external financing have eased the process of transition, maintained political support for reforms in programme countries, and persuaded non-programme countries to adopt IMF-supported programmes of accelerated reform and stabilization?

The IMF indeed can exercise some leverage in mobilizing external resources in support of reform and stabilization in transition countries. However, this leverage is, at best, limited. The bulk of official external assistance provided to developing and transition countries takes place under the auspices of a group of industrialized countries or consultative groups organized to pledge financial resources in support of programmes agreed with the IMF and the World Bank.[16] While financing from the multilateral lending agencies depends on the authorities' progress in economic reform and stabilization, much of bilateral official assistance may be motivated by considerations not related to economic reforms in a direct sense. Prospects for promoting exports, humanitarian assistance, political support, and financing for denuclearization have all been major determinants of the flow of official assistance in specific cases. Moreover, in the face of budgetary stringency in many donor countries, governments have been reluctant to place further burdens on their populations in support of reforms elsewhere. As our colleague Mr Hernandez-Catá has put it: 'One can cope for a world in which Parliamentarians and public opinion in the wealthy countries recognize that the international community is facing a challenge of historical significance – that of ensuring the transition from a totalitarian, centrally planned, and bellicose Soviet state to a new, peaceful, democratic, and free Russia – and that this extraordinary challenge requires a measure of sacrifice in the form of a temporary increase in taxes to finance temporary assistance to Russia and the other countries of the former Soviet Union. But that, unfortunately, is not the world in which we live today.'[17,18]

Furthermore, though the availability of foreign assistance undoubtedly smooths the process of transition, there is little evidence that such assistance can 'buy'reform. The delay in the provision of sizeable foreign assistance to Estonia, Latvia, and Lithuania by more than a year did not deter the three Baltic states from pushing ahead with reform and stabilization in 1992, and achieving substantial progress. As for the celebrated case of Russia, one will probably never know whether more financing would have generated more reforms, in both 1992 and 1993. We only note here that the limits to the amount of reform in Russia were set by strong political forces that showed little interest in the role of external assistance.[19]

Conclusion

The transition countries continue to face the massive challenge of transforming a previously centrally planned economy into a market-based system. This paper has discussed the ways in which the IMF has been helping these economies with technical assistance, policy advice, and financial support for reform and stabilization efforts in these countries. It has also sought to show how the IMF has taken into account the distinctive features and problems of transition economies.

The IMF has tried to respond flexibly and creatively to the unique circumstances of the countries in a number of ways. It has devoted much attention to reforms to the institutions, regulations, and behaviour of economic agents that govern the way these economies operate. It has recognized that, in the pursuit of sound macroeconomic policies, changes in the framework for designing and executing fiscal and monetary policies are needed. The IMF has devoted considerable efforts toward the establishment of new arrangements for trade and finance between former centrally planned states, as well as assisting the authorities establish new currency regimes. In all of this, technical support and training as well as financial assistance have played leading roles.

The process of transition has just begun in a number of countries, and it may be premature to draw general conclusions regarding the extent to which the IMF has been successful in its efforts. Nevertheless, the paper has argued that those countries that have adopted an ambitious approach to stabilization and reform, supported by the IMF's financial resources, are now on the road to economic recovery. A gradualist approach that delays transformation is generally not a preferred course of action. On exchange rate policy, the IMF has pursued an eclectic approach supporting a fixed or more flexible exchange rate regime as underlying circumstances warrant. While a fixed exchange rate has certain attractions, it requires adequate supportive policies; in the absence of these preconditions, the IMF has supported a flexible exchange rate strategy as the appropriate policy in many transition economies. Finally, the paper has noted the constraints to the IMF assuming even more of a leadership role in generating external assistance for the transition economies, and has argued that, while such assistance can help, the pace of the reform effort has depended on domestic political circumstances in these countries. Indeed, although we in the international community must and will continue to do everything we can to assist these countries in their efforts to transform, success will ultimately depend on the firm commitment and dedication of the people and leaders of these countries themselves.

Notes

1. In Poland, official statistics estimated the decline in GDP in 1990-91 at 18-20 per cent, while recent assessment by research institutes put the decline at 5-10 per cent in that year. See, Leszek Balczerowicz: 'Common Fallacies in the Debate on the Economic Transition in Central and Eastern Europe', EBRD, Working Paper, No. 11, October 1993.
2. Compared to counterparts in developing countries, the education level of the population, skills of the labour force, and other infrastructural facilities, such as roads and public health are better in most transition economies. Thus, the rewards from accelerated structural reform in transition economies can be expected to be swift and high.
3. For two comprehensive studies of fiscal reform issues in transition economies, see Vito Tanzi (ed.), *Fiscal Policies in Economies in Transition,* International Monetary Fund, 1992; and Vito Tanzi (ed.), *Transition to Market: Studies in Fiscal Reform,* International Monetary Fund, 1993.
4. For issues of financial sector reform, see Gerard Caprio, et al. *Building Sound Finance in Emerging Market Economies,* International Monetary Fund, 1994. See also Tomas Balino, et al. 'Payments System Reforms and Monetary Policy in Emerging Market Economies in Central and Eastern Europe', *IMF Staff Papers,* September 1994; and Hugh Brendenkamp: 'Conducting Monetary and Credit Policy in Countries of the Former Soviet Union', International Monetary Fund, WP/93/23, March 1993.

5. See Donald J. Mathieson and Richard D. Haas: 'Establishing Monetary Control of Financial Systems with Insolvent Institutions', International Monetary Fund, PPAA/94/10, June 1994.

6. See Matthew I. Saal and Lorena M. Zamalloa: 'Use of Central Bank Credit Auctions in Economies in Transition', International Monetary Fund, PPAA/94/11, June 1994.

7. See, for example, International Monetary Fund, *Economic Review Financial Relations Among Countries of the Former Soviet Union,* February 1994; and International Monetary Fund, *Economic Review: Trade Policy Reform in the Countries of the Former Soviet Union,* February 1994.

8. These include countries in Central and Eastern Europe, Russia, Transcaucasia, and Asia (Central Asia, Mongolia, China, and South–East Asia).

9. Access under the STF is subject to a limit of 50 per cent of the member's quota, and the repayment period of ten years with four and a half years of grace is longer than for Stand-By Arrangements and is more appropriate for transition countries in the initial stages of reform. The STF can also be used as a supplement to other facilities such as the Stand-By Arrangement.

10. Jeffrey D. Sachs and Wing Thye Woo: 'Structural Factors in the Economic Reforms of China, Eastern Europe and the Former Soviet Union', paper presented at the Economic Policy Panel meeting in Brussels, Belgium, October 22-23, 1993, pp. 6-7.

11. See Sachs and Woo, op. cit.

12. See Sachs and Woo, op. cit. and also John Odling-Smee and Henri Lorie: 'The Economic Reform Process in Russia', International Monetary Fund, WP/93/55, July 1993, p. 3.

13. Estonia and Lithuania introduced fixed rate regimes under currency board arrangements in June 1992 and April 1994, respectively. For a discussion of the Estonian currency board, see Adam Bennett: 'The Operation of the Estonian Currency Board, *IMF Staff Papers,* Vol. 40; for a general discussion, see Adam Bennett: 'Currency Boards: Issues and Experiences', International Monetary Fund, PPAA/94/18, September 1994.

14. It may be argued that the market exchange rates for the currencies of many transition economies are seriously undervalued because they include large risk premia that reflect uncertainties about prospective policies. But persistence of high inflation under a fixed rate regime – because of lack of supporting policies – can rapidly turn an undervalued currency into an overvalued one. For example, with inflation at the relatively low level – by transition economy standards – of 7 per cent per month, a currency undervalued by even 100 per cent becomes overvalued in less than a year's time.

15. In point of fact, the domestic currency appreciated significantly in nominal terms in the course of stabilization.

16. Moldova, Kazakhstan, and the Kirghiz Republic benefitted from the pledges made in the context of Consultative Groups, and Estonia, Latvia, and Lithuania received EU/G-24 financing for their programmes.

17. Ernesto Hernandez-Catá: 'Russia and the IMF: The Political Economy of Macro-Stabilization', PPAA/94/20, September 1994, p. 12.

18. Having said that, it is important to note that average official new money inflows in 1992–1993 accounted for over 3 per cent of the 1992 GDP in Russia and for over 4 per cent of the 1992 GDP in the Baltic states. These figures compare favourably with the Marshall Plan support received by countries in the post–World War II period. See Brau, Eduard: 'External Financial Assistance to the Baltic States, Russia, and Other States of the Former Soviet Union: The Record and the Issues', paper for Conference on Marketization of the Former Soviet Union, Adam Smith Institute, London, October 26-27.

19. See Hernandez-Catá, op. cit. pp. 6-11.

14 The International Financial Institutions and the Challenge of Transition and Reconstruction in the Former Communist Countries of Central and Eastern Europe

Otto Hieronymi

Did we understand the magnitude, and did we meet the challenge?

The collapse of the communist system has represented a unique and unexpected set of opportunities for a dynamic and peaceful development of the world economy in the coming decades. It is the thesis of this paper that there is a danger, although fortunately not yet a certainty, that a significant portion of these opportunities have been squandered by the intellectual and financial short-sightedness of the Western industrialized countries.

After World War I, the 'peace was lost' because of ill-fated economic and financial policies among the victors. After World War II, the 'peace was won' due to the political and economic leadership and solidarity that prevailed among the Western powers, victors and vanquished alike. While history never repeats itself, today there is a threat that scenarios resembling the post-World War I situation are more likely to prevail in the years to come than the general and shared prosperity that prevailed for decades among the market economies since the 1940s.[1]

Obviously, the population and the political and economic leaders of each country in Central and Eastern Europe are primarily responsible for dealing with their own problems and challenges. But in a closely integrated European and world economy, the success of the Central and Eastern European countries is in the best interests of the rest of the world. While charity begins at home: solidarity with countries facing severe reconstruction problems has proven the best long-term investment during the post-war period.

The answer to the question raised in the subtitle above has to be an unqualified no: *in the Western world, we did not understand the magnitude of the challenge and we did not meet it adequately, either at the economic or at the political level.*

Thus, it was not surprising that the late Prime Minister Antall of Hungary never missed an opportunity to remind the Western political leaders with whom he was dealing that the Western world had not been prepared, either materially or mentally, for the collapse of communism.

Why the surprise?

Ever since the bolshevik revolution, and even more since the imposition of a socialist dictatorship in Eastern European countries in the late 1940s, the great majority of Western experts and politicians had been rightly convinced of the political and economic inferiority of the communist system. Most of them had rightly argued, even during the various periods of 'détente', that the system, based on the antiquated ideas of Marx, Lenin, and Stalin, was fundamentally flawed and could not be reformed and made economically efficient and politically acceptable, without a total collapse.

Yet, the vast majority of Western politicians and Western experts, including most of those professionals who spent their life watching the 'socialist economies', did not expect the collapse of communism at the time when it did occur.

At the political level, even after the worst totalitarian excesses had ceased, the communist regimes continued to be based on the exclusive rule of the communist parties, that curtailed civic liberties and prevented the development of pluralistic political institutions and traditions. This was the case both in the Soviet Union itself and in the Eastern European communist countries.

By the 1980s, some of the communist leaders and experts came to believe, however, that it would be possible to build an efficient 'socialist market economy', while maintaining, at the same time, the communist one-party state. The 'reforms' would help liberate private initiative in the economic field: the resulting improved economic performance would reduce the pressure for radical political change and would make the continued exclusive rule of the communist parties more acceptable to the citizens of the 'socialist countries'.

To a large extent, this erroneous view was based on the belief in the efficiency of the so-called 'Hungarian model'. It is true that, compared with other more orthodox communist countries (such as the Soviet Union, East

Germany, or post-1968 Czechoslovakia), Hungary had tried to introduce a series of reforms, without openly breaking with the basic tenets of socialist economic doctrine and without abandoning the communist party's monopoly of political power.

Among those who believed in the working of the Hungarian model were not only the Hungarian leadership, but also Gorbachev. By the end of the 1980s, the 'Potemkin character' of the Hungarian model had become obvious (not the least to the then communist Hungarian leadership): the 'most liberal' socialist regime in the communist system collapsed under its own contradictions and inefficiencies, without any outside force or intervention.

The political challenge

The Central and Eastern European countries have been facing unprecedented challenges and unexpected historic opportunities since the collapse of the communist regimes in 1989-90.

In order to understand the role and performance of the international financial institutions, it is necessary to recall the nature and the order of magnitude of these challenges and opportunities.

In the political field, the challenges and opportunities can be summed up in three key points:

1   the possibility of creating or re-creating *pluralistic parliamentary democracies* based on the rule of law,

2   acquiring full *national independence from foreign (Soviet) political and military domination*, and

3   gradual *political and security integration* into the European and Atlantic community of free democratic countries.

It should be emphasized that these opportunities represented more than what the citizens of any of the communist countries had dared to hope for even six or seven years ago. Success in seizing this historic window of opportunity was essential not only from a political point of view: it also represented the precondition for success in building dynamic market economies on the ruins of several decades of the socialist or communist experience.

The economic challenge and opportunities

The economic challenge and opportunities to build a market economy appeared to be rather simple (compared to the task of creating functioning parliamentary democracies) to many people at the start.

In reality, the economic challenge has turned out to be much more complex and drawn-out, and the difficulties in meeting it have even blinded many people in and outside of Central and Eastern Europe. Consequently, they could not appreciate the results achieved in the political field. The disappointment was so great that some of the results and opportunities were given up by some countries.

For the sake of round numbers, the *economic challenges can be summarized under twelve headings*:

1   The number one task was *selecting the appropriate contemporary European model of a functioning dynamic market economy*. The author of the present article was and remains convinced that the best model was that of the *'social market economy'*, that has been so successful not only in Germany but also in a growing number of Western European countries.[2]

2   The number two challenge, closely related to the first one (as well as to the political challenges), has been the *creation of the legal and institutional framework* necessary for the proper functioning of the market economy. Where this problem has been ignored (or underestimated), or has not been successfully solved, one could not expect the other challenges to be met either.

3   The third task, the one that was most deeply ingrained in the consciousness of the citizens of the former communist countries, has been the need to *create the basis for rapid and sustained economic growth*. This was and remains the central cause and justification of the change of regime: the goal and opportunity is to catch up, within a reasonable period of time, the ground lost to the Western European countries.

4   Of equal importance as the preceding three fundamental challenges was the task which the new freely elected governments had to face from the first day in office: *to avoid an economic and financial collapse*, to maintain a functioning economy during the process of transformation.

5   One of the most severe challenges that all former communist countries had to face emerged from the rather *unexpected collapse of what had become over the decades their principal export markets.*

6   Closely linked to the preceding problem was the task of *structural change and the need to deal with the* de facto *or* de jure *bankruptcy* of significant portions of the economy and to *become competitive virtually overnight* with the most efficient Western suppliers both on domestic and on export markets.

7   While the medium-term goal is growth, all these countries had to manage economic transformation and social stability during a *period of a severe decline in production,* the order of magnitude of which was last seen in the market economies only during the Great Depression of the 1930s.

8   Building the market economy means building an economy based primarily on the private sector: *successful privatization has been and remains one of the most difficult economic, social, political, and financial challenges* in all of the former communist countries.

9   Maintaining *domestic and external macroeconomic balance* is an essential task in a market economy: it has been and remains particularly painful as a result of the open or concealed inflationary distortions inherited from the socialist regimes and as a result of the sharp decline in available resources.

10 The tenth, and by far not the least, challenge has been the one of *reconstruction:* the inheritance of the communist regime did not consist only in a generally inefficient economic and social system, but also in totally run down, wastefully managed, and neglected infrastructure. Although the collapse of communism was not the result of war, the *task of physical reconstruction* was and remains as daunting as in the aftermath of major wars.

11 One of the most obvious tasks has been to organize and speed up the *know-how transfer at all levels* between the world economy and the former communist countries: we all know that the free flow of ideas and people, technology transfer in all segments of the economy and society have been one of the principal engines of growth during the last five decades in the world economy.

12 Last but not least: *generating a non-debt-creating resource transfer* in favour of the former communist countries was and remains a key challenge for the world economy.

Building dynamic market economies: the perception of the international financial institutions

With the exception of the former East Germany, the major international financial institutions have been assigned a significant role in the transition and reconstruction process of the former communist countries in Central and Eastern Europe.

The relative importance, however, of this role must not be exaggerated. The main responsibility (again with the exception of the Eastern provinces in Germany) belongs in the first place to the countries themselves (the population and the political leadership), and in several countries also to the private sector in the OECD countries. Also the national administrations of the member countries of the Group of 24 have played a significant role in various areas of the transition process.

Still, the IMF, the World Bank, the newly created EBRD, and to a lesser extent, the European Investment Bank, are among the most visible international agents of change in the countries of the former Soviet Empire. The Bank for International Settlements, the oldest international financial institution has played a much more traditional low-profile role.

All these institutions have welcomed the challenge and have claimed a high-profile advisory role (being the 'source of ultimate wisdom'), even if the material and human resources at their disposal on the whole have fallen short of the magnitude of the task.

The gap between the need for resources and the available resources was strikingly demonstrated during the 3rd Annual Meeting of the European Bank for Reconstruction and Development in St Petersburg in April 1994. This was also obvious at the Annual Meeting of the Bretton Woods institutions in Madrid in September 1994.

Also, one should never tire of repeating the most striking illustration of this gap: i.e. the striking difference between the size of the government resource transfer in favour of the 17 million citizens of the former East Germany (well in excess of DM 500 billion so far), and the very limited official resource transfer to the well over 300 million other citizens of the former communist countries in Central and Eastern Europe.

Let me summarize my global judgement of the performance of the international financial institutions since the collapse of communism:

1   **on the positive side:** *faute de mieux,* the involvement of the international financial institutions has been useful so far;

2   **on the negative side:** however, the actual performance of the international financial institutions has fallen short of the expectations both of the industrialized countries, and of the leaders and citizens of the so-called transition countries, and *pari passu,* of the (self)-assigned role of the institutions themselves.

The reasons for this negative balance on the whole are well known. Let me mention four among the principal ones:

1   The principal and most obvious factor is that the performance of these institutions clearly mirrors the lack of a coherent strategy among the leading Western countries on how to deal with the post-communist world, and even more the lack of material solidarity with the citizens of these countries. No political sophistry and no technical arguments couched in terms of economic theory can explain away this fundamental fact.

2   The second point is that these institutions, like most of the political leaders and experts, have vastly underestimated the weight of the communist inheritance, the complexity of the domestic and international tasks and the truly historical magnitude of the challenge of transformation and reconstruction. *These institutions also shared the lack of experience of the current generation of economists and politicians with the work of systemic change and reconstruction on the scale of an entire continent.*

3   The third source of problems is the result of the weight of 'bureaucratic inertia' and the 'fights for turf and influence' within the institutions, among them, and with the national administrations in the transition countries and in the Western economies. One of the anomalies has been the weight given to the established bureaucracies in 'trying to build the market economy'. This has given excessive importance in key decisions to foreign (national and international) officials and experts in the former communist countries, and has also strengthened local, entrenched bureaucracies in the transition countries, thereby weakening

the position both of the freely elected post-communist political leadership and of the newly emerging national business community.

4   Finally, a major error and a source of delays and dispersion of efforts was the initial decision not to create more efficient structures of co-ordination dealing with the problems of each specific country (country task forces).

Meeting the specific challenges: the record of the international financial institutions

The objective   of a conference like the one organized by the Robert Triffin–Szirák Foundation in Brussels is to stimulate open critical discussion. I do not think that the international financial institutions are responsible for the current difficulties of the former communist countries. Yet, I think a number of critical comments are called for. In this section, I would like to illustrate my reasons for serious preoccupation in the light of the twelve main challenges mentioned above.

1   *Overall concept or model:* two problems should be mentioned under this heading.

    a   The first one is that the systemic approaches or models advocated by the international financial institutions do not sufficiently take into account the most successful European models. Thus, there is little or no reference in their work to the concept of the *'social market economy'* (most of their staff would have a hard time defining it).

    b   The second serious problem is that the tasks of *reconstruction* has been underestimated and still receives little attention. The approaches the institutions are most comfortable with are 'macroeconomic' balance, on the one hand, and 'economic development' strategies, on the other.

2   The importance of *creating the legal and institutional framework* necessary for the market economy is also a relatively recent discovery for the international institutions. At the same time, there is too much rivalry and too little concerted action on this account (the 'not-invented-here' syndrome).

3   All the international financial institutions are *guilty of not concentrating on the need to create the foundations for sustained economic growth*. Whereas all the OECD governments openly declare economic growth as a central objective, there is a veritable paranoia to admit that economic growth has to be the central objective of the transformation process. There is a deep-rooted confusion at work: the task is not inflationary financing of growth, but the creation of the sound bases of growth that will allow macroeconomic equilibrium.

4   The *potential danger of economic and financial collapse* has not always been fully recognized by the international financial institutions. In some countries, the time-consuming approach, the deliberate pace of the institutions may have been too slow both in recognizing key problems or dealing with crisis situations. I am afraid some of the major surprises may still lie in the future.

5   The international financial institutions *did not foresee the collapse of the export markets* of the former communist countries and did very little to prevent it, or to deal with its domestic industrial consequences. The task was not to try to create a regional payments or trading area on the OEEC/EPU model. However, the minimum that the Central and Eastern European countries expected was that the international financial institutions should match the export financing that OECD exporters enjoyed and which helped drive even their competitive products out of their former export markets.[3]

6   The international financial institutions were also very slow *to recognize the need to save the viable portion of the companies* facing collapse in the transition countries. There has been no or very little finance available for corporate restructuring (assistance that is available from the governments of virtually all OECD countries under various names and cover-ups), little or no assistance to help find new markets, new technologies, etc.

7   Like everybody else, the international financial institutions have also *failed to predict the magnitude and duration of production cut-backs*, and *the sharp decline in domestic resources* in all the former communist countries. What is so worrisome today is that they still do not seem to see the connection between the severity of the depression in these countries and the difficulties to achieve domestic financial balance.

8   Like everybody else, the international financial institutions have also recognized the importance of privatization in these countries. They have, however, *provided virtually no risk capital to speed up domestic privatization*. The few instance where they take equity positions, they always select the safest bets ('cherry-picking' in American parlance), where private capital is also available.

9   Much could be said about the macroeconomic policy advice and constraints imposed by the international financial institutions. Without accepting the popular view, two general criticisms are called for: (a) the general impression that the *macroeconomic approach they recommend is too Malthusian* and, in particular, it does not distinguish between structural causes and 'deliberate' inflationary policies; and (b) in most cases, the *resources that the institutions could mobilize to back up their tough advice have been rather limited*.

10   As noted above, the international financial institutions have paid little attention to the *challenges and the opportunities of the task of reconstruction*. The fact that the reconstruction of the former communist countries could provide extraordinary growth opportunities both for the countries themselves and for the rest of the world is recognized neither in their rhetoric nor in their actions. The failure to encourage and help the creation of 'reconstruction and investment banks' in each country is symptomatic of this problem: it was obvious from the start that the EBRD could not play the role of such domestic reconstruction banks.

11   The international organizations have made considerable efforts to speed up the know-how transfer towards the former communist countries. They have, however, concentrated almost exclusively on accounting, financial mechanisms, macroeconomic policies. While all this was very urgent, by and large they have *neglected the equally urgent need of these countries for market research, technology transfer*, and the like.

12   Finally, on the whole, the *international organizations have done little to alleviate the severe structural resource shortage or the problem of the external debt burden* of the former communist countries. In fact, they have failed to remind both their member governments and the general public that there was and there is an urgent need for non-debt-creating resource transfers, besides direct private investments, to the

former communist countries. Thus, the experts of these organizations have done little to dispel the fallacy that reconstruction can be successfully financed from private capital and from official loans. They also failed to remind the world that despite the domestic budget problems of most of the member governments, a resource transfer that could have made a difference, would not have created uncontrollable budget deficits and inflationary pressures in the world economy and even less a drop in the living standards of the industrialized or the developing countries.

A new beginning?

The globally negative perception by the political and business leaders and by the population in the 'transition economies' of the international financial institutions is well documented. This cannot be explained away by arguments of the kind that these institutions are there 'to teach economic and monetary discipline', that they are the necessary 'harbingers of bad news'.

The negative perception cannot be corrected through 'better public relations work'. The truly bad news is that the negative perception is based on the critical judgement of the effectiveness of Western advice and on the questioning of the Western willingness to co-operate in building successful, dynamic market economies on the ruins of many decades of communist experiments.

This judgement may appear too harsh to overworked international civil servants and it may not tell the full story: *yet, if nothing is done to correct this judgement, the long-term political, economic, and social consequences could be disastrous, not only for the transition countries, but also for the OECD countries and for the institutions themselves.*

The answer to this harsh reality is not a withdrawal or a freezing of the activities of the international financial institutions in Central and Eastern Europe. I would like to outline briefly three main factors that could possibly contribute significantly raising the effectiveness of the work of the international financial institutions in this crucial area:

1   adopting a *more pragmatic and, at the same time, a more dynamic strategy* (which should also include a much more effective co-opera-

tion with the private sector within and outside the transition economies),

2 a *sizable increase of the resources to be employed in carrying out their
tasks*, and finally,

3 *adopting a more modest political profile*, one that is proportionate both
to their effective experience with the tasks and the knowledge of the
countries concerned and with their material and human resources.

Notes

1. Cf. Keynes, John Maynard: *The Economic Consequences of the Peace*, London,
   Macmillan, 1919.
2. Cf. Hieronymi, Otto: *Economic Policies for the New Hungary*, Columbus, Ohio,
   Battelle Press, 1990; and the Hungarian edition, Hieronymi, Otto: *A magyar gazdaság
   megújulása – nyugati szemmel*, Budapest, *HVG/Battelle, 1990*.
3. Cf. Hieronymi, Otto: *Economic Discrimination Against the United States in Western
   Europe*, Geneva, Droz, 1973.

15 World Bank Assistance to the Countries in Transition

Marcelo Selowsky

Introduction

The assistance to the countries in transition has faced the Bank with one of its toughest challenges. Within a short period of time, the Bank had to build up capabilities to assist an increasing number of countries who became members – today twenty-six in total, of which half joined during the last two years (Table 1).

The task is complex because of the significant diversity across countries, particularly on the institutional side. Some countries, like those in Central Europe, inherited institutions and a legal framework supporting the development of markets. Achieving consensus in these countries has been easier. In the countries of the former Soviet Union (FSU), these institutions have to be built almost from scratch. Significant tensions still exist between the executive and parliamentary branches of governments as well as unclear constitutional rules regarding the rights and responsibilities of local versus central governments.

Factor endowments also differ significantly. The Russian Federation is estimated to hold 10 per cent of world's oil reserves, 40 per cent of natural gas, 10 per cent of hard coal reserves, and 20 per cent of the world's brown coal reserves. In contrast, in some energy importing countries such as Belarus and Ukraine, oil imports represent more than 20 per cent of their GDP.

This note briefly discusses the Bank's activities in these countries. First, it outlines the organizing principles behind such assistance. Then, it reviews selectively some of its present activities, in particular how the bank has adapted its instruments to different country situations. Finally, it discusses some future challenges and dilemmas.

General issues

Organizing principles: the principle of complementarity

The key principles guiding the Bank's assistance are: (a) to match instruments to country reform efforts so as to maximize the complementarity between domestic efforts and external assistance; (b) to recognize that the Bank is only one player in such assistance, and its financial resources are limited in relation to overall needs. Hence the Bank's assistance must improve the environment and the incentives for other types of external flows to come, in particular private flows and foreign direct investment, which in the medium term, may become equal or more important than official assistance.

The Bank's assistance addresses two families of constraints to the recovery of growth. The first is the lack of an environment to generate enough incentives for investment and restructuring. It is the results of macroeconomic instability, insufficient price and trade liberalization, absence of a predictable legal framework, and insufficient progress in transferring productive assets into private hands.

The second is the constraint imposed by the lack of resources to revamp key public infrastructure (crucial for private sector growth) and insufficient credit for the emerging private sector.

A proper assistance strategy must look into both of these constraints and identify a proper mix of interventions. This is not an easy task. Premature lending to revamp public infrastructure before enough progress has been made on the incentive system and privatization may lead to inappropriate selection of infrastructure projects. Needless to say, public infrastructure should respond to the new structure of final output guided by the new relative prices. Premature credit lines for the productive sector can end up in sectors which ought to contract as a response to new relative prices and a more open economy. Furthermore, lending under significant macroeconomic instability and lack of sufficient public sector reform may simply end up in capital flight and wasteful public expenditures. The result can be to pile external debt without a major impact on a country's growth prospects.

But the Bank is also concerned about the 'quality' of the economic recovery. The most vulnerable groups must be protected, particularly if in the short run these groups are at risk. The very elderly, mothers, and young

142

children do not have reserve supplies of labour – efforts to protect them must be put in place. Social assistance programmes must be retargeted and efforts must be made to avoid the collapse of basic health services. The worst environmental problems, especially those threatening basic health, must also be confronted early on as part of the Bank's assistance.

The Bank's assistance today

The cumulative commitments of the Bank to these countries during fiscal years 1990–1994 (ending up in June 1994) amounts to $13.5 billion, of which $3.6 billion were committed in 1994 (Table 2). The Bank has established 13 resident missions during the last three years, including a 'hub' type of resident mission in Hungary from which specialized technical assistance is given in some selected areas.

Assistance to the countries of the FSU

The initial assistance to these countries has relied on three instruments: rehabilitation loans, heavy technical assistance support, and selected investment loans to avoid the collapse of key infrastructure or in key sectors where a rapid supply response could emerge.

Rehabilitation loans are fast disbursement operations of one tranche (disbursed against imports) to support the first stages of the reform programme. They support the fiscal adjustment by replacing inflationary financing and hence providing the necessary 'breathing space'. It takes time to efficiently raise revenues and cut expenditures; still, inflation needs to be reduced rapidly. Hence inflationary financing must be reduced much more rapidly than the pace at which a 'high quality' fiscal adjustment might be possible. They also enhance import capacity (the external side) preventing further decline in output and welfare, particularly in the health sector, key public services, etc. This is done by agreeing on a 'specific list of imports' that have to be given first priority before financing the rest of imports (the rest is usually financed through the general foreign exchange market).

For the country to receive a rehabilitation loan, several conditions must be fulfilled. First, the country needs to show commitment to stabilization, generally by subscribing to an IMF programme (in general, rehabilitation loans go in parallel with operations out of the IMF's Systemic Transformation Facility or a Stand-By Arrangement). Second, a minimum advance is required in the areas of price liberalization and privatization. Third, a written statement of future reforms to which the government is committed in key structural areas is required, such as price liberalization, privatization, governance of state-owned enterprises, financial sector reform, legal framework for private sector development, social protection, and safety nets.

The second area of support has been loans for institution building and technical assistance. These loans have taken place even in situations where the country has not yet received a rehabilitation loan, such as in Belarus and Ukraine. In most cases, however, they have some in parallel with a rehabilitation loan (i.e. Russia, Kazakhstan).

During the first stages of transition, the lack of appropriate institutions has been an impediment for implementing stabilization policies and a major bottle-neck to modernization and restructuring. To meet the needs of a market economy, the state apparatus for civil service, the organization of public finances, and the regulatory frameworks all need reform. In this sense, support to the central government or to specific agencies in sectors or subsectors becomes an essential first step.

For instance, institution building loans in Ukraine and Belarus focused on oblasts and cities willing to accelerate reforms. In Ukraine, the Bank supported the organization of auctions for small enterprise privatization and the simplification of the regulatory framework for private business. In addition, this project provided assistance for pilot privatization of some larger firms. In Belarus, institutional building was aimed at strengthening the tax administration in the city of Minsk and, later, in the other six oblasts of the country. In addition, the project in Belarus provided support to the government in the evaluation of alternative mass privatization programmes.

The Bank had two institutional building operations in Russia during the past years; one to support the mass privatization programme and several other key complementary areas to privatization (competition policy, environmental liability issues, etc.). The other one supports employment services, programmes, preparing the way to provide such services in case unemployment increases as a result of restructuring. A project in Turkmenistan will provide technical assistance to improve the framework for private sector participation in the oil/gas sector.

Selective investment loans in key infrastructure and in areas where a quick supply response may take place have been the third instrument of support during this initial phase.

In Russia, for instance, deterring output fall in the energy sector will have a significant impact on the economy. The bank has committed $1.1 billion for that purpose. These loans were conditioned on the improvement of pricing policies and the legal regime, which are fundamental for foreign direct investment in the sector.

Efficient investment in transport and other infrastructure can also make a significant difference to the supply response. Transport needs to be reoriented toward new markets and different modes, for example, away from rail and toward more flexible road traffic. In Russia, a highway rehabilitation loan is designed to help a shift from rail to road for short-haul freight traffic. In Kazakhstan, a project focused on the restoration of public transport service in the country's three main cities.

As the reform programme deepens, adjustment operations have supported further reform steps. For example, a second rehabilitation loan to Russia (presently being processed) will support further liberalization of the trade regime, mainly in the energy sector. The Bank has worked with the Russian counterparts on agreements to auction scarce pipeline capacity rights so as to make trade in energy more efficient and transparent. An acceleration of privatization – notably the start of mass privatization programmes – and of financial sector and banking reform are now part of adjustment operations in Moldova, Kirghizia, and Kazakhstan.

Assistance to Central Europe

I will now turn to Central Europe. Again, we are trying to adapt our assistance to a variety of countries and circumstances. Hungary, Poland, and the Czech Republic are more advanced in stabilization, privatization, and overall liberalization. The private sector is growing quickly and it is generating a significant (derived) demand for public infrastructure. Crucial is to expand such an infrastructure so that it does not become a bottle-neck for private sector growth. In these countries, the Bank is being active in transport, telecommunications, and in the restructuring of educational systems. In both Hungary and Poland, there is a need for basic reform in the pension system – crucial for the sustainability of public finances. The Bank is discussing the possibility of adjustment operations to support further reforms in public finances.

In Bulgaria and Romania, where privatization has been slower, the Bank is working on financial and enterprise reform loans that will support both the acceleration of privatization and the necessary reforms of the financial sector – conducive to a larger intermediation of funds to the private sector. To support the strong reform efforts in Albania, the Bank has financed operations on a broad front: housing, schools, water supply, rural development. The objective is to provide technical assistance and to maximize the mobilization of co-financing by bilateral donors.

Finally, the Bank has supported debt reduction agreements for both Bulgaria and Poland, by providing funds to finance buy-backs and the collateralization of new government bonds being exchanged for old debt.

Sectoral issues

Let me now have another cut in discussing the Bank's assistance and focus on what we are doing in selected sectors.

Financial sector reform

Bank support in these areas aims at (a) phasing out subsidized directed credit and support the introduction of a market-determined and transparent interest policy; (b) the restructuring and privatization of state banks; (c) the resolution of the 'bad debt' problem and the issue of recapitalization of banks; (d) improving the financial sector's legal and economic infrastructure, i.e. payments system, laws of collateral and bankruptcy, prudential regulations, supervisory capacity of the Central Bank, etc.; (e) providing credit to the emerging private sector through credit lines that are broad and priced at what the market bears.

In addressing these objectives, the specific approach varies from country to country. Let me illustrate this by comparing the case of Poland, the Russian Federation, and the countries in Central Asia.

In Poland, the resolution of the bad portfolio of the banking sector relies on a decentralized process of conciliation – where incentives are given for banks to enter into work-out arrangements (including debt/equity swaps) with debtor enterprises outside the formal legal system of bankruptcy. In the process the banks have been partly recapitalized. In Russia, recapitalization of the state banks has been deemed too risky, the legal environment and prudential regulations are still incipient. The strategy is to support the emergence of a new generation of banks and to build around them a set of

regulations and incentives together with strict capital adequacy requirements (what is called the International Standard Bank concept).

In Poland, the process is being supported by a Financial Sector Operation.
In Russia, it is supported by the largest technical assistance loan ever
processed by the Bank – a $200 million Financial Institutions Technical
Assistance loan co-financed also by the EBRD. This loan is being followed
by a large credit line operation directed to the private sector through the
new banks. This operation also has an equity component financed by the
EBRD and some donor countries.

In Central Asia, the containment of the 'bad debt' problems will have to
rely on more centralized approaches, at least in the short run. Here, the
worse money-losing enterprises are being isolated from the banking system
and placed under a new restructuring agency where downsizing and/or
liquidation is one of the alternatives to be considered. Special budgetary
allocations are made in order to make any remaining subsidies transparent
and conditional on downsizing and divestiture of assets.

Legal reform

In a market economy, the legal framework defines the universe of property
rights and sets rules for exchanging those rights, it sets rules for the entry
and exit of actors into, and out of, productive activities, and it sets rules for
overseeing market structure and competition.

The legal structure in the countries in transition is evolving in many of
these areas. Countries of Central Europe have a rich legal tradition from the
pre-socialist times. But in many areas, the laws are too general – especially
in the area of property rights – leaving too wide a discretion for adminis-
trators and courts. This represents a major source of uncertainty because
there has not yet been enough time to build up a body of codes and
precedents that would guide decisions. This is particularly true in the area
of restitution, transfer of land, the role of local governments in managing
the housing stock, the legal framework for foreclosure and eviction, etc.
The disarray in the registry system and the slowness of notary systems are
additional problems.

The process of legal reform is complex, requiring a careful revision of
old legislation, the drafting of new laws, the establishment of implementation and enforcement mechanisms, the strengthening of the judiciary and
regulatory institutions, and legal training. The Bank has accelerated its

support in this area recognizing that initiative in this area may slow down the pay-off of reform in other fronts. However, one must also recognize that the role of the Bank in this field can only complement domestic initiatives.

The Legal Department of the Bank has taken the lead in many of these areas. The initial rehabilitation loans incorporated technical assistance to improve the legal environment for private sector development, putting together a competition and anti-monopoly legislation and improving the legal regime for foreign direct investment. Albania, Bulgaria, and several republics of the FSU have been beneficiaries of technical assistance funds supporting wide legal frameworks. In Belarus and Russia, the Bank has provided legal technical assistance on a sectoral basis, mostly for privatization, labour market legislation, and oil legislation (in Russia).

In addition, the Bank's staff has assisted several countries in securing grant financing for the preparation of specific pieces of legislation, such as petroleum legislation in Azerbaijan financed by the United Kingdom Know-How Fund, and assistance in bankruptcy legislation in Lithuania financed by the Central and East Europe Law Initiative.

Assistance to the social sectors

Support in this area aims at improving the targeting of social assistance including pension reform and building unemployment compensation programmes that encourage job search and job mobility. All this must be done within strict fiscal constraints, notably in the countries where stabilization has still not been achieved.

In the FSU countries, the Bank has been actively involved in supporting a better targeting of cash transfer programmes and reforming the pension system to assure a minimum pension of sufficient purchasing power to protect the very elderly. This involves increasing the present (very early) retirement age and capping specific pension programmes for some of the more politically powerful groups. This has not been easy, and not much progress has been achieved.

In the interim, there is increasing evidence that in many countries basic social services – particularly basic health – have been deteriorating rapidly during the last two years. To avoid such deterioration, the Bank has quickly geared its efforts to prepare health projects in the Kirghiz Republic, Turkmenistan, Ukraine, Georgia, Estonia, Albania, Croatia, Bulgaria, the former Yugoslav Republic of Macedonia, and in Slovakia.

A programme is being prepared for the Russian Federation to prevent the collapse of basic health and education and reorient the provision of social services from enterprises to municipalities and private sources of supply. The Bank has already reassigned funds within an existing project (supporting privatization) to transferring day-care services from enterprises to local governments.

The first explicit project to assist such a transfer of responsibilities is being prepared for Kazakhstan. The project will finance the rehabilitation of basic health and education services as they are transferred from enterprises to local governments in six selected cities. Most important, the project will finance (on a declining basis) the additional recurrent costs that the cities now have to incur by such transfer.

The energy sector

A key feature of the countries in transition – mainly in the FSU - has been the significant underpricing of energy and its effect on the energy intensity of the overall economy. As trade in energy moves toward world prices, the pay-off to expand energy production and save on the consumption side becomes more important.

The Bank lending to the energy sector amounted to about one quarter of total lending in FY94. In the oil importing countries of Central Europe, as well as Ukraine, Belarus, and the Baltic countries, the Bank has been actively involved in projects to improve efficiency in the use of energy, by rehabilitating the power sector and district heating system. In countries with an energy surplus, such as the Russian Federation, projects to rehabilitate and to avoid further reduction in oil output have been accompanied by agreements to improve the legal framework for private investment in the sector, particularly foreign investment.

Support of a better environment

Across Eastern Europe and the FSU, water and air pollution continue to undermine both livelihood and health. To stop (and reverse) environmental damage requires both know-how and financing. The Bank has been actively involved in this area both at the project level and as catalyst to attract donor support. Projects of environment clean-up have been approved initially for Poland and the Czech Republic and recently for the Russian Federation.

Additional projects are under preparation for Belarus, Lithuania, and Latvia.

In the Russian Federation, the Bank's project focuses on two areas: (a) environmental management and institutional strengthening at the federal and regional levels in three regions: the Upper Volga, the Urals, and North Caucasus; and (b) in identifying, developing, and setting country policy (and the policy instruments) dealing with environmental epidemics, water quality, water resource management, and hazardous waste management.

A major analytical report, the Environmental Action Program has provided the basis for strengthening donor co-ordination and policy advice. The Bank also participated in the design of an action plan for the Danube and, together with other donors, it has identified a portfolio of investments for the six riparian states of the Black Sea.

Other issues

Other bank group activities

The International Finance Corporation (IFC) has stepped up the number of operations in the countries in transition from two in FY90 to twenty-nine in FY94. The IFC has supported the private sector by investment in private enterprises and has provided technical assistance in the areas of privatization, capital markets, and promotion of foreign investment. Recently, it has been central in developing pioneering pilot projects in the area of privatization both in Ukraine and Belarus.

Research and training support has been given priority too. As a knowledge-based institution, the Bank offers more than just a financial product, and its research has addressed issues ranging from macroeconomic stabilization to enterprise behaviour. They include comparative studies on enterprise restructuring, the emerging legal framework, agriculture transition, and many different aspects of labour markets and poverty.

The Economic Development Institute (EDI) has, since 1990, established many joint programmes of training. A special emphasis has been given to train local teachers to train mid-level officials in local institutions and agencies, i.e. 'training of trainers'. In late 1992, a training centre at Moscow State University was established targeted to public officials and taught primarily by local staff. This model is being replicated in Ukraine and Uzbekistan, with plans for Kazakhstan, Belarus, and Moldova. Similar programmes have started in Central Europe, at the Center for Economic Research and Graduate Education in Prague, Warsaw University, and lately with the Joint Vienna Institute. Altogether 1,175 professionals have been invited to Washington or Vienna during the last three years. Most recently the EDI has begun reaching journalists, parliamentarians, and the public at large (the TV programme on the ills of inflation for the Russian Federation) on the objectives of reform programmes and lessons from country experiences.

Issues for the future

What will be the challenges for the future? We can envisage some of them.

The *diversity* in country performance may accelerate as time passes – due to the synergism between improved domestic policies and higher level of capital flows, particularly private. Countries doing well on the policy front will probably attract further foreign capital flows reinforcing the incentives for accelerating reform. Countries lagging behind or having reversals will experience further capital flight and problems in attracting external financing, even official financing. This may accentuate the incentives for further controls and inflationary financing.

The above diversity will necessarily require further flexibility in the Bank's instruments of assistance. In the former group of countries, the Bank will have to experiment in 'building bridges' toward external capital markets such as guarantees for private investment in public infrastructure. Some initiatives are today being considered in the area of motorways and pipelines in the Czech Republic and Poland respectively. In countries where lack of political consensus prevents progress on a broad front, the Bank may have to experiment with local projects of a pilot nature aimed at generating incentives at replicability by other local governments. However, these projects will require complex institutional on-lending arrangements between central and local governments.

The Bank may have to increase its capability to advise on legal reform. However, there are limits by which institutional reforms on the legal side can be speeded up through external interventions.

The Bank will probably face strong demands to finance 'active' restructuring programmes (i.e. investment programme of expansion or restructuring) for money-losing enterprises remaining in the public sector. My personal opinion is that the Bank should limit itself to support 'passive' restructuring facilitating enterprises' downsizing through the provision of budgetary support for severance payments, the divestiture of social services to local governments, and technical assistance for the enterprise to develop restructuring plans themselves.

Accelerating and finding new ways to support the social sectors and programmes of social assistance will be a key challenge for the Bank. In large countries such as Ukraine and the Russian Federation, the more realistic projects in this area will have to be done at the local level. Still, for these interventions to be replicable, it will again be necessary to advance in the constitutional clarification of rights and responsibilities between the central and local governments.

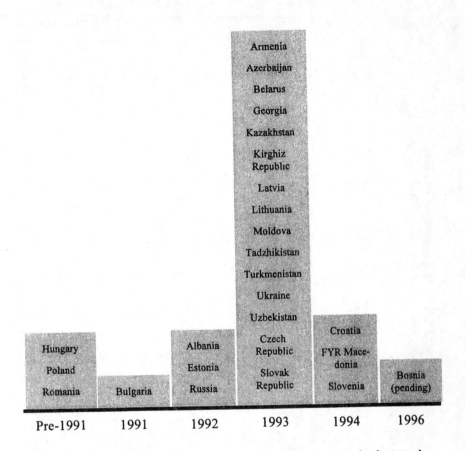

Figure 15.1 Evolution of membership in the IBRD by economies in transition (by July-June fiscal year)

Table 15.2 ECA lending operations by country commitments in US$ millions by fiscal year)

	1991	1992	1993	1994	1995	Total 1991-1995	Resident Mission
Central and Eastern Europe	2937	1777	1655	1378	776	8523	
Albania		41	44	47	67	200	Yes
Bulgaria	17	250	178	148	125	718	Yes
Croatia				128	120	248	
Czech Republic	450	246		82	2	870	
Hungary	550	200	413	129	38	1330	Yes
FYR Macedonia				80	123	203	Yes
Poland	1440	390	900	146	240	3116	Yes
Romania	180	650	120	401	60	1411	Yes
Slovak Republic				137		137	
Slovenia				80		80	
Former Yugoslavia	300					300	
Former Soviet Union			1630	2278	3507	7414	
Russia			1370	1520	1741	4631	Yes
Armenia			12	28	117	157	Yes
Belarus				170		170	Yes
Georgia					103	103	To open in 1996
Moldova			26	60	90	176	Yes
Ukraine			27	25	648	700	Yes
Estonia			30	50	30	110	Yes
Latvia			45	25	53	123	Yes
Lithuania			60	26	32	118	Yes
Azerbaijan					82	82	Yes
Kazakhstan				274	283	557	Yes
Kirghiz Republic			60	78	77	215	Yes
Tadzhikistan						0	
Turkmenistan					25	25	
Uzbekistan				21	226	247	Yes
Total, CEE and FSU	2937	1777	3285	3656	4282	15937	
Turkey	900	334	564	100	250	2148	

154

16 The Information Aspect of Foreign Capital Flows

Jan Klacek

I will try to divide my presentation into two parts. First, I would like to comment on the issues of trade flows between the Czech Republic and possibly also other Central European and OECD countries and second, on foreign capital inflows to the region.

As to the first issue, I would like to present the view that the issue of mutual trade has been the most important element of the reform process, at least in my country and, I believe, also in other countries of the region. If I were asked to give a list of preferences in the policy measures from the side of developed market economies in relation to the region, I would certainly place trade issues first followed with a long interval by other measures.

As far as foreign capital inflow is concerned, I share the opinion that the bulk of new investments required in the region is very significant. But this is a very long-term process. Just to give you one example: when voucher privatization was started in our country, someone made the calculation that it would last 200 years before the equity capital of enterprises to be privatized could be obtained if it were to be purchased at all.

The sources of capital accumulation within the region are very limited, even though I still believe that the only way out from that dilemma is to start a long-term process of capital accumulation in the country. Parallel to that process foreign private and institutionalized capital flows remain very important. By institutionalized flows, I have in mind foreign capital which is promoted or organized or channelled through international institutions.

Why is the issue of trade flows so important? Not because of the collapse of the former markets in Central and Eastern European countries, mainly the Russian market, although this is said often enough. I think this is not the most important factor behind the trade issue. Much more important is the information aspect.

The most negative element of the legacy of central planning was the completely distorted price system where prices were distorted not only in the sense economists tend to describe decision-making. A consequence of this was a complete misallocation of resources from the structural point of view, and that is why the structural adjustment, structural change, which has been started, tends to be very long-term: the process has been there for forty–fifty years. For this purpose, a market-driven, market-determined price structure in the system opens up the market of developed Western countries, and therefore, it serves a really existential purpose for the countries in transition. Countries like the Czech Republic, Hungary, Poland, and Slovakia are usually considered as relatively developed in terms of the transition process. They consider to be already in the second stage of the transition after the stabilization phase. Even these countries, if one looks at the price structure after four or five years, are still far from the relative price structures prevalent in developed Western countries.

So the issue of getting the right signals for decision-making is still with us. This from the point of view of economists is the foremost element of why trade should be opened, and why existing barriers and restrictive practices should be lifted as soon as possible.

I collected interesting data concerning the impact of the possible opening of developed market economies to exports from Central European countries, the Czech Republic, Poland, Hungary, and Slovakia. So-called sensitive exports, which are the most debated, are agricultural, textile, chemical products – these altogether represented 1.7 per cent of total imports of the OECD countries in 1990. And in terms of total output of OECD, these represented 0.4 per cent. The other calculation is showing the impact on employment. The present level of exports from these four countries to OECD represents in terms of this sensitive items, 0.5 per cent on employment in the OECD countries. And even if the present levels were increased by 100 per cent, the loss in terms of jobs would be less than 200,000 jobs in the total OECD area, while another 100,000 jobs would be created. So the overall impact would be rather small.

Now, I return to the issue of capital flows to the Czech Republic. We have experienced the following sequence of different capital flows. First, it was institutionalized capital flows to the country – in the very beginning of the transition process, in 1991-92 – and in this period they really played an important role in stabilizing the economy and providing necessary cushions when we introduced limited convertibility of the currency and dealt with the foreign debt service.

Soon after that, when the economy was stabilized, private foreign capital started to be interested in entering the country, and soon after principal agencies, rating agencies like Moodies, Standard, and Poor's upgraded the Czech Republic to the investment grade from the so-called speculative grade. Then private capital flows started to appear in the country and they were participating in the privatization process. Therefore, both direct investments and portfolio investments are already active. But having said that, I would like to stress that there are many preconditions for such a sequence.

First of all, stabilization and, generally, economic policy have to be credible and have to achieve certain tangible results. Secondly, institutionalized foreign capital flows have to be in place before and have to show that in all major investment projects, in particular in infrastructure, institutions like the World Bank, the EBRD, and others, already entered the country, showed serious interest and showed that the risks in this respect are not as great as in other countries. So there is an interlink between this institutionalized capital flow and private capital flow to the country.

17 Technical Assistance:
What More could be Done?

George Kopits*

These remarks are simply intended to supplement the presentations of my colleagues from the World Bank and the International Monetary Fund, by giving a view from the trenches. Specifically, I would like to comment on technical assistance to former centrally-planned economies in transition. Is there some scope for further assistance from bilateral, regional, or multilateral institutions? In what areas should additional assistance be provided? But first let me mention a major distinguishing characteristic wich sets these economies apart from, for example, the economies in Latin America, or post-war Europe: namely, the very weak linkage between macroeconomic policies, on the one hand, and institutional arrangements, economic behaviour and administrative practices at the microeconomic level, on the other. This week linkage is reflected in the limited effectiveness of fiscal and monetary policy tools typically used in market-oriented economies, when applied in the former centrally-planned economies.

As difficult as it may be to formulate a macroeconomic policy strategy, with the appropriate mix and sequences, or as complex as it may be to design institutions in the unfamiliar post-socialist environment, I believe these are still much simpler tasks than the ones to which I would like to draw your attention. Indeed, to design an income tax law, to abolish price subsidies – as done in a number of economies at the outset of the transition – is relatively simple. To prepare a central bank law or even to draft a constitution – following a Western model – can be rather straightforward. In contrast, practical implementation of laws, rules, and regulations is far less tractable in this environment, as illustrated by five different areas.

---

* Senior Resident Representative in Hungary, International Monetary Fund.
   The views expressed do not necessarily reflect those of the Fund.

In the area of *enterprise regulation*, both Poland and Hungary enacted bankruptcy legislation in the mid-1980s— before the advent of the transition – essentially by dusting off pre-World War II bankruptcy laws. But for a number of years, bankruptcy legislation was not enforced. When the law was invoked in Hungary, in the early 1990s, the courts lacked sufficient financial literacy to exercise judicial functions in this area. Court decisions would vary substantially between a rather strict and a very liberal interpretation of bankruptcy rules. However, many other countries in transition have not recognized yet the need to expose enterprises to bankruptcy risk – the ultimate form of hard budget constraint in a market-based economy.

Reform of *commercial banking* does not merely entail cleaning up non-performing portfolios or recapitalizing banks – to protect depositors – for bad loans extended under the previous regime, or, in some instances, to liquidate such banks. In comparison to the savings and loan rescue operation undertaken in the United States – where it was assumed that banks know how to conduct risk assessment abiding by prudential regulations – in the economies in transition, actual banking practices have yet to be learned. In these countries, for the most part, apart from collecting deposits, commercial banks have yet to master elementary banking skills. This involves acquisition of practical know-how as well as elimination of the moral hazard that still prevails in the banking system (mostly state-owned banks) in these countries.

A third area is *tax and customs administration*. Although there are manuals that explain the principles of tax audit and cost accounting, actual application of these principles requires considerable experience that is unavailable in the countries in transition. Similarly, there is an absence of experience in the use of customs valuation techniques, as under central planning only a handful of large state trading enterprises conducted all foreign trade, exempt from any explicit tax or customs liability. The combination of relatively high statutory tax rates – and, in some cases, high customs duty rates – and weak tax and customs administration, explains the booming underground economy throughout the region. Not surprisingly, according to conservative estimates, the underground economy accounts for at least one fourth of GDP.

The fourth area is *budgetary practices*. If zero-base budgeting has any meaning anywhere, it is in the economies in transition. Indeed, the shift from socialist central planning requires a systematic review of all government expenditures to ascertain their appropriateness in a market-oriented environment. Equally important is the establishment of market-oriented cash and debt management and adoption of transparent public procurement practices. To this day, only in a few progressive countries in transition, there has been a start in introducing such practices. Standard cost-benefit analysis is being applied to large infrastructure projects only when it is required by an external lender. In most countries, some Soviet-type government pro- grammes, budgetary priorities and internal provisioning are still in force after five years of transition. Incidentally, the shortcomings of tax admini- stration and budgetary practices contribute significantly to the large fiscal imbalances experienced in many economies in transition.

Finally, as regards *social safety nets,* considerable progress has been made in designing social security systems appropriate for a market economy. However, a monumental task still lies ahead: the development of cost-ef- fective delivery of health-care services, unemployment compenstaion, man- power training, social assistance, etc. In a number of countries this is not necessarily a problem of insufficient physical capacity; for instance, there is a large surplus of hospital beds being used in a highly disfunctional manner to provide social assistance for the homeless and employment for excess health-care personnel. In such cases, it is necessary, above all, to trim capacity or to transform it for efficient use. Also, proper targeting of social assistance is to be made operational.

The upshot of my remarks is that in these and other areas, there remains considerable need for technical assistance. While significant amounts of assistance has been deployed by multilateral and bilateral donors in policy formulation and institution design, technical assistance of a hands-on nature has been rather modest, particularly compared with the enormous task ahead. Assistance in customs valuation, for example, cannot be provided by a few experts who visit for, say, a couple of months a country like Ukraine. The above areas require large scale, and in some cases, prolonged assis- tance, to reach a critical mass. Obviously, political will is a necessary ingredient. To crack down on the hidden economy or to remove moral hazard from the banking system presupposes serious resolve at the highest level of government underpinned by social consensus.

18 The Specific Contributions of the EBRD to the Transition Process

Nicholas Stern

Introduction

It is a pleasure for me to be here today and an honour to participate in an event which recognizes and celebrates the invaluable contribution of Robert Triffin. The analytical problems he identified, coupled with the ingenuity and determination he showed in devising institutions and policies to respond to them, should inspire and guide us in our efforts to assist the crucial process of transition from a command to a market economy in Eastern Europe and the former Soviet Union (FSU).

Transition – A progress report

This transition, which the EBRD has been mandated to promote, is unprecedented. In an attempt to advance the understanding of this historic process, the EBRD has recently published a new report, which we have called the *Transition Report*. The report's main purpose is to advance the understanding of transition. It does this by describing, analysing, and assessing the stage of market-oriented transition in the countries of Central and Eastern Europe and the FSU.

It is important to recognize that the term *transition* refers here to a specific and unique process, and as such, it is a very different concept from those of development or stabilization. *Development* broadly relates to improving standards of living among individuals. This means: command over resources, embodied in the notions of consumption, income or wealth; health, embodied in the notions of nutrition, morbidity or mortality; and education, embodied in the notions of achievement or schooling. Transition is different: in the language of the mandate of the EBRD, it is the process of moving

161

from a command economy to an open market oriented economy. Countries have embarked on transition because they hope it will enable them to deliver higher growth and development. But in the short run, transition generally carries costs, for both growth and development.

Stabilization concerns the basic macroeconomic variables such as inflation, balance of payments, and debt. It has a strong relationship with transition. Price signals are crucial for the functioning of the market economy and are distorted by inflation. Further, very high inflation and instability inhibit the long-term commitments essential for investment. And there are relationships in the other direction too. Transition can pose major threats to the tax base and to monetary control.

Before embarking on a more detailed discussion of the transition, it is worth pausing to recognize that a particularly striking feature of reform in the region is the commonalty of the agendas of the participants. The countries have separately and willingly chosen to embark on a similar process of radical and fundamental economic and political change. In historical terms, it is surely very rare that such far-reaching and basic reforms occur over such a wide area by choice rather than by force.

At the outset of transition, the countries of the region were all middle income in terms of the standard World Bank classification based on conventional GDP per capita measures. There were generally reasonably high scores on other measures of standard of living, such as life expectancy or education. The process of transition has seen some decline in living standards in terms of income and, in some cases, such as Russia, strong decline in life expectancy, particularly for middle-aged males. Unemployment has risen sharply in many countries of the region. The transition has been a painful process for many but, as I have emphasized, its central purpose is to increase standards of living over the longer term. The gains are already appearing in many countries.

It is not easy to assess the progress of transition, not the least because many elements of transition are very difficult to measure. However, in the *Transition Report* we have attempted to do just that. Somewhat boldly, we have produced a table which seeks to measure the stage of transition in each country, through a number of key indicators relating to the three basic concepts: enterprises, markets, and financial institutions. The indicators selected relate to the privatization process, enterprise restructuring, price liberalization, changes in trade and foreign exchange systems, and banking reform. These are core elements of a market economy and, therefore, central to the transition process. For each indicator, we use a classification system which is rather crude: a country is assigned a number on a scale of 1 to 4 one point indicating little progress and four points indicating substantial progress. The findings are set out in the Table of the *Report* (attached). One striking feature stands out: the diversity across the region. The countries started the transition from very different circumstances and they have had sharply differing experiences.

Within this diversity, substantial advance in the transition has been made in many countries. Dynamic private sectors are emerging: in nine out of twenty-five countries in the region, the private sector accounts for over half of GDP. Foreign trade and domestic prices have been liberalized in most countries and most small-scale units have been privatized. Furthermore, successful stabilization programmes have ensured the containment of inflation in most of Eastern Europe and the Baltic states. Much of this region is currently experiencing positive economic growth. Some countries – Poland and Albania – already achieved this in 1993.

Unfortunately, this is not the case further east. Many of the CIS countries continue to be plagued by falling output and high inflation, and have yet to embark on serious market-oriented reform programmes. In 1993, eight of the twelve CIS countries had annual rates of inflation of more than 1,000 per cent. On the positive side, however, Russia and Kirghizia have made great strides in privatization, and have, along with Moldova and Ukraine, reduced inflation substantially this year.

It is natural and interesting to ask about the reasons for this diversity. There are many, and it is not easy to single out any as the major cause. The countries, as I have noted, had very different starting points in terms of economic structure, debt, links with the developed countries, history of reform, and so on. The political framework and recent history differed strongly. There had been large transfers between states within the region, most of which have now ceased. The period of communism was much longer in the FSU. The cultures are also very different. All these things surely must play a role in understanding the differing experiences. But we must also recognize that policy matters. Broadly speaking, those that have achieved macroeconomic stabilization and liberalization the quickest, have also shown the best performance in terms of growth and limiting the costs of transition.

One crucial shared feature, however, is the difficulty of reorienting their economies to a new trading pattern. The severe challenge of opening these economies to competitive international trade was combined with the shock experienced when the old organization of trade within the region collapsed.

While the available data are generally unreliable, it seems that trade turnover within the region shrank by more than half. This dislocation of intra-regional trade, coupled with the uneconomic structure of production in the region, has played a major role in the fall in output experienced in all countries. Nevertheless, the achievements in the reorientation of trade have been striking. It appears that those who embarked on reform earliest and most rigorously are also seeing the earliest and biggest rewards in terms of trade. The countries of the Visegrád group, South East Europe and the Baltic states have seen trade turnover with the Western market economies roughly double between 1989 and 1993. The EU market has absorbed by far the largest share of this expansion and now receives seventy per cent or more of the exports of transition economies to the OECD area.

Even for those countries which have moved furthest down the transition path – namely, the Czech Republic, Hungary, Poland, the Slovak Republic, the Baltic states, and some countries of the former Yugoslavia – deep difficulties remain. Most of these countries have started to tackle the thorny problem of large-scale privatization and the related issue of financial sector reform. All are finding it difficult. Whilst it is possible to sell fairly rapidly the more competitive state-owned enterprises to strategic investors, governments are having to deal with the old industrial giants of the command economy. Burdened with bad debt – owed to the banks and to each other – these giants are finding it difficult to rationalize cost structures and find new markets. These difficulties are also being faced by some companies which have already been privatized through voucher-based sales. Restructuring, before or after privatization, remains a major challenge. In addition to the uneconomic organization, outputs and production methods and the history of debt, this challenge includes the social responsibilities of enterprises. Many of the large enterprises were and are responsible for housing and schooling, for example. The dislocation of unemployment is severe in itself but could become catastrophic for individuals if coupled with loss of housing. It is hardly surprising that the restructuring of such enterprises has proceeded cautiously.

A further major challenge, as already emphasized in discussing expenditure, is that of creating a functioning tax system. Tax collection is at the heart of financial stability, without which private sector growth is severely constrained. Under the 'old' system, a government could command the resources it used; in a market economy, a government must finance these resources. Tax reform is, therefore, a logical requirement of transition, it is central to achieving macroeconomic stability and should be a priority. As the transition has progressed, this task has proven difficult. The old sources of revenue, particularly the profits from state enterprises, have fallen sharply. Meanwhile, bringing the new private sector into the tax net has not been easy. The result in many countries has been high deficits and high inflation – to the detriment of private sector development. The failure to match revenue and expenditure has also encouraged the growth of *ad hoc* and often confiscatory tax regimes. These countries now face the very severe challenge of introducing tax systems which are stable, broad-based, and even-handed across taxpayers.

The realization that even the most advanced countries in the transition have some deep-rooted problems must not come as a surprise, nor must it allow us to lose perspective. Much has been accomplished within a relatively short space of time.

To conclude this brief discussion of the experience of the transition economies, let me summarize some of the lessons we have learned. Macroeconomic stability is of crucial importance. As we have emphasized, the most successful countries – in terms of resumption of output growth – were those that achieved macroeconomic stability and price and trade liberalization the earliest. Controlling inflation and liberalizing prices can and should be done quickly. Whilst some elements can be put in place quickly, others, such as the privatization of large-scale enterprises, restructuring of enterprises, and the reform of the financial sector take longer. Crudely speaking, changes affecting 'nominal' variables, i.e. prices and their levels, can be carried out quickly, but the reform of institutions takes much longer. Generally, through the process of change, policy should be guided by the principles of stability of signals and transparency of government interventions. These are crucial for investors to take a long-term view.

Keeping these lessons in mind, let me now turn to the international community and, in particular, the EBRD's distinctive role.

The specific contributions of the EBRD

We must, of course, remember that the individual governments and the political processes in the countries of the region remain the key influences on the transition. Nonetheless, the international community and international financial institutions can provide valuable assistance in advancing the reforms. There are three ways in which the international community can assist the transition: by offering greater market access for East European exports, by catalyzing foreign investment into the region, and by providing financial and technical assistance through bilateral and multilateral channels.

Trade and investment are particularly important. Apart from their macroeconomic benefits, they can influence specifically some of the core problems of transition by generating pressure for behavioural and institutional adjustment, by contributing to technology transfer, and by providing skills and understanding for the market economy.

There has been much progress in the area of trade but significant obstacles remain. Market access to the key Western markets has improved greatly through the Europe Agreements (with the European Union) and a series of other trade agreements. However, some of the most important product sectors have been left out of the game and successful exports in many others face the constant threat of contingent protection. For instance, the agricultural sector, which is more important for many Eastern European economies than it generally is in the West, is largely excluded from effective market opening. Other 'sensitive' products are subject to special tariff and quota regimes which, while temporary, seem to be easily substituted by safeguard or anti-dumping action if East European exporters prove too successful. The recently publicized EU decision to make more active use of the 'countervailing duty' weapon is threatening for the transition economies since it is often easy to argue that there are, present and past, subsidies to exporting firms. On the other hand, the European Commission is elaborating proposals to speed up the harmonization of competition and state-aid regimes between Eastern Europe and the EU, and, in parallel, to phase out trade remedy instruments. Such measures, building on the valuable advances of the European Agreements deserve strong support.

Foreign investment into the region has increased substantially since the start of the transition process, but remains concentrated on a small group of countries. Perceived country risk is important in explaining this concentration but there are other reasons. For instance, intra-regional trade and access to Western markets are often viewed as not sufficiently secure to warrant region-wide production and sales strategies by multinational companies. Also, foreign investment is partly a cumulative process in which early investors draw in others. The important thing is to get the process started. The international community and international financial institutions (IFIs), in particular, should search for ways of increasing foreign direct investment into a broader group of countries. There is scope for doing this on a commercially sound basis without subsidizing the investors. One way to achieve this is by accompanying investors as partners in their projects, which may then face less political risk and which may benefit from the knowledge of institutions dealing comprehensively with these countries.

The type of investment or assistance that can be provided by IFIs, depends very much on a country's stage of transition. In countries that are in the early stages of transition, there is limited scope for direct private sector investment. This is especially the case where modest progress on structural reform is combined with significant macroeconomic imbalances. In these countries, project-financing IFIs will channel more resources through the public sector, especially for infrastructure. As transition progresses, the scope for targeting IFIs investments more directly to the private sector increases, as we have seen in the Baltics, Russia, South East Europe, and to some extent in Kirghizia. At this stage, more work can be undertaken with foreign and local investors, as well as with local financial intermediaries. At the more advanced stages of transition, and where there is macroeconomic stabilization, it becomes possible for the IFIs, in general, and the EBRD, in particular, to place greater emphasis on direct investment in the local private sector.

This pattern is clearly visible within the operations of the EBRD. The EBRD is a unique institution. Unlike most IFIs, we do not have development as an explicitly stated goal, our goal is to foster transition. Transition as an objective is spelt out unequivocally in Article 1 of the Agreement which created the Bank. This reads:

'In contributing to economic progress and reconstruction, the purpose of the Bank shall be to foster the transition towards open market oriented economies, and to promote private and entrepreneurial initiative in the Central and Eastern European countries committed to and applying the principles of multi-party democracy, pluralism, and market economies.'

How does the EBRD differ from other IFIs? When drawing up its mandate, the Bank's shareholders recognized the unprecedented and uncertain nature of the transition process. The institution created to assist transition had to be able to respond and to adapt constantly, and it had to focus on the problems facing an emerging private sector. The EBRD is able to do just that. One of the Bank's key characteristics is that the financial tools at its disposal are very flexible. In particular, we can operate in both the public and private sectors adapting our instruments as necessary. We offer non-recourse financing, can make equity placements where appropriate, employ guarantee instruments tailored to address specific risks of private counterparts, and provide the whole spectrum of debt finance from subordinated to sovereign-guaranteed loans in local or foreign currencies, at fixed or floating interest rates. Our focus is on projects. We are not heavily involved in economy-wide policy conditionality as with the World Bank's Structural Adjustment Loans or the IMF's Stand-By Agreements and Systemic Transformation Facilities. Of course, our operations are set in the context of any policy conditionalities of such loans and may be made easier as a result of them.

We are relatively small. We cannot have more investments outstanding, *in total*, than our capital of ECU 10 billion. This may be compared with a size of the economy in our region of the order of ECU 1,000–1,500 billion in terms of *annual* income (the population is 400 million and the GNP per capita in purchasing power parity is of the order of 3,000–4,000 US dollars). Thus, there has always been an understanding that our impact must reach beyond our investments. Therefore, we seek projects that can have a catalytic or 'multiplier' effect. For example, the Bank invests in projects with a strong demonstration effect both for domestic and foreign investors. By being at the 'cutting edge', we aim to show what can be achieved in the changing economies of the region. In developing infrastructure, we leverage our impact by focusing on severe bottle-necks, both financial and physical, which are holding back private sector growth, or seek projects which demonstrate how infrastructure can be made commercial or which open up opportunities for further investment. Telecommunications have been an example of particular importance to us.

How does the EBRD differ from commercial banks? The Bank has several advantages over a commercial institution. First, its cost of capital is relatively low. The Bank's shareholders provide paid-in capital on which they do not require a dividend, and its AAA status allows it to borrow cheaply. Second, as a result of its official character and preferred creditor status, the Bank is less subject to certain political risks than commercial lenders or equity holders would be. Third, whilst the Bank does not have a 'soft window' such as International Development Association (IDA), or its own technical assistance resources, it does have a special relationship with various technical assistance funds, including PHARE and TACIS. These advantages do not imply, however, that the Bank is subsidizing its clients. It must make a profit. Nevertheless the advantages do allow the Bank to pursue an objective different from profit, i.e. the promotion of transition. The backing by its shareholders allows it to be less risk averse than commercial financial institutions. Technical assistance permits it to assess and mitigate risks, among other ways by working at both the public and private levels. Often, these different factors open a space in which the Bank's projects are 'additional', i.e. they do not directly compete with private sources of funding while, at the same time, safeguarding sound banking principles.

The Bank is now in its fourth year of operations and, we believe, is making substantial headway in our endeavours. Investments of ECU 4.5 billion of debt and equity have been approved by our Board in 196 projects. At the same time, these 196 projects are 'mobilizing' a total of over ECU 13.7 billion of investment. The EBRD is associated with, as an investor, around 15 per cent of the foreign direct investment into the region.

It is our mandate which gives us our basic direction. As transition has progressed, we have also sought to adapt our activities to this process. Working closely with our shareholders, we clarified our operational priorities at the beginning of the year. Our new priorities were resoundingly endorsed by governors at the Bank's Annual Meeting in April, and we have been working on their implementation since then.

1   We have altered the balance of our geographical approach. We are striving to be active in all countries of operations. This might seem straightforward, but it is not. When the Bank was created, its activities were focused on seven countries. Now there are twenty-five. It is important to ensure that the Bank's portfolio does not become over-concentrated in certain geographical areas – areas in which we have already built up business links and in which it is easier to function. We have no option but to respond to the needs of all our twenty-five countries of operations.

2   In addition to shifting our geographical balance, we are financing different types of operations. We are trying to do more difficult things in more difficult places. In particular, we are placing increasing emphasis on local, small, and medium enterprises. They must be a central driving force in the transition. Difficult though was it is in some countries, and remembering that we are not a retail bank, the Bank is actively seeking ways of working with local business partners. This means smaller loans and more risk as well as more work through local financial intermediaries. A greater EBRD local presence will assist this new direction. Furthermore, our work with foreign industrial partners continues across the region, especially within those countries that

currently find themselves at the intermediate stage of transition. Our work in infrastructure also remains a key priority.

3   In seeking to address the real needs of the region, we have also adapted our financial tools. In response to client demand, we are making increasing use of equity products as opposed to debt products, which have been our primary business to date. We are also placing greater emphasis on the use of guarantees, because through their ability to isolate and transfer risks, they can play, by enhancing the willingness to invest, an important part in the transition process.

By shifting its emphasis, the EBRD is charting a new course for IFI assistance to the region. We are seeking to address needs or demands which are currently not being met, and to respond to opportunities which otherwise would not be taken. However, this new emphasis on smaller, riskier projects in a broader geographical spread does present us with a problem, that of profitability. We must balance our books. This will be difficult to achieve if we do not increase our productivity. We are, therefore, looking at ways of increasing our productivity, while at the same time maintaining our new direction. We are currently looking at two options, one is an increased role in trade finance, and the second is to adopt a more 'wholesale' approach in our relationships with companies who have long-term programmes in the region.

Conclusion

The EBRD is an exciting institution. It established itself in record time to address the special needs of this region. By straddling the public/private sector divide, it pursues the special goal of transition using the instruments of the modern capital market. Of course, it will always be small in relation to the economies it serves, but it can and does make an impact by demonstrating what is possible, by being at the 'cutting edge' and adapting quickly to changing circumstances in the region. It is this unique ability to respond and adapt to the transition process which makes the EBRD the IFI of the 1990s. It was founded at a time when the advantages of a dynamic private sector were uppermost in the minds of policy makers, economists, and other analysts. The intellectual climate contrasts with that surrounding the founding of the other IFIs at the time of Bretton Woods. If you want to talk about the future of IFIs, it is as well to talk about the EBRD.

The transition process itself will not be easy. There are fundamental challenges and difficulties. Institutional change cannot be instantaneous or painless. The starting point was one of great dislocation, grossly distorted economic structures, and uncertainty. The progress in five years has been remarkable, and one can be guardedly optimistic about the future, whilst recognizing and trying to limit the costs of the process. Many of those in the transition economies are making major sacrifices and adjustments as they work towards and in a new environment. We shall all share in the rewards of the success of the transition. The advanced market economies have a great responsibility to promote this process. They must offer experience, resources and, above all, open markets.

Table 18.1 Progress in transition in Eastern Europe and the former Soviet Union [1]

(see classification system for transition indicators opposite)

Countries	Private sector share of GDP Mid-94 in % (rough EBRD estimate)	Enterprises			Markets and trade		Financial Institutions
		Large-scale privatization	Small-scale privatization	Enterprise restructuring	Price liberalization and competition	Trade and foreign exchange system	Banking reform
Albania	50	1	3	2	3	4	2
Armenia	40	1	3	1	3	2	1
Azerbaijan	20	1	1	2	3	1	1
Belarus	15	2	2	2	2	1	1
Bulgaria	40	2	2	2	3	4	2
Croatia	40	3	4	2	3	4	3
Czech Republic	65	4	4	3	3	4	3
Estonia	55	3	4	3	3	4	3
FYR Macedonia	35	2	4	2	3	4	2
Georgia	20		2	1	2	1	1
Hungary	55	3	4	3	3	4	3
Kazakhstan	20	2	2	1	2	2	1
Kyrgyzstan	30	3	4	2	3	3	2
Latvia	55	2	3	2	3	4	2
Lithuania	50	3	4	2	3	4	2
Moldova	20	2	2	2	3	2	2
Poland	55	3	4	3	3	4	3
Romania	35	2	3	2	3	4	2
Russian Federation	50	3	3	2	3	3	2
Slovak Republic	55	3	4	3	3	4	3
Slovenia	30	2	4	3	3	4	3
Tajikistan	15	2	2	1	3	1	1
Turkmenistan	15	1	1	1	2	1	1
Ukraine	30	1	2	1	2	1	1
Uzbekistan	20	2	3	1	3	2	1

[1] Many Western European countries would for almost all transition elements qualify under category 4. What is being assessed in the Table is the status rather than the pace of change. Thus, for instance, the placement of Slovenia's small-scale privatization in category 4, despite the absence of a comprehensive small-scale privatization programme in that country, reflects the fact that small-scale activity in Slovenia was largely private before a comprehensive transition process was initiated.

Classification system for transition indicators[2]

Transition element	Category	Description of the category
Large-scale privatization	4	More than 50 per cent of state-owned enterprise assets privatized in a scheme that reflects support for corporate governance
	3	More than 25 per cent of large-scale state-owned enterprise assets privatized or in the process of being sold but with major unresolved issues regarding corporate governance
	2	Advanced comprehensive scheme almost ready to be implemented; some sales completed
	1	Little done
Small-scale privatization	4	Comprehensive and well-designed programme implemented
	3	Nearly comprehensive programme implemented, but design or lack of central supervision leaves important issues unresolved
	2	Substantial share privatized
	1	Little done
Enterpise restructuring	4	Restructuring programme which substantially improves corporate governance in operation; strong financial discipline at the enterprise level; large conglomerates broken up
	3	Structures created (for example through privatization combined with tight credit and subsidy policies and/or enforcement of bankruptcy legislation) to promote corporate governance; or strong action taken to break up conglomerates
	2	Moderately tight credit and subsidy policy; weak enforcement of bankruptcy legislation; little action to break up large conglomerates
	1	Lax credit and subsidy policies weakening financial discipline at the enterprise level: few other reforms to promote corporate governance
Price liberalization and competition	4	Comprehensive price liberalization and price competition; anti-trust legislation in place
	3	Comprehensive price liberalization and price competition
	2	Price controls remain for several important product categories
	1	Most prices remain formally controlled by the government

Trade and foreign exchange system	4	Few import or export quotas; insignificant direct involvement in exports and imports by ministries and state-owned former trading monopolies: almost full current account convertibility at unified exchange rate: no major non-uniformity of customs duties
	3	Few import quotas; almost full current account convertibility at unified exchange rate
	2	Few import quotas; almost full current account convertibility in principle but with a foreign exchange regime which is not fully transparent (possibly with multiple exchange rates)
	1	Widespread import controls or very limited legitimate access to foreign exchange
Banking reform	4	Well functioning banking competition and prudential supervision
	3	Substantial progress on bank recapitalization, bank auditing, and establishment of a functioning prudential supervisory system: significant presence of private banks: full interest rate liberalization with little preferential access to cheap refinancing
	2	Interest rates significantly influencing the allocation of credit
	1	Little progress beyond establishment of a two-tier system

[2] The classification system established here is crude and builds on the judgement of EBRD economists. The system may be revised and refined in future editions of the *Transition Report*.

19 Central Eastern Europe's Great Contraction

István Töröcskei

Professor Robert Mundell described in a recent presentation in Budapest the current transition period of Central Eastern Europe.

Nobody knows, when and how this great collapse will end. In all the Central Estern European countries between the end of 1989 and the end of 1993, the real GDP fell cumulatively by 22.1 per cent. An enormous decline by any standard. In the successor countries to the former Soviet Union, the decline was even more dramatic at 36 per cent. This is not a depression but a contraction.

The cumulative 22.1 per cent contraction of GDP of the Central Eastern European countries, Poland, Hungary, the Czech Republic, the Slovak Republic, Romania, and Bulgaria was on a scale not experienced almost since the black death has reduced Europe's population by 40 per cent.

When comparing the Great Contraction with the Great Depression of the 1930s, we find that output fell by 20 per cent in the United States, by 5 per cent in the UK, by 11 per cent in France and by 39 in Germany. The contraction in Eastern Europe and in the former Soviet Union was less than in Germany. We all know the consequences of the Great Depression: right and left wing extremism, and war.

Historical comparisons aside, we now must look at the future and we must try to find ways to end the Great Contraction. This is not easy because none of us has been prepared for this experience. In any case, it seems that the traditional medicine of one-sided restriction of monetary-fiscal policies might not be a sufficient solution.

This is why we are looking for the international financial institutions' patience and assistance. We should work together, arm-in-arm to find a satisfactory solution.

Apart from the cultural and the language problem which we should not underestimate, there are others. Among the greatest difficulties to integrate these countries with the European Community and the world economy are privatization and the establishment of monetary stability. These require a working financial system able to intermediate between domestic companies and the international financial market, and to finance a non-inflationary credit expansion in the private sector substituting inflationary credit by the government.

Further questions relate to the budget. How to finance stabilization and growth without inflation. There are institutional problems: fostering the growth of capitalist institutions or helping institutions and their integration in the market economy. They are very peculiar legal problems. Not only the legal norms are to be introduced but also their proper application. Banks must be privatized. A banking system matching international standards must be established. Tax structures and a workable taxing culture must be introduced. The taxing system must not be punitive. It should help the individual to pay taxes. There should be sufficient incentives for the generation of savings. We must reduce government spending and restructure the whole revenue and spending culture. Health and the pension funds might need to be privatized.

However, all these items need capital. But investment capital at reasonable interest rates is at the moment in short supply all over the world. Financing has to be done but it is not an easy exercise; especially not in the present business climate when the whole world economy seems to be under repair. By 2000, the banking system will be quite different from what we know now. There is at present a fierce struggle for capital. That is why we need the EBRD, the World Bank and the IMF. We need to encourage somehow private capital to flow to Central Europe. Without such encouragement, there will not be enough capital to finance all these changes. Several surveys show that private banks, financial institutions, companies are not inclined to be the main providers of financing the reconstruction of Eastern and Central Europe. They all think this will be a tertiary area to be financed.

Therefore, we need the EBRD's and the World Bank's support to give to private investors a kind of confidence to come to this part of the world. On the other hand, we have to encourage investors, with the possibility of higher returns, to finance the economic reconstruction of Central and Eastern Europe, after its Great Contraction.

20 The Role of the European Investment Bank in the Countries of Central and Eastern Europe

Ariane Obolensky

I have framed the subject of this paper around two key issues: the role of the international financial institutions (EIB, EBRD, and IBRD) and Eastern Europe's pursuit of closer integration into the European Union. It goes without saying that these issues in turn encompass a presentation of the activities of the European Investment Bank (EIB) in Central and Eastern Europe, a region which I take, *stricto sensu*, to embrace Poland, Hungary, the Czech Republic, Slovakia, Bulgaria, and Romania.

The approach adopted by the EIB

From the very outset, when the West first mobilized financial backing for Poland and Hungary in 1989, followed some two years later by support for these countries' neighbours, the nature of the European Union's contribution to the common effort was very much influenced by the long-term perspective. Clearly, geographical proximity and the values shared between nations whose history has intermingled over the centuries should serve to forge a relationship endorsing this exceptional affinity. Consequently, over and above purely financial and technical support for restructuring their economies, the European Union wanted to give these countries access to an institution whose immediate goal was to aid the integration process and which was bound solely by the criteria traditionally applicable to its operations within the Union.

It was clear from the outset that the transition towards market economies called for adherence to economic stabilization and reform policies, and that implementation of these policies would influence the pace of EIB financing. On the other hand, as in the case of its lending activity within the Union, the Bank clearly deferred to the national authorities in matters of domestic economic policy. The philosophy underlying this *pragmatic approach* is based on several decades of experience gained within the Union in terms of respect for differences from one country to the next, and acknowledgement of the fact that the best organized of economic systems depends not only on theory but also primarily on the commitment of the people who make such systems work. Another argument in favour of pragmatism was the recognition of substantial capital investment needs, at any rate many times greater than the financing Western countries were able to mobilize in favour of the region, not to mention far beyond the absorptive capacity of the recipient nations.

The close dialogue initiated with the authorities was aimed first and foremost at pinpointing priority actions least vulnerable to the uncertainties part and parcel of the transitional phase. All the same, if we need a school of thought for a reference point in this area, it would be appropriate to note ideas developed recently in the field of *institutional economics* whose pragmatism, dismissing outright liberalism, and excessive centralization without siding with either but forming its own amalgam of the two, favours an approach privileging existing structures and contractual relationships. Interdisciplinary by nature, inasmuch as it combines 'organizational studies' with 'applied microeconomics', and 'technical' analysis, this *common sense* line is in many ways similar to the case-by-case approach of the Bank which pays attention to the geographical, institutional, financial, economic, and technical aspects of each investment project under consideration. It also certainly accords with the *undogmatic realism* deriving *from the works of Robert Triffin,* particularly their emphasis on the regional dimension when addressing international monetary problems. Consequently, from the very start, the hallmarks of the EIB's activity in the countries of Central and Eastern Europe (CCEE) have been pragmatism and a long-term vision of their gradual integration into the Union. I should now like to sketch out a brief picture of our initial achievements before turning to the outlook in the medium term.

The lessons of the transitional phase – 1990–1994

Over the period 1990–1994, long-term financing provided by the multilateral institutions to the CCEE totalled some USD 14 billion worth of commitments, of which around 8 billion was supplied by the World Bank, USD 3 billion by the EIB and USD 2.4 by the EBRD. Deducting from the contribution made by the World Bank its structural-adjustment related lending (4 billion), the three major institutions committed some USD 8 billion to support capital investment during this critical period. Total disbursements amounted to USD 6 billion. When measured against aggregate capital spending in the region of between 30 and 40 billion dollars a year, these three institutions' input is patently a determining factor, all the more so since it is focused on a number of key areas, principally communications infrastructure, energy, and the financial sector.

These banks' joint and closely co-ordinated action helped, if not to limit the slump in investment during a period of severe economic recession, marked by an average decline in output of some 30 per cent to 40 per cent, *at least to lend vital momentum to the recovery* now discernible in most of these countries. These institutions provided long-term financing at fairly low interest rates to CCEE when these countries were virtually ostracized by international capital markets. They also provided considerable assistance in identifying and implementing viable projects during a period marked by an extraordinary degree of *uncertainty* as to the future direction and pace of the main economic variables. In comparison, the period of reconstruction in Western Europe in the wake of World War II appears almost to have simply been a case of needing, from the depths of an economic trough and without major restructuring, to mobilize and reallocate resources between sectors more or less in proportion to their previous importance. *In contrast, one of the features of the transition required of Eastern Europe was its predominantly structural dimension.* Two brief examples suffice to illustrate the practical difficulties encountered.

The disproportionate role of the railway sector in socialist economies compared with other modes of transport is well known. It was nevertheless also obvious that lack of infrastructure maintenance and the use of obsolete technology called for no time to be lost in initiating a massive drive to modernize and catch up. Without these, there was the likelihood of vital rail services virtually collapsing to the detriment of the economy as a whole. On the other hand, in the absence of a credible evaluation of long-term traffic trends, it would certainly have required a feat of mental gymnastics to have been able in 1990 to define a programme of minimum capital investment needs. *The answer, therefore, was to phase in, as much as possible, and to prioritize rehabilitation of existing facilities constituting the hard core of the network, while accompanying this capital investment with those traffic, tariff, institutional, and technical studies* essential for planning the following phases.

In the energy sector, hypertrophied by a legacy of underpricing linked to cheap supplies from the Soviet Union, production was sorely inefficient and went hand in hand with massive pollution. While two of the keys to *rehabilitating the sector* undoubtedly lay in a *drastic increase in,* and reform of, *tariffs,* it should also be appreciated that *the scale of the foreseeable consequences for the economy made it hard to envisage implementing abrupt and radical changes.* Incidentally, the widespread absence of individual electricity meters throughout the CCEE amply demonstrated the *ineffectiveness in the very short term of transposing to these countries the demand regulation methods adopted in Western Europe.* On the other hand, there were immediate opportunities for investment in schemes designed to rehabilitate the main generating facilities, including equipment for reducing pollutant emissions in 'sensitive areas', information management systems monitoring energy flows, and renovation of transmission networks so as promptly to cut back system losses and to increase supply efficiency. *Preparation of more comprehensive programmes,* based on a more precise vision of the future level and structure of demand and of the least-cost alternatives needed to meet this demand, *proved extremely time-consuming,* a factor exacerbated by the uninterrupted recession of the four previous years which meant that the basic parameters for every projection had constantly to be revised.

In both sectors, *it is clear that the pragmatic approach* which I emphasized earlier *really constituted the only conceivable way to adapt to circumstances of this kind.* It remains so today, despite the relative macroeconomic stability regained recently and renewed prospects of sustained growth in the region.

The outlook for European integration

Permit me to advance a number of statistics essential for bringing both European integration and the EIB's potential contribution to this process into perspective. In the first place, given the promising upturn in capital expenditure and exports, growth in output in the CCEE is estimated at about 2.5 per cent for 1994, and is expected to reach some 3.5 per cent in 1995. Needless to say, performance varies considerably from one country to the other; in a nutshell, between the northern CCEE, further along the road in the reform process, and the southern CCEE, burdened with a heavier heritage of communism. But *signs are at last emerging to the effect that the latter economies are taking off.* All the same, even for those countries making the best showing, we *should probably be thinking in terms of decades* rather than of a handful of years for the *process of catching up* with levels obtaining in Western Europe. The same point is driven home by estimates advanced in a number of surveys (Centre for Economic Policy Research 1991, and World Bank 1992) putting the volume of capital investment needed to reduce the time gap between East and West to one of 10 or 15 years at between 300 and 400 billion dollars, i.e. roughly the equivalent of the CEE region's GDP. A second consideration to be borne in mind, when focusing on the prospects of European integration, is the *general objective, within the Union as such, of economic convergence.* In practice, this is being translated into regional and structural policies deploying very substantial financial resources. An illustration of the decisive contribution being made by the EIB towards implementing these policies is its annual lending figure, in recent years averaging around 10 to 12 billion ECUs, in support of projects targeted at developing the least advanced regions. A third and final element not to be lost sight of is the *demographic weight of the CEE region.*

With 100 million or so inhabitants, it is home to the equivalent of almost one third of the Community's population. In other words, not only does the CCEE's *development drive* need to be seen as a long-term, if not a *very long-term*, challenge, but it is likely to prove all the more pressing insofar as it falls within the ambit of enlargement of *the Union and the latter's convergence objective.* Indeed, this implies a substantial shift in respective weights between the 'richer' and the 'poorer' regions.

In this context, at least during the initial phase of economic resurgence, I feel that we need to be modest enough to acknowledge that while *outside assistance is crucial for economies undergoing transition, it still has to be understood as something complementing, rather than substituting for, domestic initiatives.* To take one concrete example: everyone here knows that project financing necessarily obeys certain structural dictates, calling for a minimum contribution from domestic funds, and that it has to be accompanied by *ad hoc* measures, such as tariff adjustment, designed to guarantee project viability. Those who advocate opening up the throttle on financial assistance, or who see its impact as independent of other factors, sometimes forget these strings attaching to the participation of the EIB and the other IFIs. Such constraints are, however, perfectly understood by those responsible for implementing investment policies in the countries concerned, but who need to balance them with other policies, notably on the political and social fronts. Indeed, this complementarity between external financing and domestic policies extends far beyond considerations peculiar to those projects supported by the Bank. We have only to look at the acceleration over the past two years in inflows of private capital into those Eastern European countries which have achieved the most progress with their reforms. The point, then, is that *the amount of capital made available to the CCEE, including that provided by the EIB, will, first of all, depend very much on domestic policies.*

The stakes are extremely high: it can be reckoned that incremental economic growth generated by a 10 per cent increase in the current level of investment in the CCEE (20 per cent of GDP) could amount to some 1 per cent to 2 per cent a year, making a difference at the end of 10 years of between 10 per cent and 20 per cent of GDP, or 50 to 100 billion dollars. The fact that capital investment is capable of having such a marked impact on growth is due to the formidable productivity potential on tap in these countries, chiefly by virtue of a highly skilled labour force combined with still extremely low wage levels (some 200 to 300 dollars a month, compared with around 2,000 dollars in the former East Germany). Investment, principally that which ushers in modern technology from the West, helps to mobilize this potential and hence exhibits very high rates of economic return. The projects financed by the EIB and by the other IFIs often yield economic rates of return of 15 per cent to 20 per cent or more. Returns of this order suggest that an extremely high marginal efficiency of capital can be achieved and that economic growth can be achieved with only a slight additional capital input.

This additional capital input is certainly not beyond the capacity of the countries making the transition to market economies. Indeed, the multiplier effect of outside financial assistance means that, *rather than concentrating on quantitative endeavours, these countries have, in effect, to turn their energies to qualitative ends* in terms both of the pace of their reforms and their capital investment priorities. Outside assistance in the form of subsidies or grants is no substitute for domestic commitment. One point in this connection that stands repeating *ad nauseam* is that a good viable project will find a banker to finance it and will benefit the economy, something which is less easy to demonstrate for a project yielding a marginal return, even when funded by grant aid. What can be said of the first of these, that it strengthens institutions and economies at structural level, cannot be said of the second. *In concentrating its operations on projects offering the best return in a small number of key sectors*, energy, communications, and finance, *the EIB can*, as I said before, *parallel this domestic commitment with optimum effectiveness*, especially in cases where the *public sector* is involved and there is the most pressing need for greater integration. I am thinking of infrastructure schemes, trans-European networks in particular, or where market financing structures (notably, the *banking sector*) are still in their infancy and require strengthening in order to speed up the development of the private sector.

With scope for lending up to three billion ECUs for the CCEE as a whole over the period 1994–1996, a significant increase over the 1.7 billion committed from 1990 to 1993, the EIB is already paving the way for the next stage. *Its pragmatic choice of phased priority projects sets the scene for the next wave when these, the forerunners, are implemented.*

* * * * *

This last observation also offers me the opportunity to conclude by stressing *the importance which we attach to monitoring those projects financed by us, an element at least as essential as getting them off the ground in the first place.* The implementation phase is crucial both for the success of a project and for creating conditions which in turn open up fresh possibilities. *Bank activity in the CCEE over the past five years or so* is set to bring benefits often poorly appreciated by the outside world but which, may I suggest, offer *increasing returns of scale*. To cite the jargon of institutional economics to which I referred earlier, the growing degree of mutual understanding built up between the Bank and its 'customers' is synonymous with lower 'transaction' costs. These benefits are probably lent added weight by geographical proximity, shared cultural values and, last but not least, the vision of a common future. In fact, the EIB has experienced this process in countries such as Portugal whose level of development when it joined the Union some ten years ago was fairly comparable to that of the CCEE but has now come spectacularly closer to the European average. EIB-financed operations in Portugal are currently accounting for around 15 per cent of annual capital investment in that country. It is a model which should serve as an inspiration for us in the longer term, with the prospect of accession in mind.

21   The Role of Banking in Transition Countries

György Iványi

The last dramatic affair I do remember in the context of our present discussion happened some five years ago, in 1989, when historic events opened the road, or rather removed some barriers from the road, to real and full European unification.

As a banker by profession and record, I am pleased to remember that the banking community was one of the first who made real steps on this road. While private commercial banks were investigating possibilities of opening banks in Eastern Europe and actually they did, on the level of European IFIs, the establishment of the EIB and of the EBRD were milestones.

I am personally proud to remember that probably the first careful experiment the European Investment Bank has executed in Eastern Europe was a 25 million ECU credit line granted to and intermediated by the Inter-Europa Bank, an institution where I was the chief executive officer at that time. Actually, that was not only an experimental affair in the history of the European Investment Bank but also in the Inter-Europa Bank, as that was the first major international long-term credit line in the history of this emerging institution. As I remember, the appropriation and disbursement of this loan was an efficient and pleasant co-operation and till today, I believe that it is remembered as a successful operation also by the EIB.

Since that time, the EIB has appropriated almost 400 million ECUs in Hungary. Half of this portfolio has been already disbursed to infrastructural projects in accordance with the basic strategy of the EIB, as I understand it.

It is a badly needed activity to provide medium-term loans to a market which is lacking an advanced capital market and where long-term funding is incredibly short. And here is some of the dangers of the present practice and experience. While long-term lending and sovereign loans are badly needed, somehow they provide space and time for governments in Eastern Europe to delay the really necessary steps which are conceptually accepted and understood by everybody but are politically extremely painful toward the development of a capital market and toward the possibility to generate long-term funding both on the home market and internationally.

God forbid to suggest to cut long-term lending by international financial institutions just to force East European governments into painful steps. But some reconsideration of the lending methodology, policies, and practice might be necessary. The most positive development in this field is the changing behaviour of the EBRD and its growing readiness for equity financing. I remember that just after the establishment of the EBRD in London, speaking about equity involvement or equity intermediation was considered taboo. A more commercial banking approach suggests a careful copying of already well-established World Bank financing techniques.

The other positive element is a growing readiness to invest into the financial infrastructure itself. This region, Eastern Europe, may not depend forever on loans or guarantees from international financial institutions or from sovereign entities. Partly the growing budget deficits of the OECD countries are constraining their capabilities to provide sovereign loans to Eastern Europe. Sovereign guarantees are also safeguarding something very unhealthy: the involvement of the state in project financing in affairs where the state has nothing to do, having neither the abilities nor, in the East European context, the experience to be involved.

In Eastern Europe, not only granting but accepting of loans seems to be constrained now. The capacities of the economy to absorb further loans in overgeared economies and with overgeared corporate sectors cannot go on forever. This region needs equity and this region needs the capabilities to increase its own saving, multiplying by that the effects of international support. In this context, what can and should be suggested? First to reconsider the policies of using sovereign guarantees. This results in the necessity of learning to appraise the financial institutions of Eastern Europe and, at the same time, in contributing to the development of these financial institutions.

The other element is the reconsideration of some of the methodology giving a strong emphasis on financing methods which rather develop the market instead of concentrating on individual projects. This creates liquidity and will make easier for other players – private, domestic, and international – to enter the field with their own capital and savings.

22 Robert Triffin and the Kredietbank*

Marcel Cockaerts

It is my pleasure to extend a warm welcome to you at this dinner with which Kreditebank wishes to contribute to the success of the conference organized by the Robert Triffin–Szirák Foundation.

The Executive Committee of the Kredietbank is honoured by the presence of such a great number of distinguished representatives of international economic organizations and governments and of reputed economists on its own premises tonight.

The subject of the conference goes to the heart of one of the most pressing economic problems of this age. But problems are also opportunities.

The Kredietbank certainly has not failed to see these opportunities and has already taken concrete steps in this respect. Last year we opened a branch in Berlin in a move to contribute to the development of the former East Germany and this year we opened representative offices in Budapest, Prague, and Warsaw with a view to expanding our participation in the economic development of the respective countries concerned.

I certainly do not have to dwell on the importance and the impact of the problems which are posed by the economic development of Eastern Europe nor do I have to point out the importance of Robert Triffin, whose name is linked to the conference as an economist and a statesmen.

Let me just say that Kredietbank is quite honoured to have had a close and long-standing relationship with Mr Triffin, who was from 1961 to 1988 a director of Kredietbank Luxembourg, at that time a subsidiary of Kredietbank Belgium.

On an even more personal note I can refer to Professor Triffin's exceptional contribution to the *Weekly Bulletin* of Kredietbank. Some of you, or

* *Delivered at the dinner, November 17, 1994*

186

may I dare to presume, most of you know the *Weekly* of Kredietbank in which our economic research department each week treats an economic subject of a fundamental or more topical nature.

Those articles are written according to the highest professional standards, and each of the members of the economic research department has always taken great pride in being able to contribute.

While being editor-in-chief of that publication, I have only once made an exception for an outsider contribution and that was Professor Triffin's article 'Basic Considerations on International Monetary Reform', which appeared on November 24, 1972.

Reading this article again, I was struck by his far-sighted points of view at a moment when the great debate still centred on the role of gold and the USD as international reserve instruments.

The two main themes were the necessity of non-inflationary long-term growth, and the need for close monetary co-operation within the EEC on the basis of strong currencies.

But after an impressive series of speeches today and still an important contribution of Mr Bernard Snoy to come, you are not here to listen to one more speech of me. So let me just wish you an agreeable evening.

23 Robert Triffin and the Broader Dimensions of Transition in Central and Eastern Europe*

Bernard Snoy

Robert Triffin's personality

Robert Triffin was a very warm, loyal, human, wise, and tolerant person. His friends said that they knew very few people like him, who believed so deeply in what they were doing and pursuing their interests with such passion.

He made powerful intellectual and scientific contributions throughout his career. But almost all the time, his work was geared to policy, to designing, repairing, and improving institutional architecture in forms attractive to the disparate interests of the parties involved. He knew all along that the most important reforms have always been dictated ultimately by political considerations.

Robert Triffin always saw economics as a way to improve the human condition. He always welcomed the cross-fertilization of the other social sciences with economic behavioural influences and values. In fact, Robert Triffin was a keen student of politics and history as well as economics. He had also interest for philosophy and theology, particularly the views of the French Jesuit, Pierre Teilhard de Chardin.

We can guess, therefore, that if Robert Triffin had been with us listening to our discussion on Central and Eastern Europe, he would have been, at the same time, pleased and worried: pleased at the concrete and constructive proposals formulated by Minister Maystadt for creating a monetary system based on global partnership (new rules of the game, broader decision mechanisms, better adapted financial instruments) and at the genuine efforts made by international financial institutions to adapt their interventions

* *Dinner address, November 17, 1994*

to the specific needs of the countries in transition; but also he would have been worried about what was heard. Indeed, we heard a number of expressions which we should not take too lightly: disappointment, political disenchantment, social crisis, gravity of the wounds of the past, difficulty in removing the 'debris' of communism, difficulty 'in the trenches', loss of confidence in the future, cycle of despair, etc. These expressions reveal a state of mind that should be taken seriously.

Going beyond the technicalities of our discussions on the international monetary system and on the modalities of assistance by international financial institutions, Robert Triffin would have encouraged us to take a broader view and to be capable of a vision, i.e. 'the ability to comprehend issues on a large scale and over a long period'. He would have recommended us to look at the broader dimensions of the subject and to touch on the socio-political, the cultural, the moral and even the philosophical dimensions of the transition process.

Socio-political dimension

Transition to a market economy is only part of the story. Countries in Central and Eastern Europe are not only moving from central planning to a market economy, they are also moving from totalitarianism to democracy, pluralism, and open societies. One move is as important as the other.

The problem here comes from the differing time frames of economic and political liberalization. Indeed, basic constitutional change can be introduced in a matter of months whereas economic change, especially structural change, takes a long time. Economic reforms cannot be effective immediately. On the contrary, they lead without fail through a 'valley of tears'. Things are bound to get worse before they get better. The depression is not only economic; it is even more social and psychological: it makes many people feel gloomy, disappointed, sometimes cynical. It is hard to predict for each country how long the 'trek' through this valley will take but it is bound to take longer than the lifetime of the first elected Parliament. The danger, particularly in Russia, is that it could engender a degree of disillusionment which could threaten the new constitutional framework along with the economic reforms which promised so much but could not deliver on time. Another danger is xenophobia and nationalism leading to ethnic violence, as we are seeing them in former Yugoslavia and the Caucasus region.

According to political scientists, consolidation of the democratic institutions is plausible only after a country has passed two 'turnover tests', i.e. two changes of the political complexion of government legitimized by democratic elections rather than imposed by force.

The international financial institutions must take this into account and help shorten the 'valley of tears', assisting in the creation of affordable 'safety nets' and of the conditions for a more rapid supply response. Unsustainable subsidies to enterprises must be replaced by better targeted subsidies to households. Reform of the health sector and other social services is a priority. I am pleased that the World Bank has set up a regional office in Budapest advising Central and Eastern European countries on reforms of the social sector. I am pleased also that the World Bank supports decentralized assistance at the 'oblast' level in Russia aimed at building employment and social protection services.

The key to combat xenophobia, nationalism, and despair is to develop civil society. According to Ralph Dahrendorf (*Reflections on the Revolution in Europe*, Random House, 1990), civil society means 'the creation of a tight network of autonomous institutions and organizations which has not one but thousand centres and can, therefore, not easily be destroyed by a monopolist in the guise of a government or a party'. These autonomous institutions are first the families, the Churches, the schools, the universities, the artistic groups, etc.

We should encourage all forms of association, national, regional, local, professional, which are voluntary, authentic, democratic, and most of all, not controlled or manipulated by the state or any dominant party. Civil society means that the people must be 'civil', 'civilian', and 'civilized', that is polite, tolerant, as much as possible 'self-reliant', and above all non-violent. Civil society means that the society should be broken into so many parts, interests, and classes of citizens that the rights of individuals or minorities will be in little danger from the interested combinations of the majority. In other words, a multiplicity of groups and organizations and associations should provide sufficient checks and balances against any usurpation of power.

At the economic level, small and medium enterprises have a crucial role to play in creating such a civil society, and I am particularly pleased that the EBRD is making special efforts to support them with equity capital and long-term loans.

Cultural dimension

The cultural dimension is a fantastic ally in the transition process. The fall of the Iron Curtain allows the cultural reunification of the two halves of Europe and the rediscovery that we share a common cultural heritage:

- Millions of Western European tourists have discovered the medieval and baroque architectural treasures of Prague, this city where the heart of Europe is beating; the classical beauty of St Petersburg makes it also one of the greatest European cities.

- There is a new awareness of how important authors such as Pushkin, Gogol, Dostoevsky and Tolstoi are for European literature. Although still difficult to find in English or French translation, there is an increasing interest for Central European writers such as Karel Capek, Imre Madách, Miklós Radnóti, Czeslaw Milosz, E.M. Cioran, and Ismaïl Kadare, to name just a few.

- More than ever we experience the pure joy of the music by Chopin, Liszt, Smetana, Enesco, Tchaikovsky, Kodály, and Bartók, among others.

We knew all along the existence of that marvellous heritage but now we recognize much more that it springs from common cultural foundations. It is important to cultivate this heritage and to stress our common reasons to be proud of it as an antidote against depression and distress in this period of painful transformation when people might become excessively disillusioned.

Moral dimension

The moral dimension will also lift our spirit. First of all, only five years after the fall of the Iron Curtain, we should not forget the long night Central and Eastern European countries have gone through and we must pay tribute to the courageous people who never submitted to totalitarianism but all along and against all adversity sustained their intellectual integrity.

One of them is President Göncz, who has kindly given his patronage to our conference. In the foreword to a collection of short stories which he recently published under the title *Homecoming and Other Stories* (Corvina,

Budapest, 1993), President Göncz evokes what he calls 'the nameless Hungarian', i.e. a man over sixty 'who will automatically have lost six years of his life which he owed to the devil and will carry the marks of two deep creases at the corners of his mouth'. One relates to the suffering under nazism during World War II, the second reflects the suffering of the crushed 1956 revolution, the labour camps, and the deep inner migration into which dissenters such as Árpád Göncz had to go.

The moral dimension is as important today to rebuild the economy and the society and to clear the debris of communism. In September 1993, at the Annual Meeting of the IMF and the World Bank in Washington, the Minister of Finance of Hungary Mr Iván Szabó, who was chairing the meeting, made a profound impression on all participants and raised the level of the debate by stating: 'freedom needs a moral content; that is, freedom makes sense if it is directed to others, if it has a communal substance'. Mr Szabó is right. Without a moral content, without a communal substance based on shared moral values, it is impossible to reconstruct the shattered economies and societies of Central and Eastern Europe. The history of capitalism since the Renaissance in Europe demonstrates the importance of codes of conduct, of business ethic, and of moral values of the establishment of relations of trust, of confidence without which trade and investment cannot flourish. Only a mafia economy can thrive in a legal and moral vacuum. When those foundations are not there, business relations can only develop on the basis of ethnical loyalties – this is why the Chechen and the Georgian mafias appear so powerful in Russia – or of connections stemming from a common past allegiance to organizations such as the communist party or the KGB.

If moral values are crucial for the success of transition in Central and Eastern Europe, they are as crucial to the future of the Western world, and we should be careful of not lecturing our Central and Eastern European friends on this subject. Indeed, the fabric of our own societies and perhaps our capacity to overcome our own economic crisis are also threatened by the danger of a collapse of our moral and spiritual values. There are ominous signs of disunity and egoism. As the famous Polish-American Zbigniew Brzezinski argues in his latest book *Out of Control – Global Turmoil on the Eve of the 21st Century* (Scribners, 1993), we are living in a philosophical climate that is out of control. It is Brzezinski's firm belief that we must draw both moral and political lessons from the 'megadeaths' of the 20th century, a century in which at least 167 million people were slaughtered in the name of the 'politics of organized insanity' or the 'metamyths' of such dictators as Hitler, Stalin, and Mao, among others. Unless we can practise self-restraint derived from a moral commitment in the quest for global democratic interdependence, we stand destined to risk again our very own survival.

Brzezinski is right in saying that moral and social values in the West are indispensable to sustain the fabric of international co-operation necessary for the success of the transition process in the East.

Philosophical dimension

On this last dimension, I will only refer to Václav Havel, the philosopher-president of the Czech Republic, the only contemporary statesman to have called for a new definition of European identity and for a 'global recasting of the self-understanding of modern civilization' after the collapse of the socialist utopia.

In an essay, 'The End of the Modern Era', Václav Havel writes the following: 'The end of communism... is a message we have not fully deciphered and comprehended since it portends an end not just to the 19th and 20th centuries, but to the modern age as a whole.' The modern era, Havel continues, has been dominated by the belief 'that the world – and being as such – is a wholly knowable system governed by a finite number of universal laws that man can grasp and rationally direct for his own benefit... /It/ gave rise to the proud belief that man... was capable of objectively describing, explaining and controlling every thing that exists, and of possessing the one and only truth about the world. It was an era of systems, institutions, mechanisms, and statistical averages. It was an era of ideologies, doctrines, interpretations of reality, an era in which the goal was to find a universal theory of the world, and thus a universal key to unlock its prosperity. Communism was the perverse extreme of this trend... and an attempt, on the basis of a few propositions masquerading as the only scientific truth, to organize all of life according to a single model, and to subject it to central planning and control regardless of whether or not that was what life wanted. The fall of communism can be seen as a sign that modern thought – based on the premise that the world is objectively knowable, and that the knowledge so obtained can be absolutely generalized – has come to a final crisis. This era has created the first global, or planetary, technical civilization, but it has reached the point beyond which the abyss begins.'

Part III

The Transition Problem and European Integration

24 Liberal Trade Policy and Transition Strategy

Leszek Balczerowicz

My topic is trading, the trade policy dimension in the overall transition strategy. Let me start with describing what one may call the liberal approach to trade and foreign exchange reform. I will treat them together because they cannot be separated.

This approach has at least four components. First, dismantling the remnants of state monopoly of foreign trade and abolishing the monopolistic right of specialized foreign trade state organizations to foreign trade. Second, abolishing most of the quantitative, direct controls on exports and imports. Third, abolishing foreign exchange restrictions, that is to say, unifying the rate of exchange and introducing the convertibility of the domestic currency, at least within the current account transactions. And fourth, introducing moderate and possibly uniform tariffs. This is my definition of a liberal approach to trade and exchange reform. This liberal approach is important for several reasons.

It is important because it is part of a new development paradigm which stresses the need for the state to withdraw from certain functions, from detailed intervention, from being the entrepreneur and letting the market and private entrepreneurship to be more active. This new development paradigm has several main elements. Besides a liberal approach to foreign trade- and exchange regimes, it stresses the importance of private property, of competition, flexible labour markets, of limiting the burden of taxes and of social expenditures, just to mention a few elements. This new development paradigm is not new. It contains many old truths and it is largely a return to certain classical functions of the state, plus some new additions like the role of the state in environmental protection and in the supervision of financial institutions.

Basically, the new development paradigm recognizes the need for a limited state. It draws some conclusions from the excess of state intervention, which is a 20th-century aberration. This has occurred especially in socialist countries where these excesses went to the extreme, but also in many developing and Western countries.

The liberal approach to trade and exchange is extremely important in transition economies. Its power is as important as that of privatization. It is equally powerful as an instrument of change. There are several reasons for this.

First, one wanted to get rid of shortages and, in particular, to improve relative prices. This was obviously crucial. One had to complement the reform of the pricing system with the equally comprehensive reform of the foreign trade and foreign exchange mechanism. These were complementing each other. Otherwise, neither could work. And conversely, a limited price liberalization, a modest price liberalization has in many countries led to a spiral of controls. Especially on exports. Because prices were distorted and there was a pressure to control goods being exported at too low prices. We see this very clearly in some countries of the former Soviet Union and in Ukraine. The first reason for a comprehensive and liberal approach to foreign trade and exchange regime is the fact that one can talk of something which may be called the indivisibility of liberalization. Liberalization cannot be effectively made in very small pieces. It has to be almost indivisible. Otherwise, a spiral of interventions sets in.

Second, a liberal approach to the foreign trade and exchange mechanism is very important in order to remove the discrimination against the private sector and to let the private sector grow. Otherwise one would need to maintain widespread rationing. This is always done by the bureaucracy. And bureaucracy discriminates against smaller and private units. If one wants to have a quick development of the private sector which is obviously crucial, one has to do something about foreign trade and the price mechanism. By doing this, one also helps reduce concentration and the dominance of huge state enterprises. They have been maintained by rationing. They had privileged access to foreign exchange and they have rationed goods. By removing rationing, one removes the sources of discrimination in favour of large units and one makes decentralization possible.

Third, the liberal approach is important, because it is the quickest possible way to introduce competition. Demonopolization, decentralization are obviously necessary but they cannot work quickly. This may be one of the few advantages of smaller countries versus larger countries in the transition process. Smaller countries can rely, to a large extent, on foreign trade liberalization as an instrument of a quick introduction of competition.

Fourth, a liberal approach to foreign trade and exchange mechanism makes it possible for latecomers to reap one of the few advantages, like learning from more advanced countries. Otherwise, these countries would remain in isolation and could not learn quickly by imitation and adaptation. This makes it possible for the comparative advantage to be revealed.

And *fifth*, without the liberal approach to foreign trade and exchange mechanism, there would be much more corruption. Ransacking and corruption are more visible in those countries which have liberalized less than some Central European countries.

This is why the liberal approach is important in the overall strategy of most Central European countries as compared to some countries of the former Soviet Union (FSU). It has to be complemented by much more access to Western markets. Otherwise it cannot work. It cannot be effective.

After a couple of years, we can now compare the experiences of various countries. First, we notice very substantial differences in the approach to the foreign trade- and exchange mechanism. There is a group of Central European countries which largely choose this liberal approach. At the same time, most of the countries of the FSU executed much more modest reforms in this sphere.

Why is this difference?

I see at least two reasons for that. First, perhaps, because there were differences in the quality of leadership of the overall reforms. The leaders in Central European countries were mostly newcomers. They came from outside the established bureaucracy and probably had a different vision of reforms. In this vision, foreign trade liberalization formed an important part.

The second reason is that in the countries of the FSU, the negative spiral of direct controls set in. They started with usually very modest trade liberalization in Ukraine and in Belarus. Once they started such a modest price liberalization, there were fresher, further controls. They did not respect the indivisibility of liberalization.

The second observation is that there have been some relatively modest reverses even in radical reformers, like Poland, Hungary, Czechoslovakia, etc. They did not reverse the nature of the foreign trade regime, which still remains relatively liberal. There are several reasons for these relatively minor reverses, like fiscal and protectionist pressures within those countries. Also there were bad examples from the West, especially anti-market protection in agriculture. Polish farmers always refer to Western examples, particularly to the European Economic Community. Undoubtedly, this bad example is one of the greatest damages the West does to the recovery of Eastern Europe.

Those countries who were radical in their reforms of trade and of the exchange mechanism remained rather liberal. The third observation is that the differences in approach to the trade and exchange mechanism and to other reforms mattered very much because trade collapse within the former COMECON and within the FSU could be taken as given. It was not dependent on actions of smaller countries. It could depend on actions of the FSU or Russia. For other countries like Poland, Georgia, Kazakhstan, it was given.

To what extent and in what way could the smaller countries compensate for the collapse of their traditional ties? Those countries who adopted a more liberal approach were more able to reorient their trade to the West. Those countries which remained attached to more controls were less able to do so. This is why the liberal approach mattered so much in the context of an unavoidable trade collapse.

It should be recognized that the countries of the FSU had also much less possibility to reorient trade. For geographical reasons they were more dependent on Russia. Their objective possibility to reorient trade was more reduced as compared to such countries as Hungary, Poland, or Czechoslovakia.

This difference in trade policies and in objective possibilities of reorientation, explains, to some extent, the differences in the decline of the GDP in the course of transition in Central Europe on the one hand, and in the FSU, on the other.

The external dimension of liberalization, the better access to Western markets is most important. The initial response of Western countries was inadequate. There was a substantial foreign trade liberalization in at least the six countries of Central Eastern Europe placing such a policy to the top of the preference pyramid. These were followed by negotiations about association agreements. Their results fell short of expectations. I have signed them on behalf of the Polish government. Therefore, I cannot criticize them too much, but clearly, they were short of expectations and, as time went by, some deficiencies of these agreements, at least from the

Eastern point of view, became quite clear. Their shortcomings were well pointed out in the recent *Transition Report* prepared by the EBRD. Three points should be emphasized. First, that so-called sensitive products were largely excluded. They happen to constitute, on the average, about 50 per cent of total exports. One can assume that comparative advantage, at least for a while, resides in these products. On the other hand, the import of sensitive products from the former socialist countries constitute a very small percentage of total imports of the West, about one per cent. Therefore, there is a tremendous asymmetry. Fifty per cent to one per cent. What is a small concession by the West can be of enormous benefit to the Eastern countries and conversely. What is a small restriction from the Western point of view may do a lot of damage to the former socialist countries. Not only economic, but also political damage. A damage which is done by bad example. There is always a very delicately balanced dispute between reformers and anti-reformers. Anti-reformers usually have a very strong position. These bad examples, this petty protectionism, which are of negligible importance from the Western point of view, can do a lot of damage to this internal economic debate and, also, to its political results. It is not always realized in the West how much damage can be done politically by instances of petty protectionism. Other weaknesses, like the arbitrary use of the safeguard mechanism, are leading to petty *ad hoc* protectionism as well. Let me finish by saying what should be done.

I have first described differences how internal and external strategies were implemented. Now I concentrate on what should be done. These two complement each other. The dinamism of internal reforms has to be maintained whenever they were launched or completed. Where such reforms did not take place so far, there should be much more external liberalization, more access to markets. There are strong links between liberalization and access. Without the prospects and actual liberalization in the West, liberal trade reforms in the East have much less chances. These two actions have to be taken simultaneously to result in maximum benefits.

In the countries which are more radical reformers, one thing which I regard to be very important is to create safeguards against domestic protectionist pressures. Much depends on what is going to happen to the GATT agreement. This is just as important as the external commitment vis-à-vis the European Union. Both are very strong safeguards against domestic pressures.

As far as the West is concerned, conclusions can be derived from the weaknesses which had been pointed out. Most needed elements are: more liberalization with respect to sensitive products; reduction of the domestic component as far as the rules of origin are concerned; and streamlining of safeguards, thereby making more difficult for Western countries to introduce arbitrary *ad hoc* petty protectionist measures.

Western countries should not only set joining dates for Central and Eastern European countries aspiring to membership in the European Union but also formulate demanding but realistic conditions. These conditions should lead to serious negotiations. Formulating these conditions could help the reforms. It would create added incentives. These conditions should also refer to public finances. The Maastricht criteria include such conditions. Therefore, the degree of privatization, the position of the central bank along the Maastricht criteria should introduce appropriate measures. On the other hand, I would be very sceptical and cautious about social clauses. One of the problems of the former socialist economies is that they are over-socialized. They have got enormous burdens on expenditures and taxes. Therefore, to require from them, to maintain or even to increase these burdens would mean for them a very difficult start to grow.

25 Trade Policies for Transition Countries

John Flemming

I have absolutely no disagreement at all with three out of four of the elements of the liberal strategy that Mr Balczerowicz recommends. My reservation is about the fourth, which is the low to moderate-level uniform tariff. Even here, I have only one reservation, and that concerns timing. There is an argument, which I shall develop briefly, for a transitional period during which the tariff structure could eventually achieve the goal of zero tariffs; although if you look around the world, that is perhaps too much to hope for.

The transition economies themselves, particularly Poland, accepted the rapid, almost instantaneous, elimination of tariffs. This objective was relatively easily realized in a number of transition economies because protection under central planning did not rely on tariffs but on other instruments. Therefore, the liberalization of the institutions of international trade, the benefits of which are well known, created a situation of virtually free trade, which, however, in reality has not been sustained. Even in the most liberal of the transition economies, in Poland, Hungary, the then Czechoslovak Republic, and also in Bulgaria, which is perhaps less liberal but is the only other one in the sample of the EBRD's *Transition Report*, tariff rates in 1992 were on average higher than in 1991. This might give the impression that the liberals are in retreat. That impression seems to me unfortunate. It is, in my view, also documented in the *Report* that in a number of countries there is an unhappy tension. This is connected to an illiberal extension of protection in the context of negotiations over major foreign direct investment projects, particularly in the automobile industry.

What is the alternative that might have been pursued and whose merits one might want to compare with those of the strategies that have been followed? All of the institutional advantages of liberalization could have been achieved with a different tariff structure that I have suggested from time to time. A structure of trade taxes should be introduced so as to create within the country a structure of relative prices which is fairly close to what was implicit in the previous regime, with a credible commitment to phasing it out over 5-10 years. The point about that is that it would keep more enterprises alive, generating cash flows sufficient to pay their workers. I would put a limit to these trade taxes. One would not, under any circumstances, want to have more than a 100 per cent effective protection. With that limit value subtracting enterprises would have to close immediately, which should generate enough unemployment in the inefficient sectors and start the reallocation of resources.

If the commitment were credible, all investment would go into the unprotected, or even negatively protected, industries rather than to the protected ones whose protection would disappear. The methods of the credibility of such a phase-out are absolutely crucial. If the phase-out is not credible, then one should not embark on this process. Credibility could be developed either through agreements with other countries in the same position or through commitments with more developed trading partners. This could easily have been built into the Europe Agreements. Indeed, that form of asymmetric liberalization was exactly the initial bargaining position of the Commission as I understand it. They were somewhat wrong-footed by the extreme liberalism of the Visegrád countries who started disarming themselves more rapidly than they were pressed to do. I believe that it would have been worthwhile under those circumstances for the Commission and for the Community representatives to press ahead with declining ceilings of tariffs in order to strengthen the hands of the trade authorities in the transition economies. If they conceded protection subsequently, as they have done to a number of the declining industries, it would have had to be temporary.

The establishing of the credibility of a temporary protection when you are just conceding it under the pressure of unemployed people or for any other reason is extremely difficult. They may get the message that if you can get a thousand people onto the streets of the capital, you can get ten percentage points on the tariff. The implication of that is that you do not want to reduce your workforce or reduce your bargaining power. You would want to retain your thousand workers so that you can put them out on the streets again next year. A ceiling on the tariff, a declining ceiling, to which the government is effectively committed, would make that strategy less attractive to those entrepreneurs or industrial managers who were reluctant to restructure their enterprises.

I would like to turn now briefly to the other side of the story, to the question of access to Western markets. This is something that a number of us have banged on at a great length. I would just like to add more to what has already been said about the damage done by petty protection. Not only the asymmetry is important but a liberal regime costs very little to the West while bringing very large benefits to the East. I want to underline further the disincentive effect of the contingent nature of Western protectionism. The expression *ad hoc* has been used. I think the expression 'contingent' captures, in some ways, better the sense of threat that any success will be hit on the head. There is no point in investing in something in Eastern Europe in the belief that you stand a good chance of making in-roads into Western markets, if when you are successful in the commercial sense, you would lose politically by being stopped in your tracks. That is a very serious problem.

At this point, I may admit to an error in forecasting that I and a number of others have made. We have predicted that Eastern Europe would not be very attractive as an investment base on the strength of its market because the people are very poor, there are not enough of them who could afford or would choose to buy highly developed Western products and that it makes far better sense to use them as an export platform taking advantage of the very low wages.

All statistical material that have become available since then points in exactly the opposite direction. The people who are investing in Central and Eastern Europe are going now for the market. It is also true that I would not have predicted a demand for Mercedes and other luxury cars. This has, however, materialized through much of the region. This has to do with the effects of the wrong income distribution, possibly corruption, not to mention criminality. One of the reasons that there has been much more interest in supplying the local market than creating an export base is due to the damaging effect of the threatened Western contingent protection.

Four other quick points. Agriculture is setting a bad example. It would be good to see it reformed. I have sometimes seen it suggested that we cannot be serious about liberalism unless we open the EU market to agricultural products. Unfortunately, that seems to me to be implausible, it would, in any case, not be liberalization, but the extension of distortions into another region. The only thing that might possibly make sense would be enlarging levy-free quotas. That, I believe, is simply equivalent to sending money to the East because it ought to have no effect on the allocation of resources because at the margin, prices would not be affected. Intervention prices in the Union would remain unchanged, prices and production in the Union itself would not change. All that would happen is that Eastern Europeans would divert some of their production to the Union. Then these products will get diverted into intervention and then dumped on third markets. Actually, these third markets are those from where the Eastern Europeans have diverted their production in the first place. This closes the circle. The Eastern Europeans will make more money. It might be easier to write cheques than to rewrite levy-free quotas.

The second point concerns local content rules meaning the 60 per cent requirement for reimport to the Union. This concerns me also as a European Union consumer, and it is the consequence for competition in Western Europe arising from local content rules which I believe bias investment in Central and Eastern Europe towards Western European enterprises rather than enterprises from the rest of the world. The enlargement of the market that is implicit in relatively liberal access for Central and Eastern European products to Western Europe is something that provides an opportunity for having more intense competition in Western Europe without sacrificing economies of scale, which is the classic advantage of a larger market. And that ought to mean having more players, and if there were not plausible indigenous players in Central and Eastern Europe, we should welcome players from Asia, Latin America, anywhere else, but Asia most plausibly, and that is at the root of these local content rules. If you assume that an investor, foreign direct investor, wants to supply something from his home base, then there is a discrimination effectively against people whose home base is not in Western Europe. Many of the American multinationals already have bases in Western Europe, a few of the Japanese, very few of the Koreans.

The third point is conditional entry to the EU. There is a very unfortunate asymmetry in what is currently being required of transition economies. They are expected to commit themselves now to a number of institutional arrangements that conform to European Union norms without any comparable commitment in terms of ultimate membership.

The fourth point concerns social clauses. Not merely because of the danger of reinforcing what I think János Kornai has called a premature welfare state in some of the Central European economies. But also I would make the point that some of the social clauses and the role of the European Union in income distribution or redistribution between and within member states is itself proving and likely to prove a very serious obstacle of the entry of the Central and Eastern European countries to the Union because they push up the cost to the existing members. And that is one of the reasons for worrying about the asymmetry of the commitments to membership, although the language used in the Commission and in the Union in this respect has changed radically over the last three or four years. There is still a serious danger of major disappointments and backlash. We all should keep this in mind.

26 The Role of Trade in Transition

Jean Pisani-Ferry

I would like to comment briefly on three topics. First, the role of trade in transition, second, the assessment of the experience of the countries of Central and Eastern Europe so far, and third, the question of membership in the Community.

With respect to the perceptions of trade, the big difference between the conditions now and ten or twenty years ago is that the gains from participating in international trade are much more recognized now throughout the world than they were then. At that time, there was still a discussion about the right policy for countries which wanted to grow and catch up with industrial countries. There are no such discussions now. Everybody recognizes that trade is a very efficient way to accelerate the catching up and to gain from international experience. This can even be observed empirically. If you look at the different countries in the world, and in particular at the emerging economies; and if you try to assess the role of trade policy in opening to imports and in the size of exports in relation to GDP and in the growth performance of the countries, then the evidence becomes clear that trade contributes significantly to growth.

This has obviously clear implications for the kind of policy which had to be adopted by the transition countries. But also, there is another side of this experience: countries in transition are bound to face tough competition from emerging economies from different parts of the world, some in Europe, many in Asia or Latin America. In this respect, the not so liberal trade policy of the European Union has also advantages. I fully agree with its disadvantages but one must recognize that it has also some advantages for the formerly sheltered countries in Central and Eastern Europe which were previously cut off from competition from other producers in Europe and in the world at large.

Actually, I think this is a big issue for trade policy of the European Union; clearly, one could imagine two different strategies. One regional strategy would devote great efforts to assist neighbours of the current members of the European Union in the growth, development, and catching up effort. Another strategy would be to say that for the well-being of the current members of the Union, it would be more profitable to participate fully in world trade on a liberal basis and to try to attract some of the benefits of current growth in other regions in the world where European firms do not trade so much at present. This is a strategic choice. At present, the not so liberal policy of the Union has also some benefits for Central Eastern Europe.

Turning now to the second point: assessing the experience, the performance, and the trade policy of the Union so far. It has been said that everything short of free trade amounts to an empty glass. I think there is a way which we could measure, assess the evolution and it is basically to ask whether the trade engine is working or not. And in that respect, for countries, at least for the Visegrád countries, there is evidence that it is working. If you look at the overall trade figures, this is quite evident. But also, you must look at the product composition of trade. This is an important indicator. If the product composition of trade changes over time, this means that the industrial structure is changing too, and that through trade, new comparative advantages are emerging. There is evidence, for example, that for the Visegrád countries, such process is under way. A contrary example is presented by the countries of the former Soviet Union, and also by Romania, whose exports to the European Union have been virtually flat over the last five years. This is very consistent with the fact that the trade engine is not at work and that this contributes to the difficulties of the transition in this country. So we would obviously prefer the glass to be absolutely full, but I think that to observe what is actually at work is important, and to assess that trade effectively has a significant contribution.

My third point concerns the explicit criteria for joining the European Union. In 1990 or 1991, there was a discussion between those who favoured deepening before enlarging and those who favoured enlargement before any deepening. I think that we have made some progress not only *de facto* because the first enlargement is already under way, but also conceptually. We can recognize now that this apparent contradiction may not be in reality a contradiction and that enlargement or widening or deepening can be actually two sides of the same problem. Why? Because if you envisage a community of twenty-five or more members, it is unlikely that all these members will have the same preferences as regards the degree of integration and that they will actually be in a similar position as regards the ability to participate in the degree, in a given degree of integration. This is obvious from the present discussions. The recent German CDU Report about the EU's future strategy on viable geometry raises several problems. These arise in discussions among the present members of the Union. The question how to organize something like a viable geometry on a more or less permanent basis, resembles the kind of problem we have to face when discussing the enlargement to the countries of Central and Eastern Europe. This uncertainity is caused by the fact that we simply do not know where the different countries who are potential or actual candidates to be members of the Union, will be at a given point in time. This applies to the participation in a free trade area, in a customs union, or in a single market. The discipline required when joining a single market is far from trivial. The same applies to a monetary union. Basically the problem now is to find a way which makes sense both economically and institutionally for organizing a system in which different levels of integration could coexist and in which countries should or could choose the level of integration they want on the basis of an assessment of its costs and benefits. In that respect, the idea to have explicit criteria is clearly the right approach, because this means first that you made explicit the necessary conditions for participating in a given level of integration. And second, that through defining these criteria, you may correct the bias in favour of moving forward to a level of integration which, in some respects, might be excessive as regards the degree of convergence which have been achieved at a certain point in time. There are benefits in moving to the highest degree of integration, both politically and economically because of the degree of redistribution which is attached to different levels of integration. But there are also significant risks. The virtue of criteria is to correct this bias for eventually ill-chosen levels and to help defining degrees of participation that are consistent with economic realities.

27 Contribution of the Europe Agreements, of PHARE, and of TACIS

Robert Verrue

Robert Triffin was one of the main architects of the post-war international economic order and also a man of great vision. We should not forget that at the time of the Bretton Woods conference, the world was still at war. For most people, it would perhaps have been difficult to imagine that the major European belligerents could live together as peaceful neighbours, let alone as partners in an 'ever closer union'. But through a combination of foresight, courage, and ingenuity (all features which one immediately associates with men of vision like Robert Triffin), a European Union *has* indeed been established. Today, this Union is confronted by a challenge of tremendous historical importance: how to support the continuing transformation of the former communist countries of Central and Eastern Europe and the former Soviet Union and how to prepare itself for enlargement to the East.

One of the founding fathers of this Union, Robert Schuman, had a vision of rendering war in Western Europe 'not merely unthinkable, but materially impossible'. This has indeed been achieved, and also much more. Today, the European Union accounts for more than one-fifth of world merchandise trade, it has abolished all internal frontiers and hence permitted the free circulation of goods, services, capital, and people within its own boundaries. It is gradually developing a common foreign and security policy and is preparing to establish its own currency. In this last respect, the European Union owes a particular debt to the late Robert Triffin, who served as one of Jean Monnet's closest advisers and was one of the first contributors to the project of economic and monetary union.

Spurred on by our achievements and by the inspiration of men like Schuman, Monnet, and Triffin, we are already engaging in a further leap of the imagination: one in which we can envisage the countries of Central and Eastern Europe (which for decades had been artificially isolated from the rest of the continent by communist rule) eventually joining this Union. Such a leap of the imagination has already been made by the heads of state and government of the existing member states. In June 1993, the Copenhagen European Council agreed that the Central and Eastern European countries could become members of the European Union as soon as they are ready to assume the obligations of membership. To paraphrase Robert Schuman, the accession of these countries to the European Union is no longer 'unthinkable', but the challenge before us is to make it 'materially possible'.

The Central and Eastern European countries, together with the other countries of the region and the newly independent states (NIS), are currently engaged in the difficult process of structural transformation. The success of economic reform in these transforming economies will depend on the ability of policy makers in the region to meet the twin challenges of creating market-based economies which are fully integrated into the world trading system, and restoring economic growth based on dynamic and competitive export sectors.

Much has already been achieved. Throughout the region, considerable progress has been made in *liberalization*, with respect to prices, foreign trade, and exchange rates. In many countries, ongoing efforts to achieve *stabilization* are now beginning to show tangible benefits as the sharp falls in output which followed the onset of economic reform show continuing signs of gradually being reversed. To complement these measures, reforming economies are also engaging in *restructuring*, which has encompassed a range of policies including the transformation of industries to enable enterprises to meet the discipline of the market, the privatization of state-owned firms, banking reform, agricultural reform, developing legal and institutional frameworks to support a functioning market economy, rebuilding road, rail, and telecommunications networks, and creating an adequate social safety net.

The European Union has been a strong supporter of economic reform in the transforming economies. Support has been provided through the PHARE and TACIS programmes and through a variety of other means such as balance-of-payments support, humanitarian aid, and the provision of investment capital through the European Investment Bank and the European Bank for Reconstruction and Development. These initiatives are all of considerable importance in encouraging the transition to a market economy, but the Union also recognizes that trade liberalization represents perhaps the greatest contribution that it can make to supporting reform in the region. The negotiation of trade agreements has, therefore, been a key priority for the EU. Today, I would like to concentrate on the trade aspects of the European Union's relations with the transforming economies and on the PHARE and TACIS programmes.

With particular reference to Central and Eastern Europe, the EU has concluded bilateral Association Agreements or Europe Agreements with six countries: Bulgaria, the Czech Republic, Hungary, Poland, Romania, and Slovakia. The Europe Agreements are wide-ranging in scope. They include *common provisions* (on matters such as political dialogue, culture, and economic and financial co-operation). In addition, the agreements impose strong obligations on the associated countries in terms of the *approximation of laws* (in particular, in areas such as competition policy and state aids, customs law, and banking).

However, it is the trade aspects of the Europe Agreements which have received the most attention. The Agreements encompass a gradual move to establish free trade in industrial goods between the EU and each associated country, as well as mutual concessions for trade in agricultural goods. The trade objectives of the Europe Agreements are being achieved progressively, but in an asymmetric manner. The European Union is dismantling its own tariffs and non-tariff measures faster and earlier than each associated country. Following the Copenhagen European Council, the dismantling of EU trade barriers was even accelerated. The result of this is that the EU will have lifted all tariffs and non-tariff barriers on imports of industrial goods from the Czech Republic, Hungary, Poland, and Slovakia with effect from 1 January 1995 (and one year after this, for Bulgaria and Romania). The only exceptions will be certain steel products (covered by the European Coal and Steel Community Treaty) and certain textiles and clothing products. Even in these so-called 'sensitive' products, the EU has already undertaken a significant degree of trade liberalization, and further liberalization is proceeding rapidly.

In the case of *steel*, the EU immediately abolished all quantitative restrictions on imports from the associated countries with the entry into force of the trade provision of the Europe Agreements. Tariffs are being progressively reduced to zero and are currently at very low levels (around 1 per cent for imports from the Visegrád countries).

Turning to *textiles and clothing products*, it should be noted that the associated countries have already benefited from significant increases in quotas, with the result that quota utilization by these countries is now extremely low. These quotas will, in any event, disappear several years before the Uruguay Round deadline. In addition, EU tariffs on textiles imports from the associated countries were either abolished immediately or are being progressively reduced to zero.

The situation in *agriculture* is somewhat more complicated, since one of the main principles of the EU's common agricultural policy has been the concept of 'Community preference'. Nevertheless, the Europe Agreements provide for considerable mutual concessions in agricultural trade between the EU and each associated country. It should be noted that with the collapse of state distribution systems in the former communist countries, their agricultural markets have become severely disorganized and this has prevented any significant growth in agricultural trade with the EU. Over the longer term, however, several countries appear to have some potential as agricultural exporters. The question of how the common agricultural policy needs to be adapted to serve the interests of an enlarged Union also needs to be carefully examined.

The Europe Agreements have, in any event, already led to a significant degree of trade liberalization by the EU, with the ultimate goal of industrial free trade virtually within reach. It is clear that the specific measures which the EU has taken will have far-reaching effects. But against these specific measures, there is perhaps also a general concern on the part of some commentators that the substantial liberalization provided for in the Europe Agreements could be undermined by restrictive use of anti-dumping and safeguard measures by the EU. To assess whether such a concern is well-founded, one needs to examine the record of the EU in implementing the Agreements.

As far as *safeguard measures* are concerned, it should be remembered that under the Agreements either party has the right to take action in response to a sharp increase in imports from the other party, and this general principle is, of course, also enshrined in the GATT. In fact, the EU has only made very rare use of this measure. The Agreements also provide for either party to respond to unfair trading practices through recourse to *anti-dumping measures*. In this respect, the Commission now treats the countries with Europe Agreements as market economies. In principle, this means that in anti-dumping investigations, the same provisions now apply to the associated countries as those which apply to all other market economy countries. The Commission has instigated very few anti-dumping actions against firms from Central and Eastern European countries (only about 0.3 per cent of imports from these countries have been directly affected), and where dumping has been found to occur, the Commission has often decided to.

accept price or volume undertakings from firms as an alternative to imposing anti-dumping duties.

Given these considerations, it is clear that the EU has a very open trading
regime with the Central and Eastern European countries. As further evidence of this, one need only look at the significant growth in trade since
economic reform began in the region. The European Union has become, in
a very short space of time, the major trading partner of the region and now
accounts for about half of its total exports and imports. Between 1989 and
1993, the value of the European Union's imports from the six associated
countries increased by 67 per cent (in current prices). Over the same period,
exports by the EU to these countries increased by 124 per cent. The result
has been that we now have a considerable trade surplus with these countries
(of approximately 5.6 billion ECU in 1993). However, this balance should
not be taken as an indication of protectionism on the EU's part. Indeed,
given the structural savings deficit in Central and Eastern Europe, it is quite
natural that these countries would tend to have a trade deficit over the
medium term.

Furthermore, trade figures for the first quarter of 1994 show that the EU's
imports from the associated countries are now growing faster than its
exports to these countries. In the first three months of 1994, EU imports
from the six countries with Europe Agreements grew by 30 per cent (in
current prices) compared with the same period in 1993, whilst EU exports
to these countries increased by 20 per cent.

As well as trade initiatives, the European Union is providing grant finance
to support the process of economic transformation in Central and Eastern
Europe through the PHARE programme. PHARE is also helping the partner
countries to strengthen their newly-created democratic societies. PHARE
provides know-how, including policy advice and training, from a wide
range of non-commercial, public and private organizations to its partner
countries. It acts as a multiplier by unlocking funds for important projects
from other donors through studies, capital grants, guarantee schemes, and
credit lines and invests directly in infrastructure together with international
financial institutions. These investment activities will account for more
PHARE funds as the restructuring process continues in the partner countries. In addition, the Essen European Council in December 1994 is likely
to consider enhancing the relative importance of infrastructure investment
in the PHARE programme.

PHARE is in fact the largest grant assistance programme in support of
the Central and Eastern European countries. At the end of its first five years

of operation in 1994, the PHARE programme will have made available ECU 4,283 million to the eleven partner countries. PHARE has been centrally involved in all of the key areas of economic transformation. These include private sector development and enterprise support, training, agricultural restructuring, environment and nuclear safety, social development and employment, public institution and administrative reform and, of course, infrastructure. PHARE continues to make a valuable contribution to reform in Central and Eastern Europe whilst, at the same time, showing the flexibility to respond to the priorities of the different partner countries.

Turning now to the NIS, the EU's trading relationship with these countries is also being radically transformed. In 1989, the EU negotiated a Trade and Co-operation Agreement with the former Soviet Union. This agreement was non-preferential, and was based on the principle of most favoured nation status. This remains the contractual basis governing merchandise trade with the NIS (other than the Baltic states). However, the EU is currently negotiating a new generation of bilateral agreements with the NIS. The Partnership and Co-operation Agreements (PCA) are being negotiated with those republics which are able to accept the obligations inherent in such agreements: respect for democracy, the principles of international law and human rights, and the principles of the market economy.

So far, PCAs have been concluded with the Russian Federation, Ukraine, Kazakhstan, Kirghizia, and Moldova. The PCAs are non-preferential. Quantitative restrictions will be largely abolished in line with the EU's overall trade policy, and both parties agree to apply most favoured nation tariffs. However, the PCAs negotiations with Russia, Ukraine, and Moldova provide for discussions in 1998 to decide, in the light of prevailing circumstances, whether negotiations on a future free trade area should be initiated.

The PCAs will also, for the first time, incorporate chapters on political dialogue, trade and services, the establishment and operation of companies, capital transfers, and intellectual property protection. There will also be provision for consultations on competition matters. These provisions are more explicit in the case of Russia, Ukraine, and Moldova and include obligations to have and to enforce laws addressing restrictions on competition by enterprises as well as to refrain from granting export aids. The PCAs will widen the range of areas included in the economic co-operation chapters, which will cover topics such as privatization and the conversion of military industries to peaceful purposes.

As is the case for imports from the Central and Eastern European countries, the EU market is already extremely open to imports from the NIS.

Russia is by far the EU's main trading partner among the NIS, and EU tariffs on imports from Russia are very low. The Russian export structure is concentrated on products for which the EU generally applies zero tariffs (i.e. raw materials, fuel, minerals, and metals). Thus, around 80 per cent of EU imports from Russia are free of duty. Since January 1993, the NIS have been included in the EU's generalized system of preferences (GSP) scheme. At present, the weighted average EU tariff on imports from Russia is estimated to be less than 1 per cent, and this could fall even further.

The EU's TACIS programme is intended to help the NIS in the process of economic transition, and it also helps them to strengthen their democratic societies. It provides support in the form of grant finance to foster the exchange of knowledge and expertise through partnerships, links, and networks at all levels of society. TACIS is the leading programme that provides grants for the provision of know-how to the NIS. Working closely with its partner countries, it will have made available ECU 1,870 million to launch more than 2,000 projects by the end of 1994.

TACIS also works in co-ordination with other donors, international financial institutions, and other international organizations to ensure that its activities complement other assistance initiatives. Key areas of TACIS activity have included nuclear safety and the environment, the restructuring of state enterprises and private sector development, public administration reform, agriculture, energy, transport, and telecommunications. In these areas and in others, TACIS is contributing to the development of trade and investment, which are essential to economic restructuring and modernization.

Before I close, I would like to say a few words about the Commission's work in preparing a strategy for the accession of the associated countries of Central and Eastern Europe. The Commission was invited to present such a strategy by the Corfu European Council in June 1994. A recent Commission communication makes specific proposals under a number of areas. One of the most important of these is creating the framework for a deepening co-operation with the associated countries. The Council has stated that it regards a structured relationship with the associated countries as a means to involve them progressively in the EU's work in areas of common interest. The Council has also approved the Commission's intention to present a White Paper on the question of harmonization of legislation after consultation with the member states and the associated countries. This would open up the possibility of gradually extending the single market to the associated countries. It is clear that such a task will not be easy to achieve, but it does represent a tremendous prospect for the future.

To conclude, it is clear that we have achieved a great deal. Both in the area of trade relations and in the contributions made by the PHARE and TACIS programmes, the European Union's efforts to support the reforming economies have greatly contributed to the prospects for future economic growth and political stability across the region. We have also set ourselves ambitious targets for the future. If we can rise to the challenge of East-West partnership, it would indeed be a worthy testimony to the vision of men like Robert Triffin.

28 European Union (EU) Financial Instruments for Central and Eastern European Countries in their Transition Process and in their Preparation for EU Membership

Joly Dixon

I had the pleasure and great honour to work personally with Robert Triffin – mainly on issues of European monetary integration. I should like to join with all those who have saluted his great vision as one of the chief architects of the post-war international economic order. At the start of this conference, Mr Szabó-Pelsőczi, Chairman of the Foundation, aptly encapsulated the attributes at the heart of Robert Triffin's considerable achievements with the words: 'personal humility and professional pride'.

I would also like to congratulate the organizers of this conference. The theme is entirely appropriate. We need to re-examine the Bretton Woods institutions. This is not just because it is their 50th birthday; nor is it because we have not been well served by them. Their architects, including Robert Triffin, did a remarkable job. But I am not amongst those who say: 'if it is not broke, don't fix it'. It seems to me that although the system has been working relatively well, it is no longer sufficient for today's world, which is characterized by the adoption of more open policies by many developing countries, a communications and information revolution, increased environmental awareness and increasing economic integration, as shown by the rapid growth of trade, investment, and capital flows. But most of all, today's international economic order has to take account of the end of the cold war and the challenge of the East-West partnership, as is recognized by the theme of this conference. The world has changed decisively; and there will have to be changes in the Bretton Woods institutions to reflect this.

These changes, which can, of course, be evolutionary, are already underway. My colleague, Robert Verrue, has discussed the European Union's overall response to the challenge, and I will concentrate on the Union's balance-of-payments support for the countries of Central and Eastern

Europe, which has brought the Union into a very close and rapidly evolving partnership with the Bretton Woods institutions.

The start of the European Union and G-24 lending

The European Union has had a balance-of-payments lending instruments available for its own member states since the early 1970s. At the end of 1989, it was decided to extend the use of this type of instrument outside the Union to a non-member state. Procedures were put in place to lend Hungary up to ECU 870 million. The technique used was the same as for lending to a member state. That is, the Union borrows the money on the international capital markets in its own name – hence with the guarantee of the Community budget – and on-lends it, on exactly the same interest rate and maturity terms, to the recipient country. In the case of Hungary, this made a very interesting deal. At the time, although some courageous reform measures were being taken, Hungary had virtually no access to the international markets. It could, at best, borrow very short-term and with a very substantial risk premium. The Community, with its AAA status, was, however, able to raise five-year money at only just over LIBOR. It therefore, in effect, obtained these conditions for Hungary.

This European Union loan for Hungary, which was closely co-ordinated with the Bretton Woods institutions, especially the IMF, was intended to allow some more margin for manoeuvre in the design of the IMF programme and to supplement the Stand-By Arrangement.

During the course of 1990, it became increasingly apparent that Hungary was not a unique case. Other countries of the region were faced with the same triple problem:

1   The costs of the first steps of reform, liberalization, and stabilization were substantially greater than expected. This was partly because the countries concerned faced two additional external shocks: the consequences of the Gulf War crisis, including the embargo which had particularly severe effects in economies like that of Bulgaria; and the dramatic collapse of the COMECON trading system, which had been based on state directed flows of goods and artificial prices.

2   The sums available from the Bretton Woods institutions were insufficient and small relative to what is available now that quotas and access

limits have been increased, and the Systemic Transformation Facility created.

3   Flows from the private sector were virtually non-existent because of both the relative unfamiliarity with the economies concerned and the great uncertainties surrounding the first stages of the reform and transition process.

Against this background, it was decided that the European Union should extend what had been done for Hungary to other countries in the region. It was also decided that the Commission should use the so-called "G-24 process" (which had been set up after the G-7 had asked in the European Commission at the Paris Summit in July 1989 to co-ordinate assistance to the countries of Central and Eastern Europe) to get other donors to contribute in a similar way to support the Bretton Woods institutions.

A number of such support operations took place:

1   In early 1991, when a Stand-By Arrangement for an amount of $850 million was concluded for Czechoslovakia, which only became a member of the Fund in September 1990, the G-24 committed a similar amount. The World Bank subsequently concluded a structural adjustment loan of $450 million in June 1991.

2   Also in 1991, Bretton Woods institution programmes in Bulgaria and Romania were supported by the G-24, and there was a further loan to Hungary.

3   In 1992, the G-24 again gave substantial financial backing to Bretton Woods institution programmes in the Baltic States and Albania, and there were follow-up operations for Bulgaria and Romania.

In each, the pattern was repeated with the G-24, co-ordinated by the Commission, committing very similar sums to those available from the Bretton Woods institutions.

Altogether, over 1991 and 1992, about $4.5 billion – a similar amount to that committed by the Institutions themselves – was committed by the G-24 in support of international financial institution programmes in the countries of Central and Eastern Europe. The European Union itself committed over half the total G-24 amount. It seems certain that the bold stabilization programmes in the region, which have laid the basis for the growth which is now beginning to be seen, could not have been achieved without this support to the Bretton Woods institutions from the G-24 led by the European Union.

1994 actions

This year, 1994, has seen the opening of a second chapter in G-24 and European Union macroeconomic assistance to the countries of Central and Eastern Europe. The first chapter was characterized by the rapid response to an emergency situation. The main features were that very large sums of money were found to support Bretton Woods institution programmes. The European Union played a key role both as the largest single provider of these funds and through its role as the co-ordinator of the G-24 process, which ensured a wide participation in the effort with tolerable burden-sharing.

There has now been a considerable evolution. Most obviously a new instrument has been created by the IMF: the Systemic Transformation Facility. Other changes have included paying more attention to structural issues and hence to a greater co-ordination with the World Bank. From the European Union's point of view, its lending has played a more policy-oriented role. It has affected the timing and the content of programmes; and a greater synergy has been achieved within the Union between its loan-based and its grant-based instruments.

I should like to illustrate these points by briefly discussing the current operations with Bulgaria, Romania, and Slovakia. Following a "lost year" for reform, a breakthrough was achieved in late 1993, early 1994, when the governments in all three countries adopted comprehensive stabilization and reform programmes that addressed specific causes for the previous set-backs and that could be supported by the IMF. These programmes included: a strong fiscal policy and the normalization of relations with commercial creditors in Bulgaria; the reform of the foreign exchange system together with a tight monetary policy in Romania; and in Slovakia a sustained fiscal consolidation to adjust for the loss of transfers from the Czech lands, while maintaining the exchange rate as an anchor.

The European Union and the G-24 decided to respond positively to requests from these countries for macrofinancial assistance to complement the IMF and World Bank arrangements. In Bulgaria, the G-24 will make available about $350 million in support of IMF drawings under Stand-By

Arrangements and Systemic Transformation Facilities amounting in total to over $520 million. The amounts available from the World Bank are of the same order of magnitude as those from the G-24. For Romania, IMF drawings will amount to over $700 million, and the G-24 will provide $275 million. For Slovakia, it is foreseen that the G-24 will provide more than the IMF – $300 million compared with $250 million.

Although the total amounts committed by the G-24 have not been as large relatively as in the first round, the co-ordination between the Commission and the Bretton Woods institutions has been more intense. Also, the policy dialogue with the authorities in the countries concerned has been broader involving a two-stage process:

1   In a first stage, the main objective has been to ensure the rapid implementation of key policy measures, especially those identified as prior actions for IMF programmes. This is illustrated by the strong pressure exerted by the Commission on the Romanian authorities to liberalize the exchange rate regime, without which the Commission would not have been in a position to assure G-24 members that the credibility of the government programme was sufficient to warrant mobilization of financial assistance.

2   In a second stage, more emphasis was put on the strategy for structural reform, which clearly involved closer co-ordination with the World Bank. Two major fields have been involved: the privatization process and the restructuring of the enterprise sector. In each, an important point was that the government should clarify the associated institutional set-up. Thus, in Bulgaria, the Commission expressed doubts about the capacity of a nascent institution to carry through an ambitious, time-bound programme that was given high priority by the government. In Romania, the process of restructuring the largest loss-making enterprises was under the responsibility of several institutions, raising some doubts about the coherence of the whole process. For both countries, these concerns were made known to the authorities and also the necessary steps have been taken to ensure that PHARE can provide assistance to strengthen the capacity of the appropriate institutions. Consistent with this approach, the disbursement of the second tranche of European Union lending will be linked mainly to *structural issues*; especially liberalization, privatization, enterprise restructuring, financial discipline, and financial sector reform.

There is no rigid doctrine in these areas. The approach has not been to dictate to governments their policies. Instead, it has been to take stock of current commitments, to discuss their consistency and feasibility, and then to pinpoint those areas where the fulfilment of some identified targets might be a decisive step. This has been done in very close co-operation with the World Bank and in the light of current PHARE programmes.

In each case, the procedure has been to identify key issues in the process of structural reform and stabilization of the economy, and then exert pressure on the authorities and help them to take the appropriate steps so as to intensify the policy dialogue with the authorities. It is too early to judge the overall success but key elements in the general strategy have been:

a a clear understanding and acceptance by the authorities of the goals and purposes of the dialogue;

b a good co-ordination with the Bretton Woods institutions with a view both to circulate relevant information and to ensure consistency;

c a good co-ordination with PHARE;

d the awareness by the authorities of this co-ordination with both the international financial institutions and with PHARE.

Next moves

The European Union's macrofinancial lending instrument has, therefore, evolved considerably since it was first used for Hungary in 1990. In my view, it should evolve further in the light of the evolution that has taken place in the countries concerned, in the Bretton Woods institutions and most particularly in the light of the commitment to membership of the Union when circumstances are right.

The need of the Central and East European countries to adapt to the requirements of EU accession calls for them to adopt coherent medium-term policy frameworks oriented towards economic stability and restructuring. The Europe Agreements include a provision for a regular macroeconomic dialogue between the Union and the associated countries; and this dialogue, which should aim at promoting convergence of the associated countries' economic performance with that of the Union, should also provide the opportunity to map out the broad lines of the necessary policy reforms and national programmes of structural adjustment.

The implementation of such policy reforms and programmes is likely to concentrate expenditure on particular areas (enterprise restructuring, environment protection, upgrading of transport infrastructure, social protection, etc.), which will imply exceptional initial costs. These will be incurred at the same time as there are tight constraints on national budgets. All the Union's instruments are increasingly being adapted to take this into account. The strengthening and enhancement of the PHARE programme, for example, goes in this direction, especially in that a certain percentage can be used for infrastructure investment. Another example is the recent Council decision extending Community guarantees for EIB loans of up to ECU 3 billion for the Central and East European countries. This provides room for enhanced financial support through project-related lending that could complement PHARE initiatives.

However, it should be kept in mind that:

a   PHARE grants and EIB loans as well as EBRD loans are project-related and therefore slow-disbursing forms of financial support;

b   the access of the countries concerned to the international financial markets is likely to remain costly and their domestic markets are still relatively narrow;

c   the availability of resources from the Community budget will remain limited in the coming years.

In these circumstances, it seems highly likely that a loan-based instrument which can complement the project-related assistance provided through PHARE, the EIB, and the EBRD will continue to be useful. As I have discussed, such an instrument exists and it has already been evolving in the right direction.

I should like to conclude with the hope that the European Union will explore the possibility that it continues to do so. Provided that we continue to work closely with the Bretton Woods institutions, it seems to me that such an instrument is an important part of the European Union's response to the challenge of developing an ever close East-West partnership.

Part IV

Do We Need a New G-7, G-10, or G-24 Initiative?

29 Has the West Done Enough?*

Daniel Cardon de Lichtbuer

It is a great honour and, at the same time, a pleasure to address you on the second day of this important and rather unconventional conference.

Unconventional because its promotion has come from a Hungarian foundation named after my fellow countryman, the well-known Belgian-born economist Robert Triffin, who was a keen observer and prominent actor of the international monetary and financial scene for more than four decades.

This conference is unconventional also because it shows the clout of the Central European countries as experts. The idea of holding the conference in Brussels has been successfully realized by the Hungarian-American economist, Chairman of the Robert Triffin–Szirák Foundation, Mr Miklós Szabó-Pelsőczi and by the idea's Western supporters.

In the first place, amongst these, I would like to name Mr Philippe Maystadt, Minister of Finance of Belgium and Chairman of the IMF Interim Committee, who has accepted to chair the Organizing Committee.

I would also like to mention the efforts and contributions of Bernard Snoy and Professor Alfred Steinherr, who were instrumental, together with Miklós Szabó-Pelsőczi, in drawing up the programme of the Conference and who have played an active role in inviting most of the speakers. I confess that, in particular, Mr Snoy's commitment to the organization of the Conference determined the League's decision to assure its participation as a co-organizer.

Many others have contributed to the success of this 'East-West joint venture', amongst them the European Commission. Here, I would like to ask them to accept our gratitude.

* Luncheon address, November 18, 1994

229

I would express my special thanks to Mr Alfons Verplaetze, Governor of the National Bank of Belgium, for his interest in this Conference and for the help of his institution.

I was also glad to see the largely international composition of this meeting. Not only both sides of the Atlantic are represented but also Asia. The extended European family is present, both the lines coming from East and West. Central Europe is represented by eminent Hungarians among them President Bod of the Hungarian National Bank, as well as by reformers like Mr Leszek Balczerowicz, former Minister of Finance of Poland, and Mr Jan Klacek, Director of the Institute of Economics of the Czech National Bank. I would also like to greet among the participants our guests from Russia, Slovakia, and Slovenia.

After the war, the reconstruction of Western Europe has taken place with the help of the United States. Their substantial help was combined with a clear vision of the future. The presence of Ambassador Fred Latimer Hadsel, Member of the Board of the George C. Marshall Foundation, is a proof of the non-relenting interest of the United States in Europe's future and in a new 'East-West partnership for economic progress'.

Has Western Europe gone far enough in helping the reform countries? Has the European Union done enough? Have we done as much as the US did for us after World War II?

Mr Václav Havel, President of the Czech Republic, has recently expressed a note of disappointment: 'We have had and we still have the historical opportunity to redefine the new Europe. Looking at it in the perspective of the last five years, I must say that this chance is only materializing slowly and, for the time being, rather in words than in deeds. I would not like to be compelled to meditate one day on the reasons which have led our generation to fail.'

I fully understand the doubts of President Havel, and this is why I would suggest that we should not hesitate to submit our action to a critical analysis conducted around the three following questions:

1   What should be done in order to make Western assistance and Western policies better respond to existing needs, the target being to lay the foundation for self-sustaining export-led growth? For me, indeed, in economic terms, the decisive criterion is the launching of the process of self-sustaining growth in Central and Eastern Europe.

2   What is to be expected from the individual effort of the transition countries themselves in overcoming their difficulties?

3   What needs to be done in order to improve the political, economic, and trade ties, both bilaterally and multilaterally, among the 'associated countries' and, more generally, among the Central and Eastern European countries?

In each case, we should proceed to an evaluation of the shortcomings and should see that they are corrected.

I would like to finish my address by saying that this Conference is also unconventional because it is deliberately adopting the long view in looking into the future rather than just celebrating the past.

The fiftieth anniversary of Bretton Woods coincides with the fifth anniversary of the fall of the Berlin Wall – on 9 November 1989 – and, more or less simultaneously, with that of the dismantling of the Iron Curtain, in its different country components. This Wall had cut our Continent, for respectively 28 and 40 years, into two almost hermetically divided parts.

My sincere hope is that this Conference, but also our future individual and joint efforts, may contribute to the preservation of peace in Europe, without letting another divisive demarcation line or something equivalent separate us again. We must indeed succeed in bringing closer the two parts of Europe in view of the positive contribution we are expected to make to the world of the 21st century!

30 The Importance of a Well-Structured Strategy of Transitions

Alfons Verplaetze

In the question of financing transformation, the size of available funds is not the most important. It is more important to know that the funds will be well spent. We must make it sure that there is a satisfactory mixture of the types of instruments, of grants and loans we use. It is only now that we are beginning to learn to use our instruments more effectively. In this respect, the European Union and the EBRD provide us with very good examples.

During the last fifty years the world has changed a great deal. Yet, this change was more a change in the geography of our concerns, than in anything else. We started fifty years ago with the IMF and with the World Bank. The IMF intended to have a good programme of financing short-term balance-of-payments disequilibria. During the last fifty years, next to the strictly monetary activities, the social aspect has gained in importance. The World Bank became a project-oriented development bank. At the beginning of Bretton Woods, the IMF was mostly concerned with industrialized countries. They needed good programmes, they needed some assistance on a temporary basis, because after all, the IMF has many features of a central bank. West-European countries, during the period of post-war reconstruction, needed short-term funds to finance occasional balance-of-payments deficits. Since then, industrialized countries have found solutions to their problems outside the IMF.

Instead, came first the problems of the developing world and then, those of Central Eastern Europe, and of the former Soviet Union. This is why I am saying that there is a change in the geographical area of activity, but the nature of the problems remained the same.

In this new situation, we want that the IMF should be the leader in centralizing restructuring and technical assistance. Capital needs, which are much more important now than they were fifty years ago, are less likely to be covered from sovereign sources. We need better co-ordination between the World Bank and private capital markets, which are more able to provide loan and investment capital resources. The co-operation and co-ordination should include the IMF, concerning economic programmes with the best social content. If we have better co-ordination in a way I just have indicated, I do not think we will need new formations of the G-7, G-10, G-24 type.

In this context, I would like to focus on three issues. First of all, the most important among these issues is strategy. Do we need a strategy, or can we live with competing strategies?

The second question is: do we need a more rational allocation of resources, or should we be satisfied with the status quo of competing technical and financial programmes of assistance.

In the third place comes the question of resources. We need a world monetary authority. Did the IMF fall far short of that? What is the role of the BIS? We all know that Central and Eastern Europe's reconstruction needs plenty of resources. Let us mobilize them all together. The question comes down again to the issue of strategy, or to a combination of strategies of the IMF, of the World Bank, and of the Economic Commission.

In summary, I would like to stress the overall need of strategy, which would help us avoid the tremendous waste, which is now going on in many fields, due to competing and contradictory strategies emanating from well-meaning, but ill-coordinated international organizations.

At least on one issue there is general agreement. Trade is important. Western Europe has, on this point, a special responsibility. If Central and Eastern European (CEE) countries import more from Western Europe than they export, Western Europe would have no problem with that. Japan does the same thing with the Asian Tigers. CEE countries are now in a deficit with Western Europe. On the other side, one should be patient with the problem of stability in the countries of transition. It is not possible to have a single economic social fundamentalist doctrine that would be good while all the others would be bad. Let us be very pragmatic. Transition takes time. Let us not forget all the things that happened in Western Europe after World War II. Co-ordination and a common strategy are imperative also with respect to the CEE area. When we give technical and financial assistance, we should not think that we have the right to define unilaterally our strategy. That would be a waste of time. The IMF is making some laudable, rational efforts in this direction. Financial resources should come from all the richness of the industrialized countries' resources, but within the framework of a given, co-ordinated strategy. Just because one institution would give capital, it should not have the right to enforce its own strategy at the exclusion of all other advice coming from the countries of transition and from others.

There is a great difference between macro- and microeconomics. Some experts believe in the primacy of macroeconomic policy. But we also need a great deal of microeconomic policy, which could be even more important.

In any case, countries in transition must help themselves in the formation of both macro- and microeconomic policies. When they create sound macro- and microeconomic conditions, private foreign capital will willingly participate in economic reconstruction. At present, transition countries are far from the optimal allocation of their own scarce resources. Inflation is not just a continental European hobby. It is a very important problem, maybe the most important of all. If we would get that under steady control, we would be able to accomplish many other things much easier.

31 Proposal for a Marshall Plan for the Former Soviet Union

Alfred Steinherr

Introduction

Soon after the opening-up of Eastern Europe, ideas for a Marshall Plan were discussed and found not justified. The main argument against the creation of a new Marshall Plan was the conviction that the existing international institutions and the newly created European Bank for Reconstruction and Development were financially adequately endowed and that their experience and the instruments at their disposal were sufficient to cope with the needs of the newly emerging economies of Eastern Europe. In the light of experience, it is worthwhile reviewing that early assessment of the adequacy of the international support mechanisms for the former Soviet Union (FSU) and asking the question whether a different approach would not be preferable. Five years after the opening up of Eastern Europe, it may, however, be felt that it is already too late for such initiatives. Two facts argue to the contrary. First, historically speaking, the post-World War II Marshall Plan did not commence in 1945, but was created in 1947 and started operations in 1949, i.e. with a decision-lag similar to the one that would arise if a Marshall Plan II was decided in 1995, four years after the blow-up of the Soviet Union. Second, numerous difficulties and shortcomings have been experienced in the FSU with the existing support framework, so that several successor countries are still only at the beginning of the reform process.

Many observers have argued that the existing framework has not provided timely and substantial support for reformers in Russia and in other successor states of the FSU. Therefore, there has been a backlash against reformers, a reinforcement of opposition groups to rapid reforms of the political and economic system, diminishing and delaying the chances of ultimate success. This retardation has increased the costs of transition and reduced large parts of the population to abject poverty.

Indeed, Western aid has been forthcoming at a very slow pace, and one can also detect a lack of co-ordination. For example, Germany, pressed by the political objectives of speeding up the departure of Soviet troops, has provided over 50 per cent of Western assistance to Russia until 1994. The G-7 made substantial commitments to support Russian reforms in 1993, but only very small amounts have been disbursed until the end of 1994. The largest part of Western support has consisted of trade credits at market conditions, and only a very small amount of the multilateral support has been at concessionary terms. The largest concessionary element has been in the German assistance. As a result of particular political and economic interests, it can be seen that Europe as a whole has taken on the lion's share of Western financial assistance to Russia, whilst the United States and Japan have played a rather marginal role.

The simultaneous support from various national sources and from a large number of multilateral institutions has also shown a certain lack of co-ordination. In particular, this lack of co-ordination implies that there is no concentrated monitoring and thus no unified definition of the strings attached to Western support. Therefore, it is possible to argue that Western support could be improved on three accounts: (1) better co-ordination and (2) increased concessionary financing, with (3) tight strings attached. We shall argue that the best solution would be to create a new multilateral institution that integrates some existing financial support mechanisms and reflects the geographical interests of the shareholders more closely than in global institutions.

The need for better co-ordination

It is generally recognized that the benefit of the Marshall Plan after World War II was not only limited to the financial support provided to Western Europe, but also – and perhaps even mainly – due to the strings that US policy makers had attached to this assistance, namely, reforms of the post-war European economies and opening-up to foreign trade as a *quid pro quo* to Marshall Plan financial assistance. Of course, the United States were in a privileged position: they were economically and militarily dominant and the only providers of financial support. Therefore, they could easily dictate and enforce conditions and there was no need for co-ordination. In the present situation, there is no clear, single government or institution that could dictate similar reform measures. What one observes is financial assistance that serves national interests (e.g. export credits), different political objectives (early German financial support for the FSU was considered premature by the G-7), institutional positioning or institutional constraints (slow disbursement of IMF support in the FSU was unavoidable, given the IMF's statutes, but in contradiction to the needs of these countries, a view shared by some G-7 members). The institution which comes perhaps closest to the role of leader is the International Monetary Fund, but the Fund is only one institution among many and by its statutes has to concentrate on macroeconomic stabilization. On the other hand, the countries most directly affected by success or failure of reforms in the FSU are the European countries. It needs to be recognized that the European Union does not enjoy the economic and military weight that characterized the USA after the war and that the European Commission does not dispose of the technical means and experience to carry out financial assistance and its monitoring on a large scale. However, the need remains. There is no point in assisting reform countries without, at the same time, negotiating appropriate reform measures and monitoring their reform process in order to make reforms an effective condition for sustained financial support. Nor is the reverse logic – to advise without provision of the required financial means – any more compelling.

The need for concessionary support under reinforced monitoring

The previous argument, the need for financing with simultaneous monitoring, is all the more compelling when concessionary funds are provided. What appears to the receiving country as a gift is too easily used for purposes that may not be optimal for the long-term development of the country. Therefore, the use of such funds and control of execution is a necessary element of any concessionary assistance. The need for concessionary assistance for the FSU can easily be demonstrated. One argument is that these countries were hit with exceptional and once-and-for-all shocks: (i) the shock represented by the explosion of the FSU and, therefore, the destruction of their existing trading framework, (ii) the shock of transition, and (iii) the need to reform the environment and increase the security of nuclear energy. Second, the success of reforms is also in the interest of Western Europe as the direct neighbour of the states of the FSU. Successful reforms are a precondition for the preservation of peace in Europe, for the independence of countries such as Belarus and Ukraine and thus for an equilibrium balance of power. They will also prevent migration to Western Europe. On all these accounts, Western Europe is the direct beneficiary of successful reforms and should, therefore, be willing to pay more than overseas countries. Therefore, it can be argued that, in the interests of the West, there should be financial assistance and that because this interest is mainly focused in Western Europe, that Western Europe should, therefore, provide the largest share of such support. Because many of these expenditures in the end benefit Western Europe and because they do not have an immediate rate of return or at least will take a very long time to materialize, such assistance should be provided on concessionary terms and this is what a Marshall Plan II could provide.

The need for an institutional reorganization

Experience has shown that concessionary assistance can only be provided when it is in the self-interest of the donors. On a world level, which is the relevant scope of operations of the World Bank and of the IMF, it is hard to imagine that the problems will be felt on a scale and to an intensity comparable to those felt in Western Europe. The risk in political terms of failed reforms in the FSU, the risk in terms of pollution, the risks in terms of outward migration from the FSU to Western Europe, are all heavily concentrated on Western Europe. Therefore, we would argue that Western Europe has to make an effort to finance this concessionary funding and, indeed, as mentioned in the introduction, most of the financial support so far has been provided by Western Europe for exactly the reasons just outlined. We would, therefore, propose that in order to cope with the targets outlined above, namely the need to provide concessionary funding, the need to attach strong strings and intensive monitoring, and the need for better co-ordination, financial support should be carried out by a new institution that would concentrate funds which are already provided by various national and multilateral institutions and could, therefore, overcome the current problem of co-ordination.

For example, we would propose that the funding provided by the European Commission, namely the technical support under its TACIS programme, funding for nuclear safety and balance-of-payments support, should be brought within this new institution which we would call the

Organization for Economic Reconstruction in Eastern Europe (OEREE). Similarly, present national support could be carried out through this institution; also, instead of providing the multilateral banks with a concessionary window, concessionary funds could be transferred to this new institution. If the creation of such an institution were not judged feasible, then it could be made a particular department of an existing bank, such as the EBRD or the European Investment Bank, but we think it would be preferable if the European Commission, the EBRD and the EIB and perhaps some of the particularly concerned national governments became the shareholders of the OEREE.

Funding would then not be a major problem because a starting point would already be provided by re-channelling existing sources to this new institution. As to additional funds, recognition of an increased 'peace dividend' obtained from a strong leadership role in the reform process would already more than cover an annual amount of USD 6 billion or 2 per cent of Russian GDP (equivalent to the importance of Marshall Plan funds for the receiving countries in Western Europe).

The OEREE could either provide low-interest or interest-free loans or grants. An annual budget of USD 6 billion would cover the interest rate on a stock of loans of about USD 60 billion, equivalent to 20 per cent of Russian GNP or more than 10 per cent of GNP of all states of the FSU. Lending for projects (restructuration of the industrial-military complex, nuclear safety, environmental clean-up, social funds backing up reform) could be supported by TACIS technical support funding and policy programme supports from already existing EU sources.

This way the leverage of the new institution would be such as to become the major policy institution and discussion partner for Eastern European countries. It might be desirable to define the length of life of this institution right from the beginning as has been done, for example, in Germany for the Treuhand. One could, for instance, decide that the institution would be closed by the year 2005 or 2010, when one could expect that the major transition problems, even in the FSU, will have been resolved.

This institution would obviously have a much larger say in economic policies than the multilateral banks which could then focus more closely on their financing of bankable projects. The wide scope of the OEREE could be thought to conflict at times with the macroeconomic advice given by the International Monetary Fund. There would obviously be need for a certain co-ordination between the new institution and the IMF and, in view of the difficulties experienced in these countries, such a second forum as an equal partner to the IMF might not be redundant at all.

32 Systemic Change in Central and Eastern Europe

Péter Á. Bod

Transition country is an established term for an economy and society faced with the task of creating or re-creating institutions of the market and of parliamentary democracy. Others called the countries in question *reform* countries. Both expressions, 'transition' and 'reform' are, in this context, misnomers. Are not the countries of Western Europe in transition? They have embarked upon rendering a significant part of their national sovereignty to unified European institutions. Western European countries do qualify for the term 'transition', or 'reform'. In the case of Central Eastern Europe and in the former Soviet Empire, the tasks these countries are facing differ. In some countries, it is the return to market and to democracy as in the case of Hungary or Poland. In other cases, it is the creation of a national state, a national market, and of national legal and political systems. In the latter cases, 'reform' is just not the right word for systemic change. The term 'transition' implies too much of continuity.

I am not suggesting here to discard the established terms the international political and financial community is using for the systemic change, but to be aware of its discontinuous nature.

The systemic change of Central and Eastern Europe is far from a harmonious process. Even in the more developed transition countries, nations with century-long history of market development, transition led to a drastic contraction of measured economic activity. In Hungary, or in the Czech Republic, up to 20 or to 30 per cent of the GDP has been lost during the years of transition. This is a contraction more drastic than that of the Great Depression of the 1930s.

Another remark on the language used in debates is provoked by statements about 'support' provided for Central and Eastern Europe, or 'threats' in trade with the transition countries. Some commentators even speak about 'overflooding Central and Eastern Europe with grant money'. The annual external debt service of Hungary amounts to $3.5 billion; under PHARE $100 million are spent in a year on Hungarian projects. Grant money, soft loans, etc. account for less than 3 per cent of the country's hard currency debt service.

I conclude that in the past 4-5 years, Western Europe has applied a *cost minimizing and reactive*, rather than proactive, strategy vis-à-vis the regions east of it.

Whatever terms we choose to use for the countries in systemic change, the fact remains that five years after the shift from a grossly inefficient economic system to an allegedly more efficient market-based allocation of resources, per capita output is still 10 to 30 per cent lower. The depth and duration of the fall of output requires explanations. Unless we postulate that the market economy as a system is less efficient in allocating resources than the bankrupt socialism, explanations must contain elements of the following factors:

a   command economies were even more inefficient than anticipated;
b   the transition was badly administered everywhere;
c   external conditions, such as access of transition countries to Western markets, were worse than anticipated.

One cannot look but sceptically at 'mismanagement' and 'bad government' as an overall explanation for the contraction in every single country of the region. Thus, there remain two conclusions. One is that the damage done to the countries under the Soviet-type economic system now proves to be too devastating for any government with a mandate of up to four years. Environmental damage, inherited international indebtedness, bad health conditions, and work ethics are all of a long-term nature. Contraction of that size is, thus, unavoidable and cannot be fully ascribed to erroneous policies during the transition years. Curious enough, there are some left-wing governments in the region who blame the management of transition for the decline in output rather than the preceding four decades.

Now we have to look at the second explanation, that is: a reluctant West and lack of a supportive external environment for the countries concerned. If it is true, and I do believe it is, that Western Europe has had a rather reactive strategy vis-à-vis Central and Easern Europe, then now in the middle of the 1990s, the time is ripe to define a proactive strategy. A strategy is needed not only to accelerate the return to the market in Central

Eastern Europe but to accelerate the growth in Western Europe as well. Commentators seldom raise the question: can Europe remain competitive without a healthy Central Eastern Europe? The US–Mexico, Japan–Pacific rim relationships indicate that there are positive externalities from integration. The integration of our region into the developed world also offers externalities. The question is open yet as to who is going to internalize these externalities.

In the light of the past five years, one is tempted to say that Triffin would be dissatisfied with the nature and direction of resource transfer and market access concerning Central Eastern Europe, as well as with the efficiency of the international support given to transition countries.

It is true that in his time private capital flows did not play such a significant role as they do in the 1990s. Private capital flows, however, cannot fully substitute for multinational and sovereign arrangements. Hungary is perhaps the best case to look at in order to assess the role and consequences of strong foreign direct investment (FDI). In the past three years, FDIs have amounted from 5 to 7 per cent of the GDP, one third of the overall investment in my country.

The *micro*economic consequences of the strong private capital inflows are very positive. FDIs contribute to the modernization of the productive capacities and to the export potentials of the country. New growth industries emerge, and old industries disappear very fast. Efficient producers and sales networks quickly drive out less efficient market agents.

*Macro*economically the picture is mixed. Structural transformation driven by FDI also means a fast decline in employment and steep increase of labour productivity in the concerned industries, as well as dynamic import penetration. Privatized and joint venture firms and utilities tend to increase prices in order to generate enough profit to pay back the privatization fee. Profound microeconomic change thus leads to unemployment and self-sustaining import growth, at least in the first phase. Later, once dynamic businesses have acquired large enough market shares, they tend to expand externally, adding to the export growth of the country. FDI and privatization transactions have, however, a certain industrial and regional pattern. They do not represent a full alternative to a conceptually sound Europe-wide proactive strategy, including funding.

Triffin would recommend a well-coordinated effort to accelerate the integration of Central Eastern Europe into the world economy. First of all, into the unified Europe. But who should co-ordinate these efforts? The institution which is the best equipped to harmonize both micro- and macroaspects are the Bretton Woods twins. But the IMF is responsible for global management, not for the development of one particular group of countries. It would be hard to expect of a global institution to invest in specific countries, while the positive externalities out of the modernization of the countries concerned would be reaped mainly by Western Europe. According to this logic, it is the EU that should co-ordinate and fund the transition of Central Eastern Europe. However, in the Maastricht phase of Europe, it is the harmonization of monetary and fiscal policies that has become the core of the European strategy. It is not for me to judge if the effort to promote the even development of Europe versus the promotion of competitiveness of Europe would serve Europe's interests best. Monetary union would certainly improve the business climate and thus would contribute to the competitiveness of Europe. Catching up, however, requires additional structural, trade, and resource transfer policies. My strong belief is that the EU would benefit most from a successful transition in Central Eastern Europe, and should, therefore, invest into the acceleration of the process. Elements of an institutional framework to promote the catching up are already there, such as the EBRD, the EIB, and structural funds. Triffin would, no doubt, propose an even more active strategy to support the momentum.

33 Intra-CIS Payments: The 'Interstate Bank' Project – its Genesis and Demise

Daniel Gros

Abstract

As the rouble zone disintegrated in 1992-93, intra-FSU ('former Soviet Union') payments became very difficult, and payments among central banks were organized on a bilateral basis. In late 1992, ten CIS states agreed among themselves to create a multilateral payments system to be operated by a joint institution, the '*Interstate Bank*'; the agreement, however, *was never implemented*. This note summarizes the payments system that was to be run by the *Interstate Bank*, and argues that such a system could have slowed down the collapse of intra-CIS trade, with significant positive effects even for Russia.

The Interstate Bank was never created because the peripheral CIS states did not understand the importance of multilateral trade and always waited for Russia to move first. Russia never took the necessary steps to set up the Interstate Bank because it felt that it did not need such an institution since it run a surplus with most CIS countries. Moreover, there was considerable opposition from the radical reformers in the Russian government against any official payment mechanism on the ground that immediate full convertibility is the first best.

Introduction

The Soviet Union collapsed at the end of 1991. Two years later, i.e. by the end of 1993, all[1] former republics had introduced their own currencies. While this outcome had been expected by most economists from the beginning, there is still a lot of controversy on whether the speed with which the rouble zone disintegrated was inevitable, and whether it would have

244

been useful to create some transitional arrangement to minimize the disruption that came with this monetary disintegration.

There is little dispute about the fact that the way in which the rouble zone was dissolved was very costly in economic terms because during the process of disintegration, which lasted for most of 1992 and 1993, intra-FSU payments became very difficult. Enterprises and banks could not pay each other because the existing official channels, on which they had to rely at the beginning, were quickly blocked.

The difficulties that arose within the rouble zone were mainly macro-economic: Russia did not want to run surpluses with the rest of the CIS and started to block payments when it discovered in early 1992 that the accounts of the other central banks with the Central Bank of Russia (CBR) showed large imbalances. This led to a period during which most payments were organized among central banks on a bilateral basis. With immediate full convertibility, payments could just have been switched to the commercial banks. However, this did not happen immediately because convertibility was established only gradually, and for a variety of technical reasons it took commercial banks some time to establish a rudimentary intra-CIS network of correspondent banking relationships.[2]

As a response to the difficulties that arose in 1992, ten CIS states agreed among themselves towards the end of that year to create a multilateral payments system to be operated by a joint institution, the Interstate Bank. Section 2 below summarizes how this agreement came about and what it contained. Section 3 provides some of the reasons for the agreement never being implemented. The idea to create a transitional payments mechanism had always been controversial. Section 4 argues that it could have potentially made a substantial contribution. Section 5 gives a conclusion. For more details and an analysis of the overall reform process see Gros and Steinherr (1995).

The Interstate Bank: a brief history

The history of the Interstate Bank project is inextricably linked with the gradual dissolution of the rouble zone. This is not surprising as it was to fill part of the vacuum left by the disappearance of the rouble zone. The following account explains how this came about.

When the Soviet Union broke up, the rouble became the common currency of fifteen independent countries. Each country had an incentive to create as much credit in roubles as possible since the inflationary impact would be borne by the others. Russia recognized this and, in July 1992, started to control flows of funds from the other FSU republics through a system of correspondent accounts with the other central banks. As these correspondent accounts were bilateral, it became impossible to offset deficits and surpluses on a multilateral basis. Moreover, as the other FSU republics ran large deficits with Russia, the CBR felt that it had to block payments. The result was a severe payments crisis for interstate transactions, which started in 1992 and continued into 1993, with increasing dollarization, barter trade, and cash transactions.

After several failed attempts to reconstitute a true rouble zone with one common central bank, the process leading to the Interstate Bank started formally with the CIS summit held on 9 October 1992 in Bishkek (Kirghizia). During this summit, the CIS heads of state concluded an 'Agreement' on a single monetary system and a concerted monetary, credit, and exchange rate policy of the states which have retained the rouble as legal tender (hereinafter: Bishkek agreement).

The aim of this Bishkek agreement was theoretically to establish a clearly defined rouble zone. This explains why some republics insisted during the negotiations (October–December 1992) that the Interstate Bank should be a joint central bank with common decision-making on the basis of 'one state–one vote', and why the eventual 'Agreement' establishing the Interstate Bank still contains vague references to possible central bank tasks.

However, a 'Decision' taken by the heads of state, also at Bishkek on 9 October, called for the constitution of a CIS working group 'to prepare specific proposals on the activities of the Interstate Bank, *first and foremost on the creation of a payments mechanism*'. The negotiations on the Interstate Bank during the final months of 1992, in which IMF and EC experts participated, focused increasingly on the Interstate Bank as a multilateral payments mechanism, and the idea of a joint central bank was moved to the background. The clear focus on the issue of multilateral clearing and settlements enabled Ukraine, that was at the time introducing its own currency, to join the negotiations and sign the 'Agreement' establishing the Interstate Bank together with nine other countries on 22 January 1993.

The most contentious issues during the negotiations concerned five points: *the subscription quotas, the credit element, the currency, the decision-making procedure, and membership.* (See Annexe 1 for details.)

After an agreement had been reached on most of these issues at the expert level in December 1992, the 'Charter' establishing the Interstate Bank was finalized at the CIS summit of 22 January 1993. Unfortunately, however, no concrete steps were taken to actually set up the Interstate Bank for nearly a year. Ratification by national Parliaments began only in June 1993, and was never complete because the Ukrainian Parliament never got around to take a vote on the Interstate Bank. However, most other countries (including Russia, Belarus, and Kazakhstan) did ratify the Interstate Bank 'Charter' in the end.

The main reason for this delay was that the fate of the Interstate Bank was linked to that of the rouble zone. Although the clearing mechanism of the Interstate Bank had been designed carefully, so that it could work as well with separate national currencies as under a rouble zone, some people argued that as long as the reconstitution of a (possibly smaller) rouble zone remained on the agenda, the Interstate Bank should not be set up. This argument was no longer tenable after Russia had introduced its own separate banknotes in August 1993, and after the rouble zone was effectively re-moved from the political agenda, because the offer to create a 'new type rouble zone' had been rejected by all countries (except Belarus and Tadzhik-istan). The Interstate Bank could then be envisaged to solve part of the problems created by the disappearance of the rouble zone coupled with the limited convertibility of the new currencies and the lack of an efficient payments system. The first decisions implementing the Interstate Bank agreement were adopted at a meeting of the central banks of the member states in Moscow on 8 December 1993. The timetable of the official negotiations and other events related to the Interstate Bank is briefly set out in Annexe 2.

However, in 1994, no additional steps were taken to set up the Interstate Bank. Moreover, in the meantime, considerable progress towards convert-ibility and the creation of an acceptable payments system has been achieved in Russia (and some other small CIS countries). Hence the rationale for setting up the Interstate Bank is disappearing fast, and if this development continues, it makes no longer sense to set up the Interstate Bank.

The narrative has so far concentrated on the institutional aspect. What was the Interstate Bank to do? Its main purpose was to run a multilateral payments mechanism on the basis of the Russian rouble among the member states' central banks that would have sent a statement to the Interstate Bank each day containing the amount of imports from the other states of the system they wanted to pay for. The Interstate Bank would provide a multilateral clearing and inform member states of their cumulative debtor or creditor position. The system was to run on an initial credit line from the CBR (fixed at 300 billion roubles), but there would be no additional credit. Central banks that run up against their debt limit were expected to limit the amounts of imports they wanted to pay through the system to the exports declared by the other partner countries (or face expulsion). It was explicitly foreseen that the Interstate Bank would operate in parallel to the commercial banking system and would never be made obligatory. (See Annexe 3 for details.)

Reasons for the demise of the Interstate Bank

Why was the Interstate Bank never created? One reason became apparent in the work of the EES–AGIR group when the concept was discussed in late 1992. Most CIS states were only interested in obtaining further cheap credit and/or cheap oil from Russia. The leaders of the peripheral CIS states were not really interested in creating an efficient multilateral payments system.

To the extent that the advantages from an efficient payments system were dimply perceived, there was a typical free-rider problem in the sense that no individual CIS country had a large incentive to invest political capital in pushing for the Interstate Bank since the institution would work only if everybody participated and the benefits would accrue to all member countries.

Finally there was, and still is, a deep-seated tendency in many CIS countries to wait for Russia to take the initiative. However, Russia never took the necessary steps to set up the Interstate Bank because the political motive was also not very strong since Russian leaders felt, correctly, that Russia did not need such an institution since it run a surplus with all CIS countries. Finally, there was considerable opposition from some of the radical reformers[3] in the Russian government against any official payments mechanism. The basic reason for this opposition was that the Interstate Bank would lead to more pressures on Russia to extend cheap credit. This was basically a political judgement since the charter of the Interstate Bank excluded explicitly any further credit. The overall argument was that convertibility is the first best and attainable immediate solution. Therefore, there was no need to discuss anything else.

An additional reason why the Interstate Bank was not created is that it has proved extremely difficult to create any type of public institution in Russia. Given that the gain for Russia would have been small (as shown below), a weak opposition was sufficient to stop all the practical steps that would have been needed to set up the Interstate Bank.

Was the Interstate Bank a good idea?

The main rationale for the payments mechanism embodied in the Interstate Bank was quite simple: to allow enterprises and banks throughout the CIS to make payments using procedures that they already knew, so that there would be no disruption through the introduction of new currencies or other macroeconomic developments. In reality the opposite happened. At first (in late 1992 and early 1993), payments continued to be channelled via the accounts of central banks with the result that each country (except Russia) introduced various convertibility restraints on imports from other CIS countries in order to obtain a *bilateral* balance with each partner. The Interstate Bank would have eliminated the problems of partial convertibility, it would have made it easier for firms to live in this environment, and it would have provided a multilateral clearing mechanism.

The absence of a multilateral clearing mechanism thus led to additional restrictions on trade and payments, which meant in turn that many trade ties were broken. A lot of anecdotal evidence suggests that large enterprises (mainly in Russia), with dollar accounts abroad, were able to continue to do business within the CIS because they could transact in hard currency. However, most enterprises in other CIS countries, and smaller enterprises in general, were not able to follow this route. They thus faced very considerable transaction costs. In 1992 and early 1993, business papers in a number of CIS countries carried advertisements from 'financial' firms offering to make payments within the CIS (mostly to Russia). The fees were reportedly in the range of 20 to 30 per cent of the value of the transaction.

Over time, the importance of the central bank correspondence accounts declined, and one gets the impression that despite the progress achieved even by mid-1994, commercial banks were allowed to deal directly with each other. Slowly new payments channels were thus established through the nascent commercial banking system. However, this took time and implied very large transaction costs in some cases,[4] if one believes the many stories one hears from bankers in Russia. One simple additional technical reason why the Interstate Bank would have been useful is that it would have processed a large volume of payments, and this large transactions volume would have yielded economies of scale not available to the small corresponding account networks that have sprung up so far.

What were the economic costs that resulted from the absence of a clearing and payments mechanism in 1992 and 1993? It is always difficult to describe what would have happened if the Interstate Bank had been created speedily. However, two considerations suggest that the cost of the disorderly disintegration of the rouble zone was substantial.

The first consideration springs from an analysis of the causes of the output decline. There is still great controversy about this topic, but a simple analysis of the output decline across a number of Russian industries suggests that the decline in intra-FSU trade had a significant impact on the output decline. Duchĕne and Gros (1994) regress the output decline of almost 100 products/sectors of the Russian economy against a number of sectoral indicators, such as the share of oil input, the share of output going to the military, the increase in profitability resulting from a switch to world market prices, to name just the most important ones. Most of these indicators are not significantly correlated with the decline in output in 1990–1992. However, there is one indicator that shows a robust and significant relationship. This is the share of gross output going to other republics. The estimated coefficient is about 0.35 to 0.39. Since in 1990, 18 per cent of average output went to the rest of the FSU, it implies that a reduction in intra-FSU trade by 50 per cent could explain a fall in output in Russia of about 3 per cent. The actual decline in intra-FSU trade was probably much larger, but this is impossible to document. While this is only a fraction of the overall drop in output in Russia, it is still a substantial cost that might have been avoided or mitigated. For the other FSU countries, the cost must have been much higher since their economies depended much more on intra-FSU trade.

The main advantage of the Interstate Bank would have been that it would have allowed CIS countries to overcome the bilateralism, so prevalent in 1992–1993. Gros (1993) attempts to quantify the gains from multilateralism in the FSU by using data on trade flows among the republics in the FSU. This approach simply asks by how much trade would have to contract if all former republics tried to achieve bilateral balance. The main results is that the forced reduction in trade would be equivalent to about 4.5 to 6 per cent of the income of the peripheral (i.e. non-Russian) CIS countries. For Russia, the impact would be equivalent to only 1.5 per cent of income. This might

250

not appear to be large. However, if one performs the same exercise for the EC countries at the time Europe returned to convertibility, i.e. in 1958, the gain would be ten times lower in terms of GDP. Multilateral trade was thus much more important to the FSU countries than it was for the EC countries in 1958. Since the latter constituted the bulk of the European Payments Union (EPU), this implies that the Interstate Bank might have been much more important for the CIS than the EPU was for Europe in the 1950s.[5]

Finally, I would like to add that I do not agree at all with the general tendency to argue that all inter-republican trade was anyway dictated only by central planners, and should hence disappear as quickly as possible. Gros and Dautrebande (1992) show that this preconception is not warranted at all.

Conclusions

This note argued that an efficient multilateral payments system (like the one that was to be run by the Interstate Bank) could have slowed down the collapse of intra-CIS trade, with significant positive effects even for Russia, which depends less on intra-FSU trade than the other CIS countries. At any rate, the creation of the Interstate Bank could never have resulted in any harm since it would not have halted, or even slowed down, the development towards convertibility. Hence the opposition from the radical reformers in the Russian government (and some Western advisors) was mistaken. As long as the first best solution, generalized immediate convertibility, was not in the cards, a second best in the form of the Interstate Bank would have been appropriate. Moreover, the argument that the creation of the Insterstate Bank would have led to more cheap credit from Russia is also not tenable in the face of the clear rules on settlement in the Interstate Bank agreement, which included strict limits on the available amount of credit. These rules would have forced member states to bring their overall trade with the other members into balance (or face expulsion from the system), for example, by adjusting their exchange rate and/or pursuing tighter monetary and fiscal policies. This mechanism would have been preferable to the *ad hoc* technical credits given by the CBR.

The Interstate Bank, however, was never created. The main reason was that the peripheral CIS states did not really understand the importance of multilateral trade and always waited for Russia to move first. No individual CIS country was ready to use its political capital to push for the Interstate

Daniel Gros

Bank since it would have received only a small share of the economic gains.[6]
Russia never took the necessary steps to set up the Interstate Bank because
its leaders felt that it did not need such an institution since it run a surplus
with all CIS countries.

Annexe 1: The main issues during the negotiations

The following five points were the main issues that emerged during the
negotiations on the Interstate Bank 'Charter' that were conducted at the
expert level between October and December 1992 by representatives from
all CIS states (in the presence of experts from the EU [EES–AGIR]
and the IMF):

1   *the subscription quotas* to the capital of the Interstate Bank ('Agree-
    ment' Art. 4). Should the quotas be of equal size, or linked to each
    member's foreign trade turnover? This issue turned out to be not very
    important since the bank would only clear payments. It should never
    have any net position. The capital would only be used to pay for
    buildings etc. The initial capital was eventually fixed at 5 billion
    roubles ('Agreement' Art. 4).

2   *the credit element* ('Agreement' Art. 6). Credit might be extended to
    cover deficits up to a certain (cumulative) ceiling. Discussion centred
    on how the credit ceiling for each country should be set, either as a
    function of trade turnover or of actual receipts, either over one month
    or two months. Since Russia would provide most (probably all) of the
    credit, the discussion on this point was somewhat academic: if Russia
    does not want to provide credit, nobody can force it; if Russia wants to
    provide ample credit, the others will not decline the offer. The final
    wording is not clear, but there is an upper limit equal to one month of
    exports.

3   *the currency* in which settlements should take place ('Agreement' Art.
    1). Western experts advised to create a new accounting unit, most states
    (except Russia, Ukraine, and Belarus) wanted to use the 'rouble'. In
    the end, the 'rouble issued by the central bank of the Russian Federa-
    tion' was chosen.

4   *the decision-making procedure* ('Charter' Art. 7). Russia argued, for
    obvious reasons, for weighted voting (Western experts supported this);

the Central Asian representatives insisted on 'one state–one vote'. The final solution reflects the first position.

5   *membership* ('Agreement' Art. 1 and 9). The October 1992 Bishkek agreement provided for the possibility of establishing a payments union with non-rouble zone countries (Bishkek agreement, Art. 13). This happened within the context of the Insterstate Bank as non-rouble zone countries became founding members. Moreover, other non-CIS countries could participate in the multilateral clearing as non-members simply by opening an account with the Interstate Bank.

Annexe 2: Timetable of negotiations and other official acts

In 1992

Oct 9 — Bishkek agreement of CIS heads of state 'on a single monetary system and a concerted monetary, credit, and exchange rate policy of the states which have retained the rouble as legal tender' concluded at Bishkek (Kirghizia); 'Decision' of CIS heads of state taken at Bishkek to set up a working group on the Interstate Bank.

Oct-Nov — Russia, with the help of EC experts, prepares draft 'Agreement' establishing the Interstate Bank.

Nov-Dec — Russia, with help from IMF, prepares draft 'Charter' for the Interstate Bank; three meetings of CIS working group of experts with participation of IMF and EC experts result in final draft 'Agreement' and 'Charter' for the Interstate Bank (November 3–5, November 16–18, and December 7–9).

In 1993

Jan 22 — Approval by heads of state of draft agreement initialled at expert level with two changes: (1) unit of account is the 'rouble issued by the Central Bank of Russia', (2) votes on the Council are distributed as follows: Russia 50 per cent, other members' weights to be fixed on the basis of intra-FSU trade in 1990.

March — Joint IMF/EC working group begins preparations and consultations on technical aspects of clearing and settlement system.

Apr 21	Seven Contracting Parties decide to set up the 'Organizing Committee' at the level of central banks chaired by Mr Savanin of the Bank of Russia.
May 14	CIS heads of state recommend that the Interstate Bank 'Agreement' and 'Charter' be ratified in member states and preparations be made by July 10 for the Interstate Bank to begin operations on October 1.
June 30	Ratification in Russia; Belarus and Kazakhstan had already ratified; a number of other countries follow.
Aug 20	First meeting of the Interstate Bank Board in Moscow to take decisions implementing the Interstate Bank 'Charter'; no decisions taken because no qualified majority present.
Nov 15	CIS Consultative Co-ordinating Committee reiterates strong support for Interstate Bank and calls for organizational meeting of Interstate Bank Board by December 10.
Dec 8	First full organizational meeting of Interstate Bank Board in Moscow concentrates on personnel matters: Mr Gerashchenko elected chairman of the Interstate Bank Board and Mr Savanin appointed president of the Interstate Bank.

Annexe 3: The payments mechanism of the Interstate Bank

The basic principle of the multilateral payments mechanism of the Interstate Bank was that a participating country, say country A, no longer settles international payments with other participants individually but deals only directly with the Interstate Bank. The central bank of country A would send all its payments orders for imports from the other participating countries to the Interstate Bank after having converted all payments into the unit of account used by the Interstate Bank. The multilateral clearing system foreseen in the Minsk agreement would use the (Russian) rouble as the unit of account.

The role of the Interstate Bank then would have been to carry out a *clearing* of all the transactions between country A and all the other participating countries. The result of this celaring would have been recorded as one entry in the 'correspondent account' of country A each time a clearing is carried out. Each participating country was to have one such 'correspondent account' in the Interstate Bank. The clearing was to be done each day. The Interstate Bank would then, on the basis of a summary document sent

254

by the participating central banks, *each day calculate the net deficit or surplus of each country vis-r-vis the system.*

On the basis of these daily balances (flows) a *cumulative position* (a stock) can be calculated for all participating countries in the following way: at the end of the first day, the cumulative position is equal to the deficit or surplus of that day (plus the opening balance). For all following days the cumulative position at the end of the day is equal to the previous day's cumulative position plus (or minus) the daily surplus (or deficit) plus (or minus) the interest on the previous day's cumulative position.

An important aspect of the system was to be a *limit on the cumulative deficit*, or debtor position, any country could build up. The limit for the cumulative (debtor) position was to be equal to one month of export receipts (i.e. the imports from the country concerned that are declared to the Interstate Bank by the other member countries over a one-month period).

This limit became significant every 15 days, when all the payments, accumulated and cleared over the past 15 days, are settled. This 15-day period was called the 'settlement period'. If on the settlement day at the end of the settlement period, the correspondent account was in *deficit,* the country concerned could pay the amount of the deficit to the Interstate Bank or obtain so-called settlement credit up to this limit. If the deficit exceeds this limit, the excess sum *must be settled.* This means that the deficit country has to pay the excess in convertible currencies or gold by purchasing roubles for them, or borrow roubles from other countries (but not from the Interstate Bank!), etc. For *surplus* countries, the surplus will first be used to redeem settlement loans which were obtained on previous settlement days. When all such loans are repaid, the remaining surplus should be deposited in the account of the creditor country A, and could be withdrawn for other purposes.

The ultimate private sector users of the system, banks, and enterprises would not be concerned at all with this mechanism. Importers would just pay their national central bank in national currency for the export contract they wanted to pay. It was to be the task of each national central bank to set the exchange rate so that imports should approximately cover exports (plus other hard currency sources).

Notes

1. Except Tadzhikistan, which is in the midst of a civil war and continues to use the Russian rouble.
2. Even Estonian enterprises, which operated in a favourable macroeconomic framework, had initially great difficulties in organizing their payments with Russia after the introduction of the kroon.
3. ...and one of their Western advisors. Most of the middle-level opponents of the Interstate Bank remained when the 'flagship' reformers abandoned all government duties in early 1994. This does not mean that intra-CIS trade should recover to its pre-reform level. Gros and Dautrebande (1992) show that there should be a radical reorientation of trade towards the EU and the West in general.
4. The commercial banking system is not efficient enough to fully enable trade among CIS countries to recover to a 'normal' market-driven level.
5. Given the radical reorientation of trade one can expect for all CIS countries, these estimates are certainly on the high side if one takes a medium perspective. However, the purpose of the Interstate Bank was to smooth the transition, hence the short-run perspective adopted here is appropriate.
6. Politically, the Interstate Bank was not popular in a number of countries since it implied closer ties with Russia.

References

Duchène, Gerard and Gros, Daniel, 'A Comparative Study of Output Decline in Transition Economies'. Manuscript, Center for European Policy Studies (CEPS), Brussels, June, 1994.

Gros, Daniel, 'Bilateralism versus Multilateralism in the FSU – What is the Potential Gain from the Interstate Bank?'. Manuscript, Center for European Policy Studies (CEPS), Brussels, May, 1993.

Gros, Daniel and Dautrebande, Berenice, 'International Trade of Former Republics in the Long Run: An Analysis Based on the "Gravity" Approach', CEPS Working Document, No. 71, Center for European Policy Studies (CEPS), Brussels, May, 1992.

Gros, Daniel and Steinherr Alfred, *Winds of Change: Economic Transition in Central and Eastern Europe*. London, Longman, 1995.

34 A Tale of Bridging Two Europes

Jozef M. van Brabant[*]

I should like to rephrase the question that the session's heading puts to the panellists, namely 'Do we need a new G-7, G-10, or G-24 initiative?' by a different, though intimately related one: 'Do we need a new European Union (EU)[1] initiative?' Of course, I shall answer that question in the positive as opposed to a negative one to the former. By this, I do not simply want to convey the message that there is an acute need to redirect the focus of the international community's attention when it comes to devising ways and means of assisting the *post-communist economies in transition* (PETs).[2] Neither do I want to suggest that the assistance rendered over the past several years has been a waste, or that no further such assistance should be provided. I do want to intimate, though, that there remains considerable room for two things. One is to streamline the assistance that has been rendered into a more coherent, better targeted approach to easing the socio-political burden of progressing with transformation in the PETs. The other is that I personally do not see either the political will or the resource availability within any of the cited G formations to innovate soon a realistic assistance strategy substantially better suited to the tasks at hand in the PETs.

To explain my position cogently, I must first justify my decision to set aside the formal title of the session and second, inquire into the existing assistance strategy of the EU, such as it is. In a third section, I succinctly indicate why, particularly after the Essen Council Session,[3] it is now the proper time to formulate a new EU strategy which would actively facilitate

---

[*] *Principal Economic Affairs Officer of the Department of Economic and Social Information and Policy Analysis of the United Nations Secretariat in New York. The opinions expressed here do not necessarily reflect my employer's.*

moving towards full accession of some PETs, much closer co-operation with another set of these countries, and otherwise purposely attune its outlook on economic co-operation with the remainder of these countries.[4] Elements of such a strategy are set forth in the fourth section. The conclusion is preceded by a few remarks on the likelihood that such a strategy will be elaborated within the context of forging ahead with core elements of an integrating Europe. In the context of the ongoing debate on remaking Europe and the crucial forthcoming intergovernmental conference (IGC), sometime in 1996, this means deepening as a priority without ignoring widening the integration movement in Europe *tout court*. This requires solidifying the EU's *acquis* while rendering as much assistance as can reasonably be marshalled in favour of the various groups of PETs, among serving the Union's other clientelistic relationships.

Section 1: From G-n to EU as focus of the reform debate

For some time now, I have maintained that there is no coherent Western strategy on how best to assist the PETs (among others, Brabant 1991a, b; 1992b; 1993a, c; 1995a, b). Certainly, elements of such a strategy, now in place, have been emerging largely under the impact of hard-won experiences with the facile approach to transition: liberalize, privatize, and stabilize, while transferring some rudimentary market institutions and knitting some social safety net to contain the fall-out of transformation policies (Brabant 1992a; 1993b). The causal connection between these recommendations and meeting the necessary and sufficient conditions for a take-off along a sustainable growth path by PETs is not always explicitly drawn, but it is an article of the paradigm's faith. Within this scenario, the strategy of assistance, if such it was, since 1989 has consisted essentially of sustaining efforts to help the PETs come to grips with stock and flow stabilization, with internal and external liberalization, and with forging ahead speedily with the divestment of state assets. This way of proceeding often ignores the real resource base of the PETs and is far too optimistic about accomplishing the catch-up, hence buttress the growth momentum, on the basis of market forces that these countries might in principle capitalize on for some time to come, preferably with substantial inflows of private resources from developed countries, provided other governance capabilities are available and mobilized constructively (Brabant 1993a; 1994a, b; 1995a).

The critical economic moment of the transition should have been proper policies motivated by the need to identify a new, sustainable growth path in the PETs. It was earlier assumed that this could be found almost spontaneously as a result of the market-motivated behaviour of individuals acting in their own best interest, provided the 'environment' was dramatically altered. Though the latter has occurred in crowbar fashion, the former has not (yet?) materialized. It is not likely to do so any time soon, in part because markets in PETs are either lacking or remain quite primitive; even if it could be accomplished, re-establishing order spontaneously will take too long and will be too costly. In any case, markets in PETs are unlikely to materialize with the nearly pure traits of the neoclassical, let alone the neoliberal, paradigm of economic behaviour. This is particularly the case for adjustments on the supply side, which are rather sluggish in economies with poorly integrated markets (Brabant 1993a, b). Yet, it is imperative that a new, sustainable growth path for the PETs be identified soonest. It is only by delivering at long last on the, at times wildly, exaggerated promises elicited by the 1989 events, notably in terms of employment security, income growth, and improved levels of living, that the tenuous democratic legitimacy gained by the new regimes can be solidified.

Though some observers have recently been gloating over the incipient recovery in some PETs, and, indeed, I too applaud any real upturn, this positive event can hardly be ascribed to the fundamental principles postulated when the above-cited scenario for transition with Western assistance was first adopted. I am not at all persuaded that the countries exhibiting positive growth in 1994, some for the second or third year in a row, albeit at a marginal pace, are now really located on a self-sustainable growth path basically because much of the recent output gain has been consumer-driven, rather than derived from investment in new productive capacities and the successful penetration of new markets at home and abroad, in some cases on questionable comparative-advantage computations. The situation elsewhere is even more tenuous, and that of most of the successor states of the Soviet Union hardly deserves any such comment by way of justification.

The conflict between static efficiency and regaining sustainable growth for PETs is a fundamental one. It is best addressed judiciously rather than on ideological grounds. In particular, a programme for adjusting to external or domestic pressures and for monitoring performance must necessarily differ from traditional stabilization formats. There are at least three fundamental reasons for this. One refers to the pervasive legacies of central planning, the sort of specific policy and systemic antecedents of these

259

economies under planning that are readily ignored. Instead, they and their specific repercussions on the behaviour of economic agents, as changes are introduced,[5] must be clearly understood and factored into the policy deliberations and the package of measures agreed upon. Another recognizes that, in part because of these legacies, macroeconomic management must include active intervention on the supply side to sensitize economic agents into undertaking the structural changes necessary to solidify rudimentary markets without getting stuck there. Finally, real hysteresis effects are likely to prevail, thus leading to path dependency, meaning that the choice of policy sequencing is by no means indifferent (Pickel 1992).

For the near term, then, adjustment in PETs will require a much more varied and flexible policy regimen, a longer time horizon, more trial and error, and more policy flexibility than customary in market economies. This cannot be managed without a much more encompassing institutional setting than envisioned in orthodox policies, such as those propounded by the International Monetary Fund (IMF or Fund for short). I have expanded on those issues elsewhere including in the 1993 Szirák Conference (Brabant 1995b). In short, it should entail more than the market, more than demand fine-tuning, more than interventionist supply measures, a broader strategy than simply cutting out budget deficits and restoring external balance, and a much longer time horizon than the conventional medium term of Fund orthodoxy. This finding can be extended *mutatis mutandis* to the World Bank and the EU as well, but I come back to the latter shortly.

Before doing so, however, I should like to note that external resources, while in principle highly useful to mitigate the burdens of the transition, including to maintain popular support for reform, cannot be the sole, let alone the principal, factor that will lead to a resumption of growth along a sustainable path yet to be located. The critical factor in regaining growth in the PETs is, and will be, changes in domestic output, consumption, exports, and investment. Since the international community in whatever G formation keeps insisting on the nearly absolute primacy of demand management, yet is not inclined to funnel into the PETs substantial amounts of fresh money, I see little purpose in advocating a new, more constructive strategy perhaps on the order of a recovery programme, for the eastern part of Europe (UNECE 1991, 1992, 1993). Short of abandoning hope and placing one's faith simply on betting that the phoenix will eventually arise from the ashes, the only alternative for a constructive strategy for the near to medium term that I can discern at this stage is to cajole the EU into more fruitful action, largely for its own benefit if basic markers of its post-war integration achievements are to be preserved and strengthened.

Section 2: Is there an EU Eastern strategy?

Before looking into the desirability of casting a new assistance programme under the EU's aegis, it is useful to briefly review the EU's efforts in that respect since 1989 and to inquiry into whether it constitutes a coherent, long-term, strategic, and forward-looking programme of action. My answer is negative, largely for the same reasons as those underlying my apprehension about the mainstream approach advocated by the Washington financial institutions. Assistance has fallen short at three levels: (1) the mobilization of adequate assistance resources from bilateral, regional, and multilateral donors; (2) the precise targeting of that assistance given the real needs of the PETs seen within their entire societal context; and (3) more effective and more co-ordinated resource delivery given resource commitments and recipient needs.

Surely, Western Europe responded quickly to the needs of the PETs. It did so magnanimously largely in the hope of engineering a decisive turn away from communism and administrative planning, and indeed from the dependence on the Soviet Union for the smaller East European countries. But the assistance has been improvisational. Such a stance could perhaps not have been avoided at the transition's inception considering the extraordinary turn of events since 1989. I would even concede that the first reaction in terms of associating the PETs closer with the EU's predecessor was appropriate, given the limited information on which Brussels was then acting. Less inspiring was the decision to entrust the co-ordination of the efforts by the G-24 to the European Commission at a time when this organ was already overloaded with its own agenda including completing the single market, moving towards a unified currency (the ECU), continuing to absorb the adjustments entailed by the second and third expansions in membership, and looking beyond all that to tighter social and political union. Also, the Commission then sought to strengthen its hands as an autonomous mover in foreign policy including through its own assistance programmes for PETs. Moreover, at the inception of the unprecedented assistance effort, the Commission had even less of a comparative advantage in dealing with the *problématique* of the transition, let alone in co-ordinating the assistance efforts of its own members and outsiders than the minimal asset the Fund possessed. Small wonder, then, that its response has been neither 'innovative' nor 'daring' (Kramer 1993, p. 234).

Although it quickly became clear that nearly all of the premises on which assistance efforts had been predicated were far off the mark, the European Commission, as well as other assisting organs, hesitated for a long time about what could and should be done for the PETs other than the haphazard assistance programmes (except for humanitarian and emergency purposes) hastily cobbled together in 1989-1990, particularly after the August 1991 coup in the Soviet Union (Reinicke 1992, p. 94). A half-way solution was found in extending to the more developed PETs an associate status based on the Europe Agreement. Later on, other PETs were offered yet another status through the so-called Partnership Agreement (since then extended only to the successor states of the Soviet Union other than the Baltic States). But little thought was given in EU deliberations to whether and when the PETs could eventually somehow be brought under the EU's umbrella. Force of circumstance has brought on severe headaches on that score. Among the crucial factors are: the persistence of policy makers of the PETs in arguing their claim for 'Europe status'; the unexpectedly severe turn of transformation policies throughout the area; the collapse of the East's economic linkages including in now defunct federations; the disintegration of the Soviet Union; and the horror of the calamitous war in the former Yugoslavia.

The above-cited multiangular response has been partly shaping the formal architecture of relations between the EU and the PETs. It now consists of bilateral Europe Agreements (presently with Bulgaria, Czech Republic, Hungary, Poland, Romania, and Slovakia, some of which are fully in effect, others only for trade facilitations), bilateral Partnership Agreements (with Kazakhstan, Kyrgyzstan, Moldova, Russia, Ukraine, and perhaps other successor states of the Soviet Union that I am unaware of), negotiations on Europe Agreement with Slovenia and perhaps some of the Baltic States, bilateral free-trade agreements with the Baltic States (to come into effect in 1995), and second-generation trade and/or co-operation agreements with many other PETs. Unfortunately, most of these agreements have not been particularly innovative and have proved to be insufficient to come to grips with four needs: (1) to provide economic, political, and strategic security to the PETs; (2) to respond in a strategic way to formal accession requests (by Hungary and Poland in April 1994) and the intention of others (notably Czech Republic, Estonia, Slovakia, and Slovenia) to seek early accession; (3) to beef up relations with the western successor states of the former

Soviet Union; and (4) to hold a constructive dialogue on strategic co-operation in economic and other affairs with many other PETs.

Another part has been the delivery of various types of emergency, technical, financial, cultural, and commercial assistance rather in a haphazard fashion with most of the resources mobilized being captured either by the delivering institutions' formidable bureaucracies or their associated rent-seeking advisers and consultants (from East and West alike, but much more the latter than the former) but with little delivery on the ground, as it were. The record over the past five-six years, then, has not been an encouraging one. It certainly has not pleased those who had hoped for a decisive breakthrough in the remodelling of Europe, however its eastern and southern borders could be defined.

Whatever one might justify for the past, it is wholly inexcusable that fairly little in the EU's posture with respect to the eastern part of Europe appears to have changed since the late 1980s, perhaps because the organization has been in the grips of a formidable existential battle for its own *raison d'être* and future. Even so, more could have been done, and will prospectively have to be accomplished. For one thing, it is by now abundantly clear that transforming this part of the world is a much more arduous, complex, time-consuming, costly, and unpredictable process than had at first been assumed. It should also be evident that the EU cannot avoid, for strategic reasons, to keep the eastern part of Europe at bay; that it cannot bring selected parts of that world within its ambit without major adjustments in its governance structures and the financing of crucial EU operations; and that some PETs are unlikely ever to fit within the EU, yet the latter cannot afford to ignore their needs for economic, political, and strategic security as affected by the East's events since 1989.

I too have been disappointed with the EU's posture vis-à-vis the East. Yet, it would be fundamentally wrong in dealing with various matters concerning the architecture of Europe, and indeed the world, in the post-cold war period, to disregard the special responsibility of Europe and its institutions, indeed the unique obligation incumbent upon them. This applies in particular to the eastern part of Europe in plain upheaval, provided the political will to do so prevails, once the PETs will have reached a firm democratic base for decision-making and will have transformed their economies in such a way that they will be steered primarily on the basis of market incentives. It is, however, the multiple and vexing questions of how to get from here to that stage that command our special attention.

In my view, a coherent strategy is yet to be innovated, now well into the fifth year of the transition and assistance efforts. No ready solution is in sight for now. Yet, there can be no doubt that something better will have to be worked out in order to really assist the PETs and make the reciprocal adjustments of East and West towards a unified Europe digestible at a tolerable cost, with some reasonably distributed benefits for all. Membership of many PETs (perhaps up to 18 out of 27) will eventually be inevitable. It is the path of how to get to that status that is paramount in appreciating and revising Community policies with respect to PETs.

Section 3: Why is there an urgent need for an EU Eastern strategy?

I have already indicated some of the critical issues that lie ahead in building up greater confidence between the two parts of Europe. These efforts should be placed as fully as possible within the context of the ongoing EU integration *problématique*. The core issues on the agenda include four. First of all, a solution to the problems pertaining to Economic and Monetary Union (EMU) and the further realization of the other pillars of the Maastricht Treaty will need to be found soonest, particularly with enlargement to Fifteen and beyond.

Second, the EU's governance structures, policies, and instruments need to be streamlined. This task involves rectifying the democratic deficit; injecting accountability and openness into the EU's affairs; and being more to the point on subsidiarity, federalism, and solidarity, perhaps by writing a coherent EU constitution.

Third, assisting the PETs needs to be strategically rethought. The EU must play a much more aggressive, intrusive, and hands-on role in the gestation of the international assistance effort in line with the agreed-upon needs of those managing the transition; by mobilizing resources in the most effective manner while minimizing adverse impacts on donors and other claimants on such aid; and in ensuring the most effective delivery of assistance in line with the needs of the PETs, notably making it possible for these countries to capitalize on their prevailing comparative advantages in a constructive manner, i.e. being more forward looking in tackling the issues around 'sensitive products' (iron and steel, textiles and clothing, agriculture, automobiles, chemicals, etc.).

Finally, the EU must assist the PETs that will soon be claimants to membership in such a way that their entry into the EU will be eased rather than made more cumbersome by the EU's further integration and the adversities of the transition.

Regardless of the institutional and conceptual assistance frameworks envisaged, successful transformation hinges critically on the ability of the PETs to penetrate world markets on a competitive basis. That depends in part on the economic restructuring under way in the East, including the policies, instruments, and institutional supports being embraced. But it is also a function of the buoyancy of world markets, and their openness to fair competition. Much remains to be done in this respect. Some efforts have been made, notably in Western Europe, to relax trade restrictions on a discriminatory basis. It would be even more important to seize the opportunity provided by the historic turn-around in the East to restore and reinforce basic elements of a multilateral trading world including by implementing soonest the Uruguay Round achievements and building further thereupon.

One of the major bones of contention between aspiring members and the EU has been the stipulation of the conditions to be met for submitting a credible membership application. One could detail the conditions regarding political democracy and a market-based economy into eight criteria (Brabant 1995a, pp. 452-68): political pluralism, democratic maturity and stability, good neighbourly relations or peaceful coexistence, introduction and effective application of the rule of law, ability to comply with EU's rights and obligations (the so-called *acquis communautaire et politique*), acceptance of the overall ambitions of European integration, having a European identity, and market-based resource allocation. Many of these concepts are rather fuzzy in the sense that they involve a lot of subjective assessments by leading EU policy makers. Take, for example, good neighbourly relations. For better or worse, the EU has insisted that the potential applicant from the East explore the room available for regional co-operation, essentially building upon the comparative advantages inherited from the post-war period, wherever they are economically warranted by the success criteria that prevail at this juncture. This challenge has led to various regional initiatives including the so-called Visegrád process and a commitment to create a free trade area during the 1990s among the four members (Czech Republic, Hungary, Poland, and Slovakia). Some policy makers in the area reject any 'counselled' form of regional co-operation other than what would spontaneously arise from market forces, for fear that temporary arrangements will inevitably become permanent, thus driving their economies back onto the periphery of European modernization.

I am emphasizing these entry conditions because I do not believe it to be very helpful when PET policy makers claim that 'their country will be ready' to join the EU in a year or two, in some cases, as in the Czech Republic, on the spurious claim that the transition has been fully completed. Even if the Union were to endorse such an acceleration, those who air a view like this seriously underestimate the requirements and domestic implications of abiding by the rules and regulations of the EU club. The PETs' fragile economies are unlikely to be able to withstand free competition from the EU for some time to come. Though all PETs have made commitments to abide by the overt preconditions for EU membership, in some cases this has been no more than a pious pledge. In others, policy makers have been more earnest, but have found the path towards political pluralism and market-based decision-making in their multiple dimensions strewn with many treacherous obstacles that can be overcome only over time, provided the socio-political consensus on the transition can be maintained.

For now there is not a single PET that can truly claim to be a workable democracy possessing a functioning market-based economic system. But some (such as Czech Republic, Hungary, Poland, and Slovenia) would seem to be closer to fulfilling the cited political and economic preconditions for EU membership, hence more credible candidates for serious negotiations than others, once the 1996 IGC will have put in place important EU constitutional reforms. Indeed some, such as Russia and the Caucasian and Central Asian successor states of the Soviet Union, are unlikely ever to become EU members; but the latter should not be ignored altogether. Even for the most ardent advocates of quick accession, it is not always clear whether the PETs are firmly committed to the overall ambitions of European integration. At least some of the more likely applicants for membership (Klaus 1993–94) are contesting the very foundations of the EU, seemingly confounding them with ambitions of a pure free trade arrangement.

The latter stance is adopted in spite of the fact that one key aspiration of most PETs from the transformation's inception has been to (re)establish solid cultural, economic, political, security, and social interdependence with the West by gaining access to, preferably full membership of, the EU 'as soon as circumstances permit'; this nondescript formula was officially acknowledged by the leadership of the Twelve at their Copenhagen summit in June 1993. But circumstances in the latter countries, as well as in Albania and the successor states of Yugoslavia other than Slovenia, are less propitious to even pursuing the idea at this juncture, as acknowledged implicitly at the Essen Council in December 1994.

The requirements for viable candidacy of peaceful coexistence, of the rule of law, of political pluralism as a gateway to the establishment of full-fledged democracy, and of moving decisively towards a market-based allocation of resources immediately project useful tasks in their own right to be discharged by the transformation. In the context of potential EU membership, however, they take on a special dimension, if only because they narrow the costs that new membership otherwise might inflict upon the existing community. These are, therefore, counterpart conditions to be met by the EU. The potential cost of assimilating the new entrant within the EU's ambit is by no means a trivial matter as the various agricultural, cohesion, regional, social, and structural funds managed by the EU, whatever their rationale and economic justification, cannot politically be abolished any time soon, and these appropriations can be augmented only to a limited degree. As a result, they can be offered to the PETs – and the PETs could not be second-class Eurocitizens by being excluded from those funds, even if they wanted to, which I doubt to be the case – only to the extent that the latter's claims remain 'manageable'.

I doubt that the EU is ready to undertake the adjustments required to absorb PETs, even in small combinations, into the realm of its four freedoms (of movement of goods, services, people, and capital) any time soon. Yet, the PETs cannot be left in an ill-defined limbo. Concerns about the political stability in, and insecurity engendered by, the countries to the east of these PETs, have recently led to several hesitant initiatives on how best to chart the future of these PETs within a 'Western', possibly a 'European', context. This holds as much for those countries that will eventually be able to lodge a credible claim to membership as for others that cannot reasonably be expected to join the EU, as full members, in any foreseeable future.

The core problem, then, is not whether to usher the PETs into the EU's multilateral regimes. Rather, it is how closely the PETs will have to be to the 'average' or the 'worst' EU member with respect to fulfilling the extended implications of the twin economic and political conditions to be allowed to access the same privileges *and* discharge the same obligations as those now accruing to 'below-average' members. In other words, the paramount issue revolves around the three principal adjustment questions regarding new members:

1   What gross cost, even if attenuated by some gross gain, is Western Europe willing to absorb by opening its markets for goods, services, capital, and labour, together or in some more modest combination, to one or more PETs according to agreed-upon rules and regulations?

2   How quickly can this cost realistically be imposed and blotted up, given the lack of buoyancy in the integration movement and the lacklustre political will in the various EU members to embark on yet another enlargement?

3   How will that cost be distributed within the EU, given the mechanisms of governance in place or those that, on present expectations, can realistically be achieved soon?

As already indicated, these costs cannot be confined to income redistribution. True, that in itself is bound to be a critical factor in considering how best to respond to new membership applications. But other considerations must be invoked. A critical one is that the answer to all three aforementioned questions depends in part on the EU's governance with respect to realizing its longer-term aims. One can be fairly certain that there are boundaries beyond which the level of the material and other costs of adjusting structures and absorbing income redistribution, the speed at which costs ought to be absorbed, and/or the feasible distribution of the cost simply will not, and indeed cannot, be tolerated, if only because of political and economic reasons.

Section 4: Elements of an EU Eastern strategy

Once PETs enter the EU, regardless of their 'maturity', governance looms very large indeed in the sequence of policy matters to be tackled head-on. This concerns fundamentally the organization of Europe, the legislative reach of the European Parliament, the role of the European Commission as a surrogate executive for Europe, the organization of a European judiciary, and related questions. Suffice it to note for now that streamlining the EU's governance structure has been on the agenda for years, that hammering out interim compromises has invariably taken much time, and that whatever solution chosen has to date tended to depend heavily on political calculations motivated by national considerations, but not necessarily in proportion to the economic or numerical weight of the members. The turbulence about carrying the single market into the monetary sphere, and its fiscal and social-welfare ramifications, is far from over. Besides, governance issues do not stem solely from potential PET membership. They derive from fundamental problems with widening the EU as such beyond the present Fifteen, which is already a strained version of governance with the original Six.

One can schematically identify issues of high priority on the forthcoming IGC's agenda, although an official one has yet to be agreed upon, in spite of the measures elaborated at the time of the negotiations about the Maastricht Treaty. On the EU's side, there are at least four to make the enterprise culturally, economically, financially, politically, and socially acceptable:

1   the core agenda for forging ahead with integration, from mostly trading issues (with some fiscal and monetary ingredients) to critical elements of political and social sovereignty;

2   governance with Fifteen and beyond, in all of its dimensions, including the institutional architecture of the 'new Europe';

3   extending the various transfer programmes to new members, including the PETs; and

4   redistribution of 'benefits' from those most advantaged now – Greece, Ireland, Portugal, and Spain – towards economically even less fortunate potential members.

The agenda for the PETs in turn comprises, among other tasks, the nearly complete assimilation of the *acquis communautaire et politique* over a fairly brief transition phase. This includes necessarily yielding on essential elements of national economic, and increasingly political, sovereignty. This may cause problems as most of the PETs have only recently regained their national sovereignty. Yet, effective membership in the Union requires submitting national objectives to essential common goals, institutions, and policy instruments. This in and of itself may cause serious existential problems. Nonetheless, without enabling the PETs to reduce the burden of sharing eventually in the Union's benefits and to compress the cost to a level that the Union may be willing to shoulder, adhesion of the PETs to the EU's integration framework would be postponed indefinitely if adjudicated largely on normal accession criteria.

Alternatively, if membership were to be sought mainly for political reasons, the relationship of the PETs within the EU would inevitably be beset by serious adjustment problems for which at least one party of the agreement does not appear to be ready, not even at the level of basic principles. However protracted any accession negotiations begun at this stage would be, utilizing the experiences of the three previous enlargements with countries less able to afford the EU, or to be afforded by the EU, any realistic agenda for the transition – say a decade – is likely to be too onerous for some time to come. Rudimentary parliamentary democracy, an unstable socio-political environment, and a still poorly functioning market economy in even those PETs most advanced with their societal transformation all stand in the way of making it successfully across such a narrow and rutted bridge.

Although neither the EU nor any PET can afford early membership, neither can ignore the other. The PETs need credibility for their transformation agenda and geopolitical security. On the other hand, the EU has to work towards reform of governance and transfer programmes, and might just as well take the needs of PETs into account at the earliest opportunity, since it is now certain that many PETs will become EU members in staggered formation, if only because the PETs find themselves at markedly different levels of fulfilling the cited political and economic preconditions for EU membership: Central Europe (Slovakia?) and Slovenia; Baltic States, Bulgaria, Croatia (once peace is restored), and Romania; and Albania, Belarus, Moldova, and Ukraine(?). Furthermore, 'better' agreements with Russia and Caucasian and Central Asian successor states and the PETs that cannot be in the vanguard of membership will have to be hammered out over time. The crucial question at this stage, then, is when and how and at what cost, i.e. the three 'ECU-and-centimes' core conditions posed earlier, these tasks can be accomplished.

A dispassionate analysis of the feasible and the desirable should take cognizance of the fact that the PETs cannot quickly be brought into the liberal economic, political, and social frameworks of Western Europe. But this does not mean that nothing should be put in train now. Indeed, it would be desirable for the EU to help prepare full accession by making it easier for the potential applicant to enter eventually without causing too much of an adjustment burden (Maillet 1993). Details of any such accommodation can only be worked out in direct negotiations between the EU and individual PETs. Not only would it be facetious on my part to attempt to predict, let alone prescribe, the terms of reference for such negotiations. It would also be too premature to do so at this stage. However, a broad framework, as well as some concrete details of the most likely policy agenda to be crafted, can be delineated in the following terms.[6]

In order to put some structure into what can reasonably be undertaken, without aiming at exhaustiveness, I group my comments under seven headings.

First, as regards commerce in the sense of facilitating market access for exports from PETs to the EU, it should be beyond doubt that providing trading outlets for products that the PETs can offer on a competitive basis constitutes one critical prop to transformation policies. This is arguably the most effective assistance that the West can render the PETs. At the same time, its true economic cost will be the least – weighing present and future as well as the interests of consumers and producers. Because the export base of the PETs for now is rather shallow, concentrated on products that have been treated as somehow 'sensitive' in recent trade management, the PETs are at a distinct disadvantage. Little change is likely to occur soon in the core export capacity of PETs based largely on comparatively cheap labour and in some raw materials. Gaining market access for the former products in particular may displace EU production in areas that can exert strong and vocal electoral pressure as demonstrated, in a broader context, since the early 1970s.

Nonetheless, strong and dependable trade outlets for products from the PETs must be found one way or the other if these countries are to experience sustainable recovery. It would be useful in formulating the Union's commercial policy with respect to the PETs if account could be taken of the unusual cost situation of many producers in PETs for some time to come. This applies notably to the state-owned enterprises that produce sensitive products. It is fruitless to attach to the Europe Agreement strenuous contingent-protectionist clauses, such as on antidumping action or to threaten the imposition of strict countervailing duties, simply to protect EU procedures. Market access must in this case be combined with all efforts to clean up the state-owned enterprises, be it through divestment, restructuring the production process, or putting in place the vestiges of standard corporate-governance frameworks as well as transparent accounting principles.

Second, official financial transfers, other than for emergency and humanitarian assistance, from the EU to PETs and various means of reinforcing the PETs' economic, political, and social environments to bolster private financial inflows should be aimed primarily at propping up the capacity of the PETs to resume positive growth after transformation. I insist upon this as a separate task if only because most such assistance has been 'granted' in the form of loans at near-market terms that must be serviced. Unless the bulk of these resources will be earmarked for 'crowding-in' projects, the environment for private capital formation and for raising factor productivity is unlikely to improve substantially, certainly not to the degree that this would seem to be needed to stimulate self-sustainable growth soon. To forestall the emergence of another external debt crisis, the EU should take the lead in formulating projects as integral parts of the PETs' transformation strategies that can subsequently be financed through one of the regional and global official financial organizations, and perhaps even by some bilateral donors.

Third, both the PETs and the EU are in for a considerable restructuring effort, regardless of the concrete shape that their relationship may take in the decades to come. In this connection it should be recalled that the EU has had some experience with graduated adjustment, such as in the iron and steel industry, the coal sector, textile and clothing, and agriculture. None has been a neat exercise conducted at minimum cost. Even so, if only because useful lessons have been garnered from these efforts, EU decision makers ought to be aware of the major political, social, and technical obstacles and costs to be reckoned with. It would then stand to reason to search for ways and means by which the PETs as non-members might already at an early stage be included in any such prospective structural-adjustment programme, including sharing in some of the funds (grants as well as other financial provisions) earmarked to support the programmes notably in the case of the troubled iron and steel sectors. Would it not be constructive to explore ways in which the relevant enterprises from key PETs might already now be included in any such adjustment programme in return for obtaining proportionately greater access to EU markets on competitive terms for these sensitive products? This applies in particular to the state-owned enterprises that may currently be more concerned about liquidity than net asset values. This does not mean, however, that the large state-owned enterprises in PETs are 'absolutely unprepared for our methods of management in the context of a market economy' (Robin 1993, p. 566).

A similar argument can be made with respect to a number of other activities, including the construction of integrated energy systems, such as electricity (Schalast, 1993) and fuel pipelines; attempts to bring cross-border and other types of pollution under control; the construction of integrated transportation networks, such as high-speed roads and railroads; communication and computer linkages; and a host of other endeavours that can be readily imagined. Some, notably at the meeting of foreign ministers on 4 October 1994 and the Essen Council in December 1994, were recently singled out for deliberations within the context of the Europe Agreement. But nothing has as yet been envisioned for other PETs, it would seem.

Fourth, many market institutions are not yet present in the PETs. With respect to engaging in external economic relations on a level playing field, several obstacles linger. The absence of efficient clearing institutions, export insurance and guarantee agencies, crediting facilities, and the like in PETs cannot simply be glossed over. This is perhaps less important in contracts with Western partners where such institutions all exist, although they are often being manipulated, with or without government intervention, to the benefit of the Western partner or his/her direct clients. But it forms a considerable obstacle in reviving economic relations among the PETs, and indeed in competing on an equal basis with Western firms in the East. Furthermore, *ex ante* foreign exchange constraints, particularly among the PETs themselves, continue to inhibit the build-up of reciprocal relations. There is no certainty that the conditions for bolstering intragroup trade will improve in the near term.

The EU must take a more active role in bolstering this economic co-op-eration for its own interests if membership extension is to succeed, perhaps through some kind of payment facility (Brabant 1991a). All this should provide a more solid anchor for genuine current transaction convertibility, a much more 'liberal' format than the present 'internal convertibility'. It would be useful to synchronize the EU's involvement with this rounding off of market-based resource allocation in the PETs in such a way that the hurdles to be jumped - the gap between the EU's sophistication and that of the PETs during the phase leading up to credible accession negotiations – not be raised by the progress with integration achieved by the Union in the interim.

Fifth, a critical ingredient of the transition agenda in any PET is gaining credibility so that the adjustment burden to be worked off by the local population will remain acceptable[7] while the PET is restructuring, as rapidly as circumstances permit, in part by promoting economic stability and expanding exports. For the latter, trade and foreign exchange liberali-zation needs to be fostered with great determination. A closer association with at least the spirit, if perhaps for now not the mechanics, of the 'ECU regime' would be highly desirable once macroeconomic stabilization has been achieved and inflation has been compressed to single-digit levels. Being closely associated with mechanisms and policies that are thoroughly within the 'spirit' of key EU features would inevitably impart a constructive psychological fillip. I argue this case in spite of the fact that the events of late 1992 and mid-1993 have proved that managing the European Monetary System is a difficult proposition for a number of reasons, including the absence of political union or concordance on political and socio-economic priorities. This could provide some credible guarantee that the process of moving towards such closer association with the (Western) European integration endeavours will not get deliberately stalled, and that reviving regional co-operation on economic grounds would not be inhibited for flagrant partisan political reasons. Of course, such a choice would make it all the more attractive – and urgent – for the EU to assume a major role in financing directly and indirectly a good part of the reconstruction costs of the PETs, until the latter can attract private capital flows and generate sufficient savings at home for productive investments.

Sixth, without denigrating the claims laid by policy makers of the PETs to their 'Europeanness', there can be no doubt that a good deal of their posturing has been based on rather naive assumptions on how pluralistic democracies come about and function, and indeed on the nature of the market, which is not 'a machine that goes all by itself with its own laws and requirements' but a 'voluntary mechanism for negotiation where people enjoy the freedom to interact; the outcome may be success or failure, but the system works provided the rules governing the interaction are good ones' (Pavan 1993, p. 59). Educating the electorate in the PETs so that broad layers of their populations will gain some perspective on and familiarity with 'European standards' should rank high on the list of priorities for providing technical and other assistance. Aside from measurable financial transfers to facilitate accession, the EU can set other, more qualitative steps to bring the PETs and their respective populations psychologically closer to Europe.[8]

It may be appropriate to note right here an elementary contribution that could easily be arranged: disseminating information about the EU in the relevant local languages of the PETs. Consultation meetings with PET politicians could only benefit matters. This applies in particular to the elaboration of the purposes of the institutional machinery for monitoring and fine-tuning the Europe Agreement as a framework instrument for orchestrating this transfer of values. These are now slated for agriculture, foreign affairs, finance, and transportation between the EU and Europe Agreement partners. That such consultative meetings will inevitably be beset by some acrimony, stemming largely from uninformed claims on entitlement to full membership at the earliest point in time, cannot be avoided. It will set the tone for later debates about integration proper. Likewise, claims on being exempted from the EU's 'petty economic apartheid' (Bressand 1992, p. 15), for example as embodied in textile, steel, agriculture, shipping, trucking, and other quotas, cannot be avoided and should be digested with a sense of humour and *savoir-faire*. Much greater transparency and openness in clarifying the realistic room for proper negotiations in both East and West would go a long way towards dissipating lingering but ill-founded suspicions.

Thus, the *acquis communautaire* calls for modifying the existing legal framework in the PETs to conform to nearly 10,000 EU laws and regulations (Reinicke 1992, p. 96). True, some can, as a rule, be introduced during the transition phase negotiated as a normal part of the accession deliberations. But it should be recalled that in earlier enlargements not the entire body of the *acquis communautaire* required substantive revisions of existing rules and regulations and, indeed, institutions. The task ahead in the PETs is bound to be vastly more formidable, given their post-war experience. Yet, without such a body of rules and appropriate institutions, it would be very difficult for the PETs to credibly commit themselves to abide by the given 'club rules' of the EU.

In the same vein, a logical argument can be made to enhance the political dialogue in the context of the framework provided by the Europe Agreement, hopefully after harmonizing the provisions into a multilateral deliberative body. Imparting a clearer view to the PETs on the role of 'market institutions' in the EU, their historical evolvement, their present functioning, as well as the advantages and drawbacks encountered at the present stage, would offer PET decision makers and the broader public a more realistic perspective on what needs to be done, including in terms of creating the governance institutions that neither belong to the state nor those whose results are scrutinized in the market-place. A pointed dialogue between such Western institutions and the emerging civil societies in the PETs would be helpful in this respect (Reinicke 1992, p. 105). Bringing PET decision makers closer to the political EU institutions, especially the European Parliament and the Commission, would contribute to disseminating information from West to East, as well as to ensuring some reciprocity. The Union should take into account the interests of the PETs to a much greater degree than this has been the case over the past several years. Foreign policy matters and security aspects of their situation immediately spring to mind in this connection (Timmermann 1993).

Promotion of the cultural patrimony as being 'European'would help in a number of ways. Similarly, bringing a considerable number of youngsters as students or interns into the European institutions at large would help fashion a European culture that other EU members have moulded over a considerable period of time. This must necessarily be a two-way street. Though the feeling of being European first and, say, French or German second is not yet particularly widespread among the citizenry of the EU, there can be no doubt that the gap has narrowed to an astonishing degree as compared to what it was, say, three or four decades ago. This change in psychology, in personal values, and in behaviour of the citizenry at large has to some extent benefited from close economic integration and co-operation, from financial transfers, and indeed from the accompanying measures from the banal to high European political and cultural manifestations, including most notably the wider educational opportunities now available. But ignorance about the history and culture of the PETs continues to be widespread in Western Europe, and the Commission could help to defuse potential hostility with respect to the 'Eastern cultures', however fundamentally rooted their European base may actually be.

Finally, whether in the comprehensive package of useful assistance measures room should be reserved for assisting the PETs with their 'reciprocal dialogue' (Maillet 1993, p. 493) has been a highly controversial element. But I deem it something definitely worth investigating not only in trade relations. Others have strongly argued against this on the ground that it would mean, putting it dramatically, political suicide (Brabant 1991a). In any case, many argue that vibrant intragroup ties, not only in the economic but also in the political and socio-cultural spheres, will eventually emerge from within the realm of being together within the EU, not the other way around, which is said to divert attention from what is deemed to be the most desirable and optimal foreign policy course to pursue. It would certainly not be useful to set up this investigation solely with the goal of deflecting actual or potential trade away from the West. Instead, it should focus primarily on how these countries individually and collectively can improve their specialization and thus mitigate the presently existing drawbacks they encounter in eventually entering the EU.

The core of Western Europe constitutes a natural centre for exerting 'subtle' pressures on the PETs, to the extent the PETs can be persuaded of the usefulness of such a course of action, perhaps in exchange for obtaining a commitment to broader assistance from, and collaboration with, the Union. This could most fruitfully be formulated to shore up and impart an impetus to intragroup co-operation, while smoothing whatever rough edges there are for now, linked directly to the integration of the PETs into the global community in general, and into 'Europe' in particular. Providing the wherewithal to support intragroup co-operation through financial transfers, through macroeconomic surveillance, and through technical assistance of the most diverse kinds from the outside would itself provide a crucial measure of credibility to intragroup co-operation, prior to merging more fully into the Union's core framework. Believers in the desirability of fostering the purest market relations may object to such 'intervention', particularly since it emanates from the outside. I consider it an integral component of good regional governance and, indeed, of good policy-making in the PETs themselves (Brabant 1993a; 1994a, b; 1995a). Positive intervention, where warranted by the adversities and distortions of the transitions, not to forget by the various instances of EU discrimination, would be particularly appropriate in the context of easing the PETs into the Union.

Of course, such should not even be contemplated simply for the benefit of reviving intragroup co-operation. Rather, it should be an integral element in the strategy for strengthening democracy and market-based decision-making in the East and preparing these countries for moving eventually more fully into the global economy in general, and in particular the EU for economic security, and NATO for political and military security. It should be unambiguous, however, that any conceivable assistance package, including its domestic prerequisites, cannot be foisted upon any PET. But intransigence on the latter's part should, then, diminish the claim for assistance to the level of perceived 'national security' that Western Europe may wish to safeguard.

Section 5: Deepening versus widening and the 1996 IGC

One of the most controversial among the many contentious issues on integration within the EU framework, and even more so in relations with outsiders, has been the debate on deepening versus widening (Western) European integration. This debate is neither new nor genuinely concerned about the delicate issues at stake. The earlier experiences with widening provide little guidance to resolving the multiple hindrances at this juncture. I genuinely feel that the present options on deepening and widening, at least from the perspective of real policy-making, are *sui generis*, and need to be dealt with as such.

Deepening means in essence working further towards full integration within the Union, reaching well beyond the economic sphere, which itself needs to be solidified, towards the more social and political aspects of working together. Widening means in essence broadening the membership and spreading the EU gospel chapter and verse with few, if any, overt amendments to accommodate other countries. The first tends to inhibit the latter, and vice versa, not only by design but also by the very nature of the conflict that may pit widening against deepening as policy priorities. This contrast is admittedly artificial. It certainly is much too stark. It is nonetheless useful to be aware of the implications of this debate, for it has real consequences for the potential association of the PETs with the Union. I shall here consider only cases in which those advocating the primacy of deepening are genuinely motivated by solidifying integration among the existing membership (see Brabant 1995a, pp. 511-24). Those that are not so listed have even more pernicious repercussions.

After the expansion in 1986 (to absorb Portugal and Spain), until approval of the Maastricht Treaty in 1991, the Twelve clearly favoured deepening integration. New negotiations for accession were either gingerly deferred or, as in the case of the European Economic Area, obliquely entered into. This was a deliberate stance, one that was, however, severely jeopardized by the events in the East, most notably German reunification on whose implications for enlargement the EU had no choice, and the disarray in the smaller PETs; and later by the calamitous disintegration of the Soviet Union. Several EU members felt strongly especially about hardening Germany's interest in European integration through deepening, before further widening could possibly dilute the *acquis* and the common policy stances in the areas identified earlier. In spite of all its problems and compromises, even on vital constitutional issues, and in ensuring the fundamental infrastructure for good governance (Boulouis 1992), this was essentially the message that the Maastricht Treaty sought to convey. However, in spite of the accent placed on deepening, the EU could only obtain support for it by accommodating at least some pressure for widening, without overly eroding the commitment to 'Europe'. In the process, the criteria for further membership expansion, as indicated earlier, have become somewhat clearer (Bempt 1993; Lippert and Wessels 1993).

Though one can logically consider the advantages and disadvantages of the four combinations of deepening and widening, notably as regards funnelling the PETs into the Union, in practice there is no choice but to combine the two, with the emphasis on one, rather than the other (Brabant 1995a). But which accent on what task? Eastern Europe adrift has presented the EU with the need to reformulate its working horizon in terms of 'all-Europe', something that had been very remote from Eurothinking for all too many decades. This is necessary to strengthen the political transitions in the PETs by shoring up the foundations of the underlying economies for moving towards market-based resource allocation. One pillar was slated to be through sizable Western assistance to be delivered effectively as a prop to the East's transformation, which was postulated to be within reach after a comparatively confined period of time. Thereafter, it was taken for granted, these societies would embark on substantial self-sustainable growth, and thus begin to bridge the enormous gaps between their wealth and productive capacity and those of the (Western) European countries, largely on their own strength.

Little thought was then given to the need to usher the PETs into the EU framework, in spite of claims to the 'return to Europe' repeated *ad nauseam* by policy makers of all ilk. It was generally assumed that if such an expansion were to occur, it would take place at best after these countries had embarked on an endogenous growth dynamic unleashed by the freeing-up of these societies. It was taken as an axiom that eventually the PETs would come to resemble Western democracies, perhaps at the lower end of the levels of wealth in the EU, but nonetheless vibrant market-based economies with a solid democratic anchor. Their integration into the EU framework would then (but not yet) be arranged in the same way that enlargements had typically been engineered in the past.

Nonetheless, the remaking of Europe is an unprecedented historical event. Forging ahead quickly, and in an orderly fashion, should rank high on the agenda of policy makers, particularly in the EU. This is feasible only if the European Commission reconceptualizes its near-term agenda by focusing squarely on the remaking of all of Europe, while proceeding with the realization of the Maastricht Treaty and beyond. That includes the thorough preparation of the constitutional changes to be tackled at the 1996 IGC, so that the Union can properly govern at least its own transformation processes.

One of the most important tasks ahead, then, will be to broaden the Union's policy co-ordination with respect to the East. Avoiding excessive bilateralism, which the Commission has stressed in a rather unfortunate fashion since it was first entrusted with co-ordinating assistance to the

PETs, is of crucial importance. A more co-ordinated approach towards assisting the PETs could be instituted by adopting a group-wide plan of action and by ensuring that effective surveillance over the transformations under way in the East can be, and is being, exercised. The need for self-help should be emphasized in the intragroup context as well, for which active EU sponsorship is required. This entails not only financial support. It also necessitates inevitably tight, but flexible surveillance of the proper kind, given the extraordinary circumstances prevailing in the PETs. Indeed, the EU's involvement in realistically reconstructing the PETs should mandate active involvement both in designing and in implementing the transition strategies, provided broad socio-political consensus exists in the PETs on the kind of market economy to be targeted. Only with such a comprehensive approach to the delivery of assistance can the EU realistically hope to secure – and justify for the respective electorates – steady fiscal support for this appropriation of funds, and mitigate apprehension about adverse effects for other countries.

Conclusion

Although I do not wish to interpret events in an *ex cathedra* fashion, I do insist upon the increasing dissatisfaction with the way in which international assistance has been extended to the PETs in general and the approaches that the EU has seen fit to undergird since 1990 in particular. If Europe is serious about its own architecture, it cannot disregard the PETs, regardless of their eventual suitability for membership. Likewise, if PETs are firmly bent on joining 'Europe', they have to formulate new approaches to laying out an acceptable path towards forging ahead with the foundations of such a transition phase leading up to full membership. A realistic compromise may then be in the offing.

I have offered my views on what could be done, indeed should preferably be accomplished, even prior to negotiating for full membership. I am aware that the PET leadership is not very happy about pursuing such a two-track approach. Neither is the EU happy about 'outsiders' proffering suggestions that, insiders sometimes claim, are already being implemented or have been fully considered within the EU's framework. That may well be the case. Unfortunately, we know all too little about what the precise strategic thinking within the Commission may be. Knitting a tighter safety net for the PETs has a load of diplomatic and political bearings that cannot be thrown around at will. Whereas I can appreciate the need for hiding behind such a veil, I do not find it a very constructive way of proceeding even under the most favourable circumstances. Those for the PETs are by far not promising. Hence the issues deserve to be aired as widely and as openly as the ill-defined boundaries of diplomatic discretion permit. It is in that vein that I have laid out my views on the core issues at stake, as I see them.

Notes

1. In what follows, I do use EU and European Commission throughout, unless proper citations require otherwise, although these designations became official only in November 1993, upon completion of the ratification process of the Maastricht Treaty.
2. I focus here on the European countries that used to be dominated by a single Communist Party and managed through some kind of administrative planning.
3. This article was written before that meeting. Had I written it afterwards, I probably would have put my case in even sharper relief: at Essen little beyond cosmetics was accomplished because the debate on the potentially momentous summitry of 1996 seems to have become stuck before it got well under way.
4. As I explain later, the strategy should preferably be modulated according to various 'waves' of PETs, beginning with Central Europe and Slovenia; some of the other Balkan and the Baltic States; and the remaining Balkan countries, the western tier of the successor states of the Soviet Union other than the Baltic ones, and the other successor states of the Soviet Union. The core elements should be targeted according to whether the PETs in the group are credible candidates for accession at some point in time.
5. The latter is real hysteresis. It comes in addition to the obstacles emanating from the legacies of communist-style administration, and should not be confounded (as it is in Yavlinsky and Braguinsky 1994) with the interaction effects that may play havoc with borrowed paradigms.
6. An alternative comprehensive solution has recently been advanced by Richard Baldwin (1992, 1994). I shall have no time to discuss it here (but see Brabant 1995a, pp. 539-67), aside from noting that we advanced many similar ideas, but also some fundamentally different ones, notably on institutional set-ups to accommodate the proffered suggestions and the very range of tasks in which the EU and the PETs should get enmeshed at the earliest opportunity.
7. As recent events in the East have demonstrated, the tolerance of these societies for protracted austerity and sustained downward adjustment in levels of living is low. Many of the achievements booked so far, including by those having held on to a stable exchange rate, 'are more likely to impress professional economists and international officials than the long-suffering electorates of the countries concerned' (UNECE 1994, p. 1).
8. Incidentally, much similar activities could be undertaken with great justification for its own members, as suggested for the even more pregnant case of the more effective integration of the five eastern *Länder* into the EU (Eppe 1993); but the lack of disseminated and assimilated information about European integration extends well beyond that particularly acute problem.

Bibliography

Baldwin, Richard E.: *An Eastern Enlargement of EFTA: Why the East Europeans should Join and the EFTANs should Want Them*, London, CEPR, 1992.

——, *Towards an Integrated Europe*, London, CEPR, 1994.

Bempt, Paul van den: 'L'adhésion des pays d'Europe Centrale et Orientale à l'Union Européenne: espoirs et problèmes', *Revue du Marché Commun et de l'Union Européenne*, No. 369 (1993), pp. 579-86.

Boulouis, Jean: 'A propos des dispositions institutionnelles du traité sur l'Union Européenne', *Revue des Affaires Européennes*, 1992, 4, pp. 5-8.

Brabant, Jozef M. van: *Integrating Eastern Europe into the Global Economy – Convertibility through a Payments Union*, Dordrecht, Boston, MA, and London, Kluwer Academic Publishers, 1991a.

——, 'Renewing Economic Cooperation in Eastern Europe and Foreign Assistance', *Economic Systems*, 15/2 (1991b), pp. 243-64.

——, *Privatizing Eastern Europe – the Role of Markets and Ownership in the Transition*, Dordrecht, Boston, MA, and London, Kluwer Academic Publishers, 1992a.

——, 'Integrating the New Eastern Europe into the Global Economy', *Structural Change and Economic Dynamics*, 1992b, 1, pp. 17-35.

——, *Industrial Policy in Eastern Europe – Governing the Transition*, Dordrecht, Boston, MA, and London, Kluwer Academic Publishers, 1993a.

——, 'Lessons from the Wholesale Transformations in the East', *Comparative Economic Studies*, 1993b, 4, pp. 73-102.

——, 'The New East in Multilateral Economic Organizations', in *The New Eastern Europe in the Global Economy*, edited by Jozef M. van Brabant, Boulder, CO, and London, Westview Press, 1993c, pp. 79-109.

——, 'Privatization, Industrial Policy and Governing the Transitions', *MOCT-MOST*, 1994a, 1, pp. 63-85.

——, 'Governance, Evolution, and the Transformation of Eastern Europe', in *The Transformation of Eastern Europe and Evolutionary Economics*, edited by Kazimierz Poznanski, Boulder, CO and London, Westview Press, 1994b. pp. 157-82.

——, *The Transformation of Eastern Europe – Joining the European Integration Movement*, Commack, NY, Nova Science Publishers, 1995a.

——, 'Western Assistance to PETs, the Monetary System, and Global Integration', in *The Global Monetary System After the Fall of the Soviet Empire*, edited by Miklós Szabó-Pelsőczi, Avebury, Aldershot, UK in association with The Robert Triffin–Szirák Foundation, Budapest, 1995b, pp. 11-33.

Bressand, Albert: 'A Pan-European Community in the Making?' in *European Reunification in the Age of Global Networks*, edited by Albert Bressand and György Csáki, Budapest, Institute for World Economics of the Hungarian Academy of Sciences, 1992, pp. 7-17.

Eppe, Franz: 'Les difficultés de l'intégration de l'ex-RDA dans la Communauté', *Revue du Marché Commun et de l'Union Européenne*, No. 368 (1993), pp. 405-9.

Klaus, Václav: 'The Czech Republic and European Integration', *Perspectives – Review of Central European Affairs*, 1993/94, 2, pp. 7-11.

Kramer, Heinz: 'The European Community's Response to the "New Eastern Europe" ', *Journal of Common Market Studies*, 1993, 2, pp. 213-44.

Lippert, Barbara and Wessels Wolfgang: 'Erweiterungskonzepte und Erweiterungsmöglichkeiten', in *Gesamteuropa – Analysen, Probleme und Entwicklungsper-*

spektiven, edited by Cord Jakobeit and Alparslan Yenal, Bonn, Bundeszentrale für politische Bildung, 1993, pp. 439-57.

Maillet, Pierre: 'La CEE et la transition en Europe centrale', *Revue du Marché Commun et de l'Union Européenne*, No. 369 (1993), pp. 490-6.

Pavan, Antonio: 'Europe and the Transition in the Eastern Countries: Democracy and Development', *Aula – Society and Economy*, 1993,2, pp. 54-61.

Pickel, Andreas: 'Jump-starting a Market Economy: a Critique of a Radical Strategy for Economic Reform in Light of the East German Experience', *Studies in Comparative Communism*, 1992,2, pp. 177-91.

Reinicke, Wolfgang H.: *Building a New Europe – the Challenge of System Transformation and Systemic Reform*, Washington DC, The Brookings Institution, 1992.

Robin, Albert: 'Les grndes entreprises des pays d'Europe centrale: leur avenir? quel concours leur apporter?' *Revue du Marché Commun et de l'Union Européenne*, No. 369 (1993), pp. 565-7.

Schalast, Christoph: 'Die Diskussion über die Ordnung der Energiewirtschaft in der Europäischen Gemeinschaft im Hinblick auf die Umstrukturierung in den Staaten Osteuropas', *Osteuropa-Wirtschaft*, 1993,4, pp. 277-80.

Timmermann, Heinz: 'Europa – der zentrale Bezugspunkt für die Länder des Ostens – Erwartungen, Möglichkeiten, Konzeptionen', *Osteuropa*, 1993,8, pp. 713-25.

UNECE, Economic Bulletin for Europe, Vol. 43, New York, United Nations publication, sales No. E.91.II.E.39, 1991.

——, Economic Survey of Europe in 1991–1992, New York, United Nations publication, sales No. E.92.II.E.1, 1992.

——, Economic Survey of Europe in 1992–1993, New York, United Nations publication, sales No. E.93.II.E.1, 1993.

——, Economic Survey of Europe in 1993–1994, New York, United Nations publication, sales No. E.94.II.E.1, 1994.

Yavlinsky, Grigory and Braguinsky Sergey: 'The Inefficiency of laissez-faire in Russia: Hysteresis Effects and the Need for Policy-led Transformation', *Journal of Comparative Economics*, 1994,1, pp. 88-116.

35 Russia and the Bretton Woods Institutions

Dmitry Smyslov

I take the liberty of reminding the veterans of the Szirák Conferences that my first contribution in 1986 was devoted to the co-operation between East and West in building up a single, universal international monetary system. I was extremely pleased that the next year, *Euromoney* referred to my statement and summarized it in the following phrase: 'The Soviet delegate, D.V. Smyslov from Moscow's Institute of World Economics, signalled his nation's desire to join the IMF.' Nowadays, eight years later, at the Sixth Conference, not a Soviet but a Russian delegate has an opportunity of appreciating the results of two and a half years' Russian membership in the Bretton Woods institutions.

There is no doubt that the International Monetary Fund and the World Bank have really contributed to the market reforming of the Russian economy. Russia has already received a financial support totalling about 5 billion dollars from them. According to the *Financial Times,* Russia is expecting to obtain approximately 14-16 billion dollar more from the IMF. Besides that, Mr Preston, President of the World Bank, in the course of his recent trip to Russia, promised to allocate loans amounting to 3 billion dollars. In accordance with the latest governmental anti-inflationary approach announced by Prime Minister Chernomirdin, these resources, together with the issue of internal state obligations of 45 billion roubles, intended to finance the budgetary deficit and to absorb excess purchasing power.

One cannot be sure that this ambitious financial package will be realized in its entirety. There is uncertainty because the issues of creating a supplementary tranche for the Systemic Transformation Facility and of a new SDR allocation, particularly for the countries which had joined the IMF after 1981, have not been solved. Generally, I think that the potential of the

SDRs, actually a creation of Robert Triffin, is evidently not utilized in a proper way. Nevertheless, there is a hope that sooner or later these problems will find their solutions.

Coming back to Russia, one can suppose that in any case, in the near future, it will – apparently – seek larger financial assistance from the IMF and the World Bank, though this would certainly aggravate its foreign debt servicing burden. I would also like to emphasize the importance of collaboration of the authorities with the IMF in formulating Russia's macroeconomic policy aimed at the stabilization of the national economy.

In spite of all the evident advantages for Russia of its membership in the Bretton Woods institutions, the attitude of the Russian public opinion towards them is very controversial. These institutions, especially the IMF, are criticized not only by the left-wing parties, but also by many prominent figures which were among the initiators of market reforms. How could this fact be explained? In this context, I would like to refer to the *The Market Shock*, a book published in 1992 by the widely-known AGENDA-group. The authors expressed, in particular, their apprehensions that the present transformation programmes inspired by international lending institutions were focused primarily 'on abstract targets such as economic stabilization, balanced budgets, current account balance, and convertible currency, irrespective of the consequences of these policies on output, investment, employment, and private consumption'. As regards the Russian case, this scenario has come true practically in full measure.

Indeed, inflation was reduced by the end of the summer to some 4-5 per cent per month; trade- and current balance account have considerable surpluses; an internal convertibility for current transactions on the basis of a floating exchange rate of the rouble has been established. On the other hand, the GDP decreased in comparison to 1990 in real terms more than during the most severe years of World War II; unemployment permanently rises; the living standard of the greater part of the population has sharply fallen.

Now, the question arises: is there a link between these two phenomena? Apparently, there is, and a very immediate one. That is why the mass consciousness tends to connect all the negative economic and social processes with the influence of the IMF as an initiator and a sponsor of the policy of 'shock therapy'.

The IMF and the World Bank are still not fully taking into account all the specific and unique features of today's Russia. In this context, I would like to draw your attention to three particular points which, in my opinion, serve as sources of collisions between the Bretton Woods institutions and a very considerable stratum of Russian society.

First, an impression emerges that inflation is treated by the IMF as a monetary phenomenon, and is reduced to only 'demand-pull inflation'. Meanwhile, in Russia, it represents an extraordinary complicated, complex, and many-sided process, involving also 'cost-push inflation'. Current inflation has, to a considerable extent, an institutional, structural nature and is stimulated by the fact that monopolies command many important sectors of the Russian economy. As a matter of fact, the typical mechanism of stagflation, which was mainly provoked in the '70s by the oil crises, is now functioning in Russia in full bloom. Furthermore, since from 40 to 50 per cent of internal consumption is provided at present through imports, Russian inflation has also a very strong import component. It seems to me that the macroeconomic recommendations of the IMF to Russia would prove, in the long run, less painful for the population and more fruitful for the economic machinery, provided they reflect a more balanced notion about the specific factors giving rise to inflation.

Second, one can discover some differences of approach concerning an optimum combination of reliance on market forces and the use of state management during the transitional period. Should we decentralize the decision-making mechanism immediately which is, as one can judge, the position of the IMF, or would it be wiser to do this more gradually? In this context, I will review the pattern of Russia's foreign trade, excluding trade with the former Soviet Union countries.

A commodity structure of *imports* is characterized by a sharply increased share of consumer goods notable for a very high degree of commercial profitability (foodstuffs, alcohol, tobacco, etc.). They have supplanted the corresponding domestic products and, accordingly, contributed to the overall decline of national production. This phenomenon has resulted immediately from the hasty liberalization of foreign trade and the introduction of currency convertibility which has been accompanied by a great fall of the rouble's rate of exchange.

As regards *exports*, the traditionally large share of energy products has increased still more. It accounts now for roughly half – together with other mineral and metal products for two thirds – of the total value of exports. At the same time, the share of machinery and equipment dropped from 18 per cent in 1990, and 9 per cent in 1992 to 4.5 per cent in the first half of the present year. Thus, the surplus of the balance of trade is actually based on a permanent and ever-increasing loss of the nation's natural resources.

Mr O. Davydov, the newly appointed vice-chairman of the government, responsible for foreign economic relations, noted recently: 'We can hold out on the raw materials exports only for three-four years more.' And one could agree with this statement. However, could the freer functioning of market forces alone for such a short period bring about a necessary restructuring of the composition of exports? This would require a tremendous redistribution of the nation's resources, a creation of adequate import-substituting and export-oriented industries, a substantial increase of the share of machinery in foreign trade turn-over. There are important reasons to believe that such an approach would result in a market failure. Evidently, the achievement of this goal is conditional on executing a strong and targeted govermental industrial and structural policy. In my opinion, it would be very helpful if the IMF could find it possible to support such a policy.

Finally, my *third point* relates to social and ideological matters. One should only appreciate that now the Bretton Woods institutions pay more attention to the fight against poverty and advocating the formation of the social safety net. However, as far as Russia is concerned, recent sociological studies reveal that a very large part of the population is discouraged not only by an overall decline of living standards, but also by a rapidly growing gap between poverty and wealth. If during 1991, the incomes of 10 per cent of the richest group of the population exceeded the incomes of 10 per cent of the poorest one by 4.5 times, in the present year this gap broadened to 12 times.

A belief is deeply rooted in Russian public opinion according to which the market is not an end and a value in itself, but a means for improving the quality of life of the people as a whole. Those who share this belief are consciously or unconsciously embarrassed by the sterile capitalistic approach of the IMF. It appears to me that the International Monetary Fund and the World Bank would facilitate the world economic and social progress still more efficiently, provided that they start from a more polyphonic and many-coloured view of the historical perspective.

36 Stabilization of the International Monetary System and Central and Eastern Europe

Yoshiaki Toda

It is an honor for me to speak at this conference held in Belgium, the birthplace of Professor Robert Triffin, on the 50th anniversary of Bretton Woods. I am pleased to offer my congratulations to this esteemed gathering. My only regret is that the number of participants from Japan, one of the three big economic powers in the world together with the United States and the European Union, is rather small. As one of the participants from Japan, I wish to do my best to contribute to this conference.

As you know, Japan achieved 'miracle' economic growth after its defeat in World War II in 1945, and today accounts for 16 per cent of world GNP. This growth is mainly attributable to the continuing efforts of the Japanese people, aid from the United States, and large loans for economic reconstruction from the World Bank, just after the war.

At the same time, however, I wish to comment on another important factor. The post-war world has been sustained by the free trade system and the stable international monetary system represented by GATT and the IMF, respectively. In this context, the Japanese economy has been greatly influenced by such events as the termination of US dollar convertibility into gold in 1971 and the shift to a floating currency system in 1973. In addition, the oil crises and the end of the cold war have had major effects on the Japanese economy.

Although the fundamentals of the Japanese economy have not shown a significant recovery in recent years, the yen has appreciated substantially against the US dollar. The rapid rise in the yen is delaying the Japanese economy's recovery from its worst and longest recession. This is a substantial disadvantage not only to the Japanese economy but also to the world economy. Moreover, it is a great pity that in this economic situation, Japan's economic co-operation or aid for the transformation of Central and Eastern Europe has not been sufficient.

The leaders of Japanese industry are deeply interested in the contents of the report from the Bretton Woods Commissions, *Bretton Woods: Looking to the Future* (see insert) issued in July this year, and the contents of the discussion, 'The Future of the IMF and the World Bank' held in Madrid in September. This is because, as mentioned before, the stability of the foreign exchange markets as well as the maintenance of a free trade system is considered to be extremely important for the Japanese economy to move out of its worst recession in the post-war era.

From the *Report* of the Bretton Woods Commission (July 1994)

The main suggestion concerning the reformation of the international monetary system would be, as stated in the *Commission Report* is that 'The governments of the major industrial countries should take two successive steps: first, strengthen their macroeconomic policies, and achieve greater economic convergence, and second, establish a more formal system of co-ordination to support these policy improvements and avoid excessive exchange rate misalignment and volatility.' There seems to be a lot of argument regarding the relationship between 'greater economic convergence' and 'a more formal system of co-ordination' here, especially that which of the two should be pursued first. This seems to be the 'chicken or the eggs case'. It does not help deciding which should be first.

It is believed that the confidential agreements reached after the Plaza (1985) and Louvre (1987) Accords among the G-3 (the United States, Japan, and Germany) to intervene to stabilize foreign exchange markets under the so-called '*de facto* target zone system' have been losing, for the past few years, their effectiveness. The problem could be that the concerted action among the leading countries including the G-3 was less than desirable. In particular, US political leaders tend to make remarks to hint at a weaker US dollar rather than to show deep concern for a strong or stable US dollar.

As long as all countries in the world want to maintain non-inflationary and sustained growth, it is impossible to imagine that political leaders desire the continuous devaluation of their currencies. Therefore, I must say that it is regrettable that US statesmen, as leaders of a core G-3 member, should express such views, explicitly or implicitly, in contradiction to this principle. A weaker US dollar might be an advantage for US industry for the time being, but the bill must be paid in the end. In fact, US industry is suffering from a rise in long-term interest rates and a slump in the bond market. In this connection, an understanding of the importance of a stable foreign exchange system is the first step towards the reformation of the international monetary system.

On the other hand, I regret to say that Japan has not always acted responsibly either as one of the three leading economic powers. For the sake of a stable currency market, it is basically necessary for each leading country to maintain internal and external economic balances. In this connection, the fact that Japan has been recording large surpluses in its balance of payments since the latter part of the 1960s is, frankly speaking, a big problem.

Two factors serve as the background for this situation. First, domestic savings are in excess of domestic investments and flow overseas instead of being spent within the country. Second, in the case of Japan, leading industries, such as machinery and transport equipment makers, rely on exports rather than on domestic sales and possess a strong international competitiveness. Although more and more people have come to recognize this situation as a potential source of international conflicts, and are trying to correct it, the problem cannot be easily or quickly solved. Judging from our recent experience, strong economic recovery leads to increased import demand. Income elasticity of imports has increased from an average of 0.5 for the 12-year period from 1973 to 1985 to an average of 1.32 for the 6-year period from 1986 to 1992. Thus, the trade imbalance can be improved quickly to a large extent only through economic recovery.

There is another important task for Japan. It is to further develop the function of Tokyo as an international financial centre. As is widely known, not only The National Bank of Hungary, but also many of the governmental institutions of Turkey, Greece, Korea, etc. have been raising funds in the form of bond issues or syndicated loans in the Tokyo market in recent years. Yet the number of such cases and the amounts are small compared to those of London or New York. To develop and make the Tokyo market more attractive, many measures should be taken in terms of the system itself, or with respect to taxation. But so far, it is difficult to say that sufficient measures have been adopted. If the Tokyo market is activated by such measures and more investors use it, the yen will support the US dollar and contribute to the stabilization of the international monetary system.

I would now like to discuss the last of the three big economic powers, the European Union. The EU is undergoing the steady process of economic and monetary integration. The first step of free movement of people, goods, capital, and services has already been achieved. The second step is the founding of the European Monetary Institute and the strengthening of collaboration with respect to the macroeconomic policies of each country. This will lead to the third step of a fixed exchange rate system, the introduction of a single currency and the foundation of the European Central Bank. Although, there are many obstacles to overcome in achieving this agenda, it is a grand experiment and deserves to be highly appreciated. We had better pay attention to the fact, among others, that the EU is deeply interested in geographical extension and contributes much to the transformation of Central and Eastern Europe, while it is deepening the quality of its integration.

Japan has been contributing to the transformation of Central and Eastern European countries through such international organizations as the World Bank, the IMF, and the EBRD. But its direct economic co-operation is not necessarily adequate. In addition, the Japanese businessmen's main concern is targeted on Japan's Asian neighbours where labour costs are relatively lower in the 'emerging markets'. They are making active direct investment and transfers of production bases to these countries. It is needless to say that the Central and Eastern European countries need to develop the economic, social, and legal base for the introduction of foreign investment. They must also publicize this in order to attract investment, not only through international organizations, but also from direct foreign investors.

In conclusion, I would like to repeat the important effect of a stable international monetary system on world economic growth, which may not seem to have a deep relationship at a glance. According to the Bretton Woods *Commission Report*, since the early 1970s, when the international monetary system became unstable, the average long-term economic growth rate of the major developed countries fell from an annual 5 per cent to 2.5 per cent. The important issue of the distribution of international liquidity, through instruments such as SDRs to Central and Eastern European countries is often discussed at G-7 or G-10 meetings. But at the same time, the discussion and an approach that is focused on the stabilization of the international monetary system are also urgent and imperative to ensure the stable and sustained growth of the world economy including, of course, Central and Eastern Europe.

EPILOGUE: Towards Global Partnership

Miklós Szabó-Pelsőczi

Introduction

Lytton Strachey has remarked (*Portraits in Miniature*, 1931) about Gibbon that he was a great historian because he was a great classical artist. Order, lucidity, balance, precision permitted him to bring order out of the chaos of the tumultuous events of almost fifteen centuries, from the reign of the 'five good emperors' (AD 98-180) to the final conquest of Constantinople by the Turks (1453).

How was this minor human miracle, a micromiracle on a historically and geographically macroscale accomplished? 'By style' – says Strachey. Style here does not mean only the formal cadences of a typical Gibbonian phrase, but much more the inner elegance and simplicity with which centuries of struggles could be linked – and separated – by one single sentence. Example: 'The mutual obligations of the popes and the Carlovingian family form the important link of ancient and modern, of civil and ecclesiastical history' (Ch. XLIX).

Rereading the volume of the papers presented at the Sixth Conference of the Robert Triffin–Szirák Foundation held during November 1994 in Brussels, I was struck by its Gibbonian style. Not the formal style: economists during the second-half of the twentieth century have no particular use for eighteenth century literary form whether of Edward Gibbon or of Adam Smith.

But the search for truth is there – and this is what counts. This search for truth gives the unity of the volume written by more than one-and-a-half score of men and women of different backgrounds, experiences and strong individual views on specific issues.

To paraphrase Gibbon: the *de facto* abandoning in 1971 of the rule of law in international monetary relations forms the link between a quarter century of relatively encouraging high quality growth in the non-communist part of the world, and the gradual global return to the rule of the jungle during the following period.

Economics: exercise in morality

The search for truth in matters economic is the search for norms, commitments, and contracts leading to optimal economic results within the framework of democracy and free markets. The Articles of Agreement of the International Monetary Fund enacted more than half-a-century ago, are codifying the purposes not only of the organization, but implicitly of all economic activity. These should aim to: 'the expansion and balanced growth of international trade... to the promotion and maintenance of high levels of employment and real income... to [avoid] measures destructive of national and international prosperity... [and] to shorten the duration and lessen the degree of disequilibrium in the international balances of payments...' (Article I).

There is no indication in the papers that the autenthicity of the Purposes would have been questioned.

On the contrary. Moral and cultural values have been often referred to during the Conference, especially, by Mr Snoy, whether he highlighted the deeply moral motivation of Robert Triffin in his approach to economics, or when he quoted the Hungarian Minister of Finance Iván Szabó at the 1993 Annual Meeting of the Fund and the Bank as saying: 'freedom needs a moral content... [and] a communal substance'. Mr Snoy went on to say: 'The moral dimension is equally important today to rebuild the economy and the society and to clear the debris of communism.' And he referred to President Göncz's writings, especially to *Homecoming and Other Stories* (Corvina, 1993) in which he defends 'the dignity and valour of a nameless Hungarian, a proxy for 100 million Europeans in Central Europe, who suffered in body and soul for almost two generations, from the rise of nazism to the fall of communism the economic and cultural indignities inflicted upon them by successive police states'.

'If moral values are crucial for the success of transition in Central and Eastern Europe, they are as crucial to the Western world.... Indeed, the fabric of [Western] societies and perhaps [their] own capacity to overcome [their] own economic crisis is also threatened by the danger of a collapse of their moral and spiritual values' – writes Mr Snoy. And he refers to Zbigniew Brzezinski's work, *Out of Control – Global Turmoil on the Eve of the 21st Century* (Scribners, 1993), and to President Havel's essay, *The End of the Modern Era* in which they observe, that 'we are living in a philosophical vacuum that is out of control... unless we practise severe restraint derived from a moral commitment in the quest for global democratic interdependence, we are destined to risk again our very own survival' (Brzezinski), and that the 'modern era has created the first global, or planetary, technical civilization, but it has reached the point, beyond which the abyss begins' (Havel).

It is clearly documented that this volume's *style,* in the Gibbonian sense, is firmly anchored in the ideas of the economic and moral humanism Robert Triffin's oeuvre represents.

Economics: exercise in global partnership (A)

Triffin's economic world-outlook was well balanced. He was a free-market economist: there is not the slightest evidence in his opus that he imagined that the economic affairs of a free society could be ever transacted in any other way, except on a free market. But he was equally convinced that markets, especially international currency markets, can never be free from distortions and misalignments unless they are subject to appropriate market controls. In this sense, he was an institutionalist and a supporter of the international financial institutions.

'IMF Managing Director Camdessus's full support and insistence on the Fund's central role in promoting "high quality" growth', as characterized in Minister Maystadt keynote address, is therefore, fully consonant with Triffin's ideas.

But Mr Maystadt went even further. He has linked the emerging monetary problems of transition countries to the general reform of existing international monetary and economic institutions. 'With the end of Soviet imperialism, the environment for monetary co-operation has radically changed... Partnership rather than power relations seems the key to the future of monetary co-operation, even more so since on the top of the emerging East-West integration, we are witnessing a wider reshuffling of vested interests and positions with world-wide implications.'

The high purposes of international monetary co-operation must be translated into reality. Global institutions created for this end are the principal transmission belts representing the most complex techniques between the world of ideas and the world of reality. Institutions, in terms of their original purposes, must be constantly reconstructed so that they should be able to perform their original tasks in an ever-changing environment. Managing Director Camdessus and Minister Maystadt deserve high praise for recognizing, perhaps among the first of global monetary leaders, that the fall of the Soviet Empire represent not an unpleasant disturbance and an urge for unwelcome dislocations for the established international financial institutions, but a fresh challenge to develop them into the high-performing engines of global monetary stability and economic growth which are their *raison d'être*.

Until the end of his life, Robert Triffin opposed the Second Amendment of the IMF, which he considered contrary to the IMF's original principles. Techniques like floating rates, which are *ab ovo* unfit to bring about monetary stability should not be accepted among the Fund's key provisions, he thought.

The developments of the last two decades have proven these anticipations as correct. The indirect freeing of central banks' reserve creation from an international standard caused central bank reserves, which, between 1949 and 1969, have increased only from $49 to $79 billion, to increase by a factor of 18 from $79 billion to $1,436 billion by 1993. 'It is clear that once the system was cut off from the gold-anchor in 1973, there was an explosion of liquidity'(Witteveen).

But even more dangerous is that Eurocurrency lending as shown in the BIS net-international bank lending tables have increased from $60 billion (1969) to $3,600 billion in 1991. The market suffers almost constantly from a demand-determined oversupply of liquidity, partly from off-shore Eurocurrency markets partly from internationalized domestic monetary creation. Both can have serious inflationary consequences. The spurts of liquidity are not due to any increased availability of savings, gold shipments from Latin-America as in the 16th century, or even to any discoveries of new gold deposits as in the 19th century. Overliquidity is now germane to the system originally created to stabilize international currency markets. National banks of course could neutralize excess monetary creation if they would decide to do so. But this is rather the exception than the rule. Furthermore, the development of almost instantaneous global money transfers and the

unanticipated large volume of derivatives trading are making it more difficult for central banks to control their own clients.

The only real solution of excess liquidity would be 'for the world's
monetary authorities to work together in order to manage the development
of international liquidity... [This would require] for the US authorities to
finance their deficits in the world capital markets... [and] off-shore markets
to be bought under the influence of the monetary instruments of their central
banks' (Witteveen). These developments could lead us back to the use of
the SDR as the principal reserve asset of the international monetary system.
We would be back then where we were 25 years ago.

To achieve this, to overcome the unintended consequences of a quarter-
century relapse to the rule of the jungle in international monetary affairs,
we now need to make a very great effort to create a true monetary partnership.

Economics: exercise of joining East and West

Robert Triffin has considered that the Bretton Woods institutions were
flawed from the start. The IBRD was more a long-term investment bank for
projects, than a development agency, although its role in this field changed
greatly over the decades and it is still largely undetermined. Although the
IMF did have a chance at the start to assume a permanent responsibility for
exchange rate stability and world liquidity, these roles were shed after 1971,
when the IMF became a mere source for short-term credits to cover balance-
of-payments needs. True enough, during the past half-a-century, under the
pressure of contrary events, much have happened to fill the gaps caused to
a large extent by the lacunae of the original structures, the Bretton Woods
institutions have left uncovered much of the territory where there is need
for international development and special financial institutions.

The Marshall Plan was created in 1947 to respond to such a well-defined
need. Ambassador Hadsel's paper recalls in this collection of presentations
an excellent, brief, unadorned, but because of this very effective account of
the Plan's genesis. To gain American support for his proposals, Marshall
explained that 'Only through grasping clearly the crisis in Europe, would
the people of the United States escape the danger of isolationism and make
the proper decisions on which "the whole world of the future" depended.
Toward Europe, Marshall extended his proposal of an American commitment to break the cycle of despair, and restore the confidence of the

Continent .... [His] principal points [were]: assistance should be a basic cure, not piecemeal. It should be open to all countries crippled by the war, not just a few. The initiative should be European, not just American. At the same time, any country opposing the programme could not expect help. Efforts to undermine this assistance would be opposed.'

The rest is history. A complex and drawn-out history, but one, which merits our tribute to the creative genius of the United States and Western Europe. It was Marshall Plan Funds which enabled Triffin to create the European Payments Union.

So far I have mentioned four authors who contributed papers to this volume. It would be impossible to attempt equal treatment or to essay even a summary of the others, no matter how immensely important they are. Without their excellence the volume could not explain the often heroic road the peoples of the transition countries covered during the last five years toward democracy and free markets, nor the often not much less strenuous efforts their governments and the international financial institutions exerted in good faith on their behalf.

But the writer of an Epilogue must draw his own conclusions.

During the five years 1990–1994, the transition countries made great strides to transform their political, economic, and social system into democracy, free markets, and a civil society. The support of the international financial institutions, and the governments standing behind them, should not be underestimated.

Yet, during the Conference the question has been often raised explicitly: 'Have we done enough?' (Mr Cardon de Lichtbuer); and implied in the statement to the effect that 'at the critical moment of transition, proper policies should have been at hand [already], motivated by the need to identify a new, sustainable growth path for the transition countries' (Mr Brabant).

The above question refers to the insufficiency of funds, with which industrial countries have assisted the transformation in East Central Europe; the above statement, to the shortage of ideas, with which transition should have been guided.

A proper analysis of either underfinancing or providing insufficient guidance would lead us too far. Yet, the issues once raised, must be answered, especially since they interlock.

Both issues beg the question: 'enough – compared to what?'

The answer seems to me: compared to the best potential product provided by the 'state of the art' of economic statesmanship. In this respect, the 'state of the art' of the Marshall Plan philosophy is still unsurpassed. In his paper, Mr Steinherr recommends that it still should be put to work, at least with respect to the FSU countries. Political realities apart, it still remains to be answered why 23 industrial countries could not have financed a non-refundable Second Economic Recovery Programme (Szabó-Pelsőczi, Szirák Conference Papers, 1991; and *Annual Report*, Szirák Foundation, 1991), which would have placed *ceteris paribus* comparable burdens on donor countries, and would have awarded comparable benefits to recipient countries as the Marshall Plan did almost half a century ago, and which would have been administered in the same way.

There is one major answer to this question. By 1989, the economies of the 23 industrial countries were not as elastic as the United States' economy was in 1947, or any time up to 1971. Therefore, by 1989, the 23 industrial countries could not respond to the new challenge as flexibly as the United States did in 1947 and during the early 1950s.

This lack of elasticity inhibited a capability of quick response. Non-debt-creating resource transfers remained significant but insufficient to motivate policies 'to identify a new, sustainable growth path for the transition countries' (Brabant).

The still prevailing inelasticity of GDP to price is a result of the IMF renouncing in 1971 (and formally in 1979) its original responsibility for managing international liquidity and for maintaining stable international exchange rates. This move has turned out to be a *cul-de-sac*. To assume these responsibilities, better co-operation among the G-3 (G-7?) is needed to maintain stable exchange rates, manage their mutual net debtor and creditor positions on international markets, and to better control central banks' reserves, off-shore and derivative trading.

In the meantime, transition countries must finance the bulk of the cost of their own transition. These costs are not low. Inherited external indebtedness, speeded up price, trade and exchange liberalization, forced privatization have caused a 20 per cent GDP drop on the average in transition countries, a decline in life expectancy, and many adverse developments in cultural and social conditions with, so far, unforeseeable consequences.

The best evaluation of the last five years is that transition countries had paid a higher price for reconstruction, than a best-state-of-the-art solution would have required. The worst evaluation of the future is that Chechenians and Yugoslavians will repeat themselves until doomsday.

Economics: exercise in global partnership (B)

To escape the worst scenario, a window of opportunity presents itself in the idea of a global monetary partnership, the seeds of which were shown by the keynote address to the Brussels Conference by Minister Maystadt. The creation of such a partnership deserves our overriding consideration.

Without this, even our efforts, to rebuild Central and Eastern Europe, will not succeed. Even if after all the adjustments, of which many of the most brilliant papers in this volume speak, were successfully completed, we might still not be in safe harbour. The docking might be perfect, but if the engines of Flagship Europe fail, then the price of our efforts will still elude us.

Mr Snoy's opening address quotes 'Jacques de Larosière... recently echoing Robert Triffin's views, when he declared in Madrid, that "the world has not yet finished paying for the consequences of 15 years' disregard of the external stability of currencies".'

Secretary McNamara has recently published his memoirs about the Vietnam war. There is an eerie quality about this writing. It seems as if the United States were a victim of unintended consequences. He often states with great candour that the United States did not want war in Vietnam, but once started, it felt obliged to continue. A characteristic sentence reads: 'By now [June 1967], it was clear to me that our policies and programmes in Indochina had involved us in ways we had neither anticipated nor intended, and that the costs – human, political, social, and economic – had grown far greater than anyone has had imagined...' (*In Retrospect*, Random House, New York, 1995).

Economic policy makers must prevent that global economic policy making should get onto the threadmill of unintended consequences. From Sarajevo in 1914 to Sarajevo in 1995, we can witness a baffling series of miscalculations: two world wars, the 1925 sterling-overvaluation, the Great Depression, dictatorships, oil-crises, large scale inbalances in G-3 external accounts, and the greatly reduced ability of the industrial countries to guide, generously and in their own enlightened long-term self-interest, with the highest state-of-the-art competence, the transformation process in Central and Eastern Europe.

After a long period of crises, the international community must take a conscious policy choice between continuing the present course of unmanaged liquidity and unmanaged currency instability: this would be tantamount of accepting the very high probability of a disaster of historic proportions. Or the policy decision could go in the other direction. The international community could choose a limited degree of unpleasantness always associated with a catharsis. In that case, democracy, free markets, stability, sustained real growth could emerge as winners.

Global partnership would be a decisive choice for the latter. This is important, in a period when the cherished moral values of Robert Triffin, which many of us share, are exposed to new challenges both from within the industrial countries, and from without. Instead of confrontation, a constructive partnership should develop between the industrial and developing countries of the Globe leading to stability, sustainable growth and, after decades or centuries, to a meaningful equalization of the presently still crass differences between rich and poor countries. A global monetary and economic partnership should serve this ideal.

Towards the end of Gibbon's monumental work (Chapter LXXI), there is a melancholy picture of the crumbling ruins of Rome drawn after more than one thousand years of declining splendour.

Economists who have seen the Golden Age of their applied discipline during the quarter century following World War II should warn their communities that unless they consciously start building a global partnership soon, they will be guilty of falling asleep on their watch.

Summer 1995

Notes on Participants

Báger, Gusztáv, General Director, Ministry of Finance, Budapest

Balczerowicz, Leszek, Former Minister of Finance, Foundation for Economic Education, Warsaw

Bod, Péter Ákos, President, National Bank of Hungary

Brabant, Jozef M. van, Principal Economic Affairs Officer, UN, New York

Cardon de Lichtbuer, Daniel, President, Banque Brussel Lambert, Brussels; President, European League for Economic Cooperation

Chaffart, Ferdinand, President and CEO, Generale Bank, Brussels

Cockaerts, Marcel, President and CEO, Kredietbank, Brussels

Dixon, Joly, Director, Direction Générale II D Commission Européenne, Brussels

Flemming, John, Warden, Wadham College, Oxford

Gros, Daniel, Senior Research Fellow, Centre for European Policy Studies, Brussels

Hadsel, Fred L., Former Director, George C. Marshall Foundation, USA

Hieronymi, Otto, Senior Economist, Battelle, Centre de Recherche de Genève, Geneva

Iványi, György, Senior Counsellor, State Property Agency, Budapest

Kierskowsky, Henryk, Professor, The Graduate Institute of International Studies, University of Genève, Geneva

Klacek, Jan, Director, Institute of Economics of the Czech National Bank, Prague

Kopits, George, Senior Resident Representative in Hungary, IMF, Budapest

Krul, Nicolas, Economist, London

Maystadt, Philippe, Minister of Finance, Brussels

Obolensky, Ariane, Vice President, European Investment Bank, Luxembourg
Odling-Smee, John, Director, IMF, Washington
Papadia, Francesco, Foreign Department, Banca d'Italia
Pisani-Ferry, Jean, Director, CEPII, Paris
Praet, Peter, Chief Economist, Generale Bank, Brussels
Selowsky, Marcelo, Chief Economist, Europe and Central Asia Region, The World Bank, Washington
Smyslov, Dmitry, Doctor of Econ. Sciences, Inst. of World Economy and International Relations, Academy of Sciences of Russia, Moscow
Snoy, Bernard, Director, EBRD, London
Steinherr, Alfred, Chief Economist, European Investment Bank, Luxembourg
Stern, Nicholas, Chief Economist, EBRD, London
Szabó-Pelsőczi, Miklós, Chairman, Robert Triffin–Szirák Foundation, Budapest
Toda, Yoshiaki, Deputy Chairman, The Nippon Credit Bank, Tokyo
Töröcskei, István Chairman, Hungarian Credit Bank, Budapest
Verrue, Robert, Deputy Director General, DG I Commission of the European Union, Brussels
Verplaetze, Alfons, Governor, National Bank of Belgium, Brussels
Witteveen, H.J., Former Managing Director, IMF, Netherlands
Zecchini, Salvatore, Assistant Secretary General, OECD, France

Common Abbreviations

BIS	Bank for International Settlements
CTA	Co-financing Trust Accounts
CMEA	Council for Mutual Economic Aid
CIS	Commonwealth of Independent States
CEPR	Centre for Economic Policy Research
EBRD	European Bank for Reconstruction and Development
EMI	European Monetary Institute
EMU	European Monetary Union
EIB	European Investment Bank
EDI	Economic Development Institute
ELEC	The European League for Economic Co-operation
EPU	European Payments Union
EU	European Union
EMS	European Monetary System
EC	European Commission
EEC	European Economic Community
EA	Europe Agreements
GATT	General Agreement on Tariffs and Trade
IBRD	International Bank for Reconstruction and Development (same as World Bank)
IDA	International Development Association
IFC	International Finance Corporation
IMF	International Monetary Fund
ILO	International Labour Organization
LIBOR	London Inter-Bank Offer Rate
OECD	Organization for Economic Co-operation and Development
OEEC	Organization for European Economic Co-operation (predecessor of OECD)

SAF	Structural Adjustment Facility
SAL	Structural Adjustment Laws
SDR	Special Drawing Right
SBA	Stand-By Arrangements
STF	Systemic Transformation Facility
WB	World Bank (same as IBRD)
WTO	The World Trade Organization